ANCHORING
YOUR
WELL BEING

Christian Wholeness in a Fractured World

A Spiritually Centered Wellness Workbook
for Individuals, Families, and Congregations

Howard Clinebell, Ph.D.

UPPER
ROOM BOOKS
NASHVILLE

Cover Art Direction: Michele Wetherbee
Cover Design: Michele Wetherbee
Interior Design and Layout: Nancy Cole
First Printing: December 1997

Library of Congress Cataloging-in-Publication Data

Clinebell, Howard John, 1922–
    Anchoring your well being : Christian wholeness in a fractured world /
Howard Clinebell.
        p.   cm.
    Includes bibliographical references.
    ISBN 0-8358-0821-1
    1. Christian life. 2. Church group work. 3. Self-care, Health. I. Title.
    BV4501.2.C586   1997
    248.4—dc21   97-11005
                                                                     CIP

Printed in the United States of America

Dedication

To your health!
To the health of those you love!
To the health of your faith community!
To the health of your broken, birthing world!

This workbook is also dedicated to the clergy and lay leaders of congregations who are discovering the special challenges, opportunities, and joys of participating in Christian ministries that enhance the whole-person wellness of their people, their communities, their society, and, in the process, themselves!

Author's note: To express respect for God's creation, this book was printed on recycled paper with nontoxic ink. But the paper that was recycled to produce a book this length originally required harvesting approximately ninety trees. To thank these trees, the earth that sustained them, and the Creator, the author has contributed to reforesting organizations—The Rainforest Action Network and the Tree People of Los Angeles—the cost of planting two trees for each one used. If you would like to express your gratitude to God for the gifts from the earth that made this and other books possible, send contributions to The Rainforest Action Network, 450 Sansome, Suite 700, San Francisco, CA 94111, USA, or to groups such as these in your community. Future generations and the cleaner air you breathe will thank you!

Contents

Frontispiece

This logo* was created by artist Joella Jean Mahoney for the Institute for Religion and Wholeness in Claremont, California. (That institute became a part of the Clinebell Institute in 1988.) The logo has three components that express major motifs in this workbook:

The *lamp* with its ascending flame represents the divine Spirit of love and light, justice and truth. This spirit of God, which Christians find expressed most fully in Jesus, the Christ, is the ultimate wellspring of all healing and wholeness, all growth in well being.

The *flying bird* is a lively symbol of that shalom that is true well being. It depicts the soaring hopes that people around the planet have for this blessing for their families, their people, and themselves. By flying through the flame, the bird also symbolizes continuing renewal, as the phoenix of hope rises in the midst of the fires of violence in our world. This particular bird is an Arctic tern, a creature of graceful flight and acrobatic wing feats. It has special symbolic meaning for well being because it is a lover of light. Its incredible annual 22,000-mile migration, much of it over the ocean, is enabled by its amazing inner guidance system. These birds nest in the Arctic tundra, where both males and females incubate the eggs and nurture their babies. As the Arctic autumn comes, both generations fly far south, crossing the equator as they follow the sun, often to near the Antarctic region.

The *circle* surrounding the bird and the flaming lamp is a universal symbol of wholeness found in many cultures. The opening in the base of this circle suggests that openness to the world is essential to all genuine well being.

---

*Used by permission of the Clinebell Institute.

Foreword

We live in a confused and fractured world. Although science and technology have made many strides in helping us find solutions to some of the issues and problems facing humanity, alone they are limited. Something else is needed to help us find our way to discovering wholeness and well being for our fractured world and to help us experience the abundant life that God intends for each of us. From a Christian perspective, I believe that Jesus Christ's threefold ministry of preaching, teaching, and healing provides the "something else."

Howard Clinebell's new workbook, *Anchoring Your Well Being: Christian Wholeness in a Fractured World*, is a timely written resource that will help the church rethink its understanding of health and wholeness. It will also provide the necessary tools to make the paradigm shifts to promote a holistic approach to health, wholeness, and salvation.

I first met Howard Clinebell, Ph.D., an internationally known counselor and teacher, at a workshop on well being he was conducting at a local church in Nashville. Clinebell's workshop was based on his excellent book by the same title, *Well Being*, published by Harper Collins Publishers, 1992.

Upon completing the weekly sessions of the wellness workshops, I shared with him my vision of developing a new healing model for The Upper Room's healing ministry. I related that this new model would be based on the concept of "raising healing and wholeness to a lifestyle." It would build on the biblical and theological foundation laid in the original *An Adventure in Healing and Wholeness*, developed by Dr. James K. Wagner of The Upper Room and introduced to the public in 1988.

This healing model also would explore the multidimensional nature of Christian healing and wholeness, lifestyles that promote wholeness for self and others, and ways to be a healing presence in the world. I felt this new model would fit well with the seven dimensions of life he had explored in *Well Being*.

When I asked Clinebell to consider writing the workbook for The Upper Room's new model based on *Well Being*, he expressed that he had more than enough writing commitments at that time. Because of his strong conviction toward holistic health and his intense interest in the healing of the planet earth, however, he accepted the invitation to talk further about this possible writing project. After some later conversations around this concept of raising healing and wholeness to a lifestyle, Clinebell graciously agreed to undertake the writing of this much-needed resource.

Anchoring Your Well Being: Christian Wholeness in a Fractured World is designed in two books, a participant's workbook and a leader's guide. It consists of eight sessions designed to help us raise healing and wholeness to a lifestyle. This ten-hour local congregation experience challenges participants to take a fresh look at the whole issue of healing and wholeness that encompasses all aspects of health, including the planet earth.

It is apparent from the depth of spiritual wisdom written in the pages of this unique resource that Clinebell has drawn from the wealth of his life's experience as a pastor, seminary professor, pastoral counselor, father, grandfather, and husband. The Upper Room feels privileged to provide this excellent resource for congregations and leaders as we seek to be faithful to Christ's mandate to go into the world to preach the gospel of salvation, to make disciples, and to bring healing and wholeness to our fractured world.

Clinebell believes that every organization, workplace, and congregation has a unique opportunity to support whole-person well being. He also believes that the church must play a significant role in providing the spiritual and moral leadership to help people experience wellness in all of life—wellness that promotes holistic health and brings each of the seven dimensions of one's life (spirit, body, mind, relationships, work, play, and the earth) into harmony or balance. Clinebell states, "The fundamental purpose of the Christian life is enabling people to develop lifestyles of spiritually empowered wholeness throughout their life journeys and helping create a world society where life in all its fullness is possible for all members of the human family."

Anchoring Your Well Being is a study-action resource aimed at helping participants discover new meanings for themselves as they seek to live the abundant life that Christ came to give. This healing model will challenge every Christian to think about health holistically and to understand that health is more than the absence of disease; it encompasses all aspects of life. It will help our churches and health care institutions to make the paradigm shift to approach health from a preventive perspective, rather than from a curative means only.

This model involves people in their own health care, but it does not stop there. It involves the care of their neighbors and members of their congregations. It recognizes the true role of the church as a healing community that promotes the health not only of the physical body but also of the soul and spirit within our social context. This healing model is one whose time has come.

Thank you, Howard Clinebell, for providing this wonderful and practical healing resource that will help the church make the paradigm shift to a new understanding of health, wholeness, and salvation.

— JOHN I. PENN
Director of Spiritual Formation and Healing
The Upper Room

Introduction

Getting Acquainted with
This Workbook of Christian Well Being

A heartfelt welcome to a learning experience that could increase your zest for living and loving as a Christian! And congratulations on your interest in improving your well being! I hope you will find this workbook a user-friendly guide to discovering new ways to enjoy Christian self-care for healing and wholeness. I hope and also expect that reading and reflecting on this book will be a good investment in your future health and your joy in Christian living. Whether you are using this book by yourself, with another person, or in a group, it could provide an opportunity for God and you, working together, to enhance your wholeness in important areas of your life. So welcome aboard for this journey of well being!

In case you're wondering if this wellness study-action approach really is for you, let me say that it is if one or more of these hopes are part of your personal agenda as a Christian:

• Learning new ways to use the Christian "good news" to guide and empower a healthy, spiritually centered lifestyle for you and your loved ones.

• Staying fully alive and fit in all dimensions of your life, throughout the stages of your life's journey.

• Encouraging the folks you care about to do the same.

• Contributing to the well being of your community, church, and society.

• Enabling your congregation (or other religious organization) to become an innovative center of Christian healing and wholeness for people of all ages and circumstances.

In this workbook you'll find practical ideas and tools that you can use to increase your own wellness, either on your own or with a family member or friend or in a church group. Church leaders—ordained and lay—and groups of all types in religious organizations can use the book to increase the wellness of the people they touch. As individuals and in groups, Christians can thus translate their faith into healing and wholeness on a day-by-day basis.

This wellness approach to Christian living has never been more timely than in contemporary society. Ours is a frantic, fractured, violence-plagued world. Soaring health-care needs and costs haunt many people's lives. For religious organizations, this health-care crisis opens two challenging doorways of opportunity.

On the one hand, wellness definitely is "in" for more and more Christian people, though many more clearly need to hear the message. Many know that their lifestyle choices are shaping the quality, creativity, and perhaps even the lengths of their lives, minute by minute, hour by hour, and day by day. As a result, increasing numbers of Christians are becoming open to discovering new ways to use their faith and values to enhance their general health. Many are seeing that loving God involves caring for their bodies, minds, and relationships, their community and natural environment—not just their souls more lovingly.

The second doorway of opportunity is the growing openness of many religious organizations to consider the implications of our society's health-care crisis for their ministries of healing and wellness. The need for spiritually centered preventive education is enormous, and religious organizations are the best-equipped institutions to respond to this need. Not since religious bodies pioneered in establishing the first hospitals and hospices during the Middle Ages have Christian people and institutions had such inviting opportunities to be pivotal players in providing whole-person healing and wellness.

By walking through these two doors of opportunity, faith communities can become transforming places that enable people to experience healing at all levels of their being and that teach people how to make self-care and caring for those in need central commitments.

Religious organizations have an incredible potential to help bridge the huge health-care gap in our country. Think of this reality: There are about 350,000 congregations of all faith groups in the United States. One hundred fifty million people go to some house of worship on typical days of worship. Congregations are the largest network of voluntary associations in our society. What an exciting opportunity they have at their very fingertips to bring healing and wholeness to people!

Many religious leaders have yet to see that their organizations have unprecedented power to respond to this crying need in our society. Some leaders have tunnel vision on this issue, caused by traditional understandings of a congregation's role. An updated perspective that takes into account several new factors in our society can enable congregations to offer exciting new health ministries both with their own people and with their wider communities. The factors that open wide the doors of opportunity include the following:

• a growing national consensus that something must be done to meet the unmet health needs of millions of our people;

• the awareness by many in government that their agencies and budgets cannot possibly supply either all the healing or all the prevention that is desperately needed;

• the consequent interest in rethinking the roles of voluntary organizations, including congregations, in health care;

• the openness of an increasing number of health-care professionals to recognizing spiritual and ethical issues as crucial factors in healing and health care, and the "new medicine" that emphasizes health professionals' role as teachers of self-care and integrates mainstream scientific medical theory and methods with complementary approaches to healing such as acupuncture, osteopathy, chiropractic, homeopathy, biofeedback, nutrition therapy, herbal therapy, massage therapy, and yoga.[1]

• the vitality and people power of many congregations, fueled by the commitment of their members;

• the awakening appreciation in some congregations of their advantages that can allow them to make unique contributions to wellness;

• the rich pool of experienced health-care providers and institutions in the major faith groups.[2]

Numerous congregations, religious schools, and health agencies are discovering that of all their spiritual outreach programs, those that increase wellness awaken the most widespread and appreciative responses in their communities, as well as among their own people. Furthermore, as individuals learn how to enhance their own and their family's well being, some become potential candidates for helping to organize and lead the classes and other wellness outreach programs in their congregations.

This workbook follows on the heels of another, more comprehensive book I wrote on self-care for wellness entitled *Well Being: A Personal Plan for Exploring and Enriching the Seven Dimensions of Life: Mind, Body, Spirit, Love, Work, Play, Earth* (HarperSan Francisco, 1992). It was described by one reviewer as "a cornucopia of wellness ideas, inventories, exercises, and guided imaging tools." It is a mini library of things you can do to enhance your overall health. It will deepen and broaden the pool from which you draw your lifestyle enhancement tools. That book elaborates on most of the major points in this book. It thus provides resources for taking steps toward greater wholeness. It's to your advantage to have both books at your fingertips to use on a daily basis, if you choose. But you do not need the book *Well Being* in order to use this workbook. Each can be used alone, if you choose.

I'm pleased that The Upper Room's ministry of Spiritual Formation and Healing is sponsoring what is called the Adventure II program and that both *Well Being* and this book are texts for this training program in holistic well being. The challenging theme of this program is "Raising Whole-Person Wellness to a Christian Lifestyle." The texts for the previous Adventure I program, authored by James K. Wagner, were *An Adventure in Healing and Wholeness: The Healing Ministry of Christ in the Church Today* (Upper Room Books, 1991) and *Blessed to Be a Blessing: How to Have an Intentional Healing Ministry in Your Church* (Upper Room Books, 1980).

These books provide an understanding of biblical modes of physical, mental, spiritual, and relationship healing. They discuss how congregations can hold healing services using traditional methods such as praying for the sick, laying on of hands, anointing with oil, and the sacrament of Holy Communion.[3] Both these traditional healing methods and contemporary approaches are valuable for Christians today. This workbook and *Well Being* don't discuss healing approaches from the New Testament because these are covered well in the Adventure I texts. Adventure II builds on that foundation.[4]

Overview

This workbook supplies ideas and methods for persons who wish to enhance the well being of themselves and others in one or more of the seven dimensions of life—spirit, mind, body, relationships, work, play, and the earth. It also focuses on how to sustain wellness during the crises and losses of life. The eight sessions constitute a basic guide for developing your Christian self-care plan—a plan that includes contributing to a healthier society on a healthier planet. An accompanying leader's guide gives suggestions for developing well being programs in congregations and other religious settings, using the resources described in this workbook.

If you decide to start a wellness program in your setting, the leader's guide provides suggestions for doing so effectively. It offers instructions for leading wellness seminars; religious education classes; wellness weeks; renewal retreats; family camps; training and growth groups; and youth, singles, and couples groups. One could use the guide in the practice of pastoral care and counseling or in congregations, religious schools, chaplaincies, church hospitals, agencies, and other religious settings. It is a kind of road map for use by those who have profited from this workbook and are inspired to make such experiences available more widely.

For Whom Is This Workbook Written?

This book is for any of the following:
- church members, clergy, and Christian educators;
- chaplains in all types of health and human service agencies;
- seminary teachers and students;
- denominational and ecumenical leaders;
- pastoral counselors and counseling center staff persons;
- staff members and volunteers on lay caring teams in congregations, hospices, and hospitals;
- health professionals interested in exploring the spiritual and ethical dimensions of whole-person healing and health and leading wellness programs in their congregations.[5]

Most of the ideas and methods in this workbook were developed and tested over more than four decades as I sought to empower clients, parishioners, seminary students, clergy, and other workshop participants to experience more of the grace-full gifts of God's healing and wholeness. The book contains insights and techniques I have used over the years. These include numerous strategies that also have proved useful in my personal struggles to increase my self-care in my often too-busy life. (Reluctantly, I need to admit that I've been better at preaching than practicing some of the more demanding self-care recommendations in these pages.)

In both texts, you'll discover the author's passion for helping people discover the joys of higher-level wellness. T. S. Eliot says somewhere in his writings, "Old men should be explorers." Although I don't yet feel old, despite my ripe chronological age, this book is a journal from my exploring. I hope that it will become a guidebook for you as you walk the trail of adventure into improved self-care and enhanced health!

How Can You Derive Maximum Wellness from This Book?

Here are some recommendations for using this book:

1. *Take time to use all three types of healing, problem-solving, growth-producing methods you'll encounter:* (a) the left-brain, self-help approaches such as the well being checkups and the practical concepts you find useful; (b) the right-brain, intuitive, nonverbal, experiential exercises such as the guided imaging meditations; (c) the action-reflection approaches that involve doing healthful things and then learning from these by reflecting on your experiences. Each of these involves using different parts of your mind that can enable learning and growth in different ways. When you come to an experiential learning exercise, please resist the temptation to skip it. If you prefer to read a whole chapter at once, make a date with yourself in the book's margin, noting when you'll come back and try the exercise. The well being checkups can be very helpful to you in two ways. They offer quick self-evaluations in each area of your living. They also provide a variety of action-options—things you can do to enhance your well being in areas where you discover that is needed.

2. *Keep a self-care journal.* Jot down in a notebook ideas that grab you and/or scribble in the margins of this workbook your questions and thoughts, agreements and disagreements, and your plans for taking action. Underline or highlight relevant or provocative ideas about which you want to think further and on which you might take some action. The more you interact with ideas in the texts, the more likely it is that they will come alive for you and result in long-term lifestyle improvements.

3. *Create a self-care plan to enhance your well being.* As you work with each session, make tentative plans concerning what you'll

do to enhance your well being in that particular area. Add to your plan bit by bit as you go along. Such an incremental change strategy often works for people who bog down when they try to make big changes in their habits all at once. It's also important to begin collecting the benefits of changes by implementing small, realistic parts of your plan *that you really want* to make happen. This will help you create some momentum in moving toward your chosen self-care objectives. You'll find instructions on this process at the end of each session.

4. If you began using this book alone, consider inviting one or more family members or friends to join you as "wellness partners" in using it. This increases the probability that each of you will follow through and find more healing and well being together. If you have come across this book on your own, talk to someone who might be interested in trying its wellness program. Or come up with a strategy to use the book in your congregation, school, agency, or workplace.

5. *Let this workbook also become a playbook for you.* Use it playfully and with a sense of humor. You'll probably learn more, remember what you learn longer, and use it to greater purpose if you take wellness learning seriously but not solemnly. Your playful inner child will love it if you regularly give her or him times to play. Play is an important form of self-care that can also be caring for and with others. Whatever you do, avoid sinking into the "no pain, no gain" swamp in which many people's health-care intentions become hopelessly mired down. Don't confuse the essential commitment and self-discipline of growth with "if it doesn't hurt it can't really be good for me."

You'll find suggestions and resources for playfulness in Session 6 of this book and lots more in Chapter 7 of *Well Being*. There is also what I hope is a smile-awakening supply of cartoons, bumper stickers, and one liners sprinkled throughout that book. Enjoy!

6. *Use affirmations to help you implement what you decide to do to enhance your self-care for wellness.* Some folks find it helpful to post visual reminder notes in prominent places (like the bathroom mirror, refrigerator, or car visor), stating in positive terms what they will do that day to increase their health-care benefits in one or more of the seven dimensions of life. Repeating these to oneself at the beginning of and during the day may increase the likelihood that health-enhancing actions that are easy to neglect or postpone "until tomorrow" will be done regularly. It is important to keep the affirmations short, simple, positive, and spiritually focused. Examples: "Give my body, mind, and spirit a health gift—a brief, brisk lunchtime walk." "Enjoy loving and energizing my whole self by breathing more deeply, avoiding junk food, giving myself a spiritual minivacation by meditating or praying." "Improve family warmth (and reduce conflicts) by limiting criticisms and expressing more appreciation."

7. *Pray without ceasing as you use this book.* Of course I don't mean mumbling prayers while you're reading and doing the program. What I have in mind is what I believe Paul meant when he wrote these words. It is an attitude characterized by a joyful and thankful awareness of the presence of the loving God who is the source of all healing, all grace, and all growth. Bathe both your struggling toward wellness and your health-care failures and accomplishments in the healing energy of that divine Spirit. Do this by opening your windows of spiritual awareness. This will baptize the whole experience with joy and blessing.

A few moments of prayerful meditation at the beginning and again at the end of sessions can help keep these windows of awareness wide open for you and for those people who may be sharing this adventure with you.

What Are Potential Rewards of Participating in Well Being Sessions?

Good question! Here are some benefits people have reported receiving. I suggest that you put a check mark in front of the ones that seem important to you. Learning:

❏ 1. Self-care methods for living a healthy, loving, Christian lifestyle.

❏ 2. Strategies for outwitting the busyness syndrome and overcoming the two big R's (resistance and rationalization) that sabotage your good intentions to do what you know you *need* to do to improve your well being.

❏ 3. Practical insights about enlivening your spiritual and ethical life as a Christian so that they energize and guide your lifestyle.

❏ 4. Ways to increase the healthy nutrition, exercise, and rest that your body needs for its well being.

❏ 5. Techniques for using your intelligence and creativity for healing your body and enjoying your mind more.

❏ 6. New ways to cope with crises, losses, and life transitions so as to cope better and even use these as opportunities to grow.

❏ 7. Strategies to reawaken zest in your work and prevent burnout by balancing work with playfulness.

❏ 8. Techniques for nurturing mutual esteem, love, and outreach to others so that Christian *self-care becomes self-other care.*

❏ 9. Ways to stretch your horizons and heal yourself by working with others in healing a wounded planet and the injustice and violence in the institutions of your own community.

❏ 10. Strategies for sharing wellness insights and methods with others through study-action classes, retreats, and workshops in your congregation.

It's heartwarming to express my thanks to those who gave valuable input in the writing of this workbook. John Penn, director of The Spiritual Formation and Healing programs at the Upper Room, and George Donigian, acquisitions editor of Upper Room Books, gave useful guidance in the entire writing process. Joyce Buekers of Phoenix shared important insights, as well as the course outlines she created while using the book *Well Being* in teaching a variety of workshops in various congregations and in ecumenical settings. Her contagious enthusiasm for developing innovative wellness programs in religious and health-care institutions was an invaluable contribution.

I'm also grateful to the clergy who asked for guidance in developing well being programs in their congregations and subsequently shared their experiences in leading these groups. They told me what they had learned from the problems they encountered and their excitement in discovering how to become better channels of God's healing and wholeness. (I welcome feedback about your experiences in using this workbook and *Well Being*.)

I affirm the prayerful hope for his readers expressed so well by James Wagner in an Adventure I text: "My prayer for you is that the Holy Spirit will have some pleasant and life-enhancing surprises for you."[6] In a similar vein, I hope and also expect that the Lord will give you challenging, joyful surprises as you use this workbook. May this experience be an adventure for you too!

Howard Clinebell
2990 Kenmore Place
Santa Barbara, CA 93105-USA
Fax: 805-687-7777
E-mail: ClinebellH@aol.com

Walking the Sevenfold Path of Christian Well Being

Note: In-depth discussions of topics that particularly interest you can be found readily in the other text *Well Being*. If your study time is too limited to cover everything offered in this session, delete the items marked with double asterisks (**).

A Biblical Perspective

 The Gospel according to John, the most lyrical version of the Christian good news, describes a healing miracle in which Jesus restores a blind man's sight. Then Jesus draws a parallel with another type of blindness that deeply concerned him—spiritual blindness. In the context of a discussion of shepherding, Jesus identifies himself as the good shepherd who cares lovingly for his sheep. Jesus highlights the purpose of his ministry: "I came that they may have life, and have it abundantly" (John 10:10).

The New English Bible translates this Greek phrase as "life . . . in all its fullness." The abundant life or life in all its fullness is what is called spiritually empowered "well being," "wholeness," or "wellness" in the contemporary language of this workbook. The fundamental purpose of the Christian life is to enable people to develop lifestyles of spiritually empowered wholeness throughout their life journeys and to help create a society in which life in all its fullness is possible for all members of the human family.

Self-Care/Health Care in Stormy Seas

 In the days of the tall ships, sailors had to learn a lifesaving lesson early in their careers. One firm rule prevailed. Whenever sailors went aloft to change the sails, they had to do whatever was required with only one hand and arm. The other hand was reserved for themselves, so they could hold on while doing their tasks. One arm for the ship. One arm for themselves. When this rule was ignored, particularly in turbulent weather, the consequences could be disastrous. The sailors jeopardized not only their own lives but also the morale of their shipmates.

Are you or someone you love in stormy seas now? If so, it's well to remember that self-care is a key to coping constructively with life's unwelcome storms. Self-caring lifestyles are desperately needed, though often neglected, in these turbulent times of chaotic social change, painful economic crises, widespread violence, and natural and unnatural disasters. Times like ours are periods of extreme stress when people need to remember to keep "one arm for self-care." Stress-rooted illnesses, family burn-up, and work burnout soar whenever this strategy for living is forgotten.

Equally important, the most effective way to prepare for pressure-cooker times is simply to learn better self-care before they happen. On the positive side, other benefits can flow from making self-care for wellness your

Christian lifestyle. These benefits go far beyond survival. Enhancing your self-care is the most direct path to developing a healthier lifestyle that makes possible a life that is rewarding, joyful, and filled with meaningful service to others.

Do you ever feel in your day-to-day life as though you are trying to sail in stormy seas without a compass and a tiller? If so, following the one-arm-for-self-care principle is both enlightened and prudent health care. During severe crises and losses when you feel as though you're struggling to stay afloat, this guiding principle will increase your ability to cope, help save your health, and enable you to grow in these dark times.

Naming Yourself and Your Hopes

Use crayons or colored pencils to print your favorite name—the one you like to be called by friends—on a three-by-five index card. (Note: Whenever a slash mark (/) appears, it means to pause and take time to do what has been described.) / Think about what you'd like to gain in this experience for your well being. Then, below your name, quickly sketch a symbol that expresses these personal hopes. This isn't an art class, so don't worry about how it looks. Just relax and let your imagination flow through your fingers.[1] /

If you're doing this well being series solo, take a few minutes to jot down in the margins of this workbook, or in your journal, notes about things you want to remember or about which you want to think. Use your name card as a bookmark in this workbook. It will remind you where you hope to go on this study-action trip.

If you're working with a partner or in a group, tell each other what your name and symbol means to you. Say one or two sentences that express your hopes for this adventure in well being. / Plan to bring your name card to subsequent sessions.

Major Objectives and Themes

In this session you will have the opportunity to learn the following:
- A foundational understanding of the overall meaning of Christian well being.
- Key definitions and concepts that will be useful throughout this workbook.
- Two visual symbols and a quick overview of the seven dimensions of your well being.
- Tips for using guided meditations, a valuable self-caring method that combines deep relaxation and active imaging to nurture your well being.
- Suggestions for starting a self-care plan to fit your particular lifestyle and health needs.
- Some enthusiasm about the challenges and rewards that are available to you in this study-action program.

What Do Key Words Mean?

Well being, *wholeness*, and *wellness* are used more or less interchangeably in these pages. They all mean whole-person health.[2] This involves balanced, mutually enhancing interplay among your mind, body, and spirit; between your work and play; and in your key relationships with other people and your community; with plants and animals in the natural world; and, most important of all, with God. Well being is comparable to light. Rather than being merely the absence of darkness, light is the presence of energy moving at certain frequencies that our eyes can see.

In a parallel way, robust health is not just the absence of major sickness but is the presence of the energy of aliveness in all dimensions of people's lives. To have well being involves continuing to discover and develop your unused, God-given gifts and possibilities through each of the unfolding stages of your life.

Let's look more closely at the meaning of health. The charter of the United Nations' World Health Organization has this definition: "Health is a state of complete physical, mental, and social well being and not merely the absence of disease or infirmity." Although the positive, whole-person-in-society thrust of this definition is consistent with what well being means, the word *complete* feels unrealistic, even utopian. Human health and well being never seem to be complete. Like sickness, they're always a matter of degree.

I like Rene Dubos's nonperfectionistic description of health because it rings true in the experience of most people: "A method of living which enables imperfect persons to achieve a rewarding and not too painful existence while they cope with a very imperfect world."[3]

What is the heart of well being? You have well being to the degree that the center of your life is integrated and energized by two things—healthy love and healthy spirituality (including healthy morality). Having these at the center of your life enhances the well being of all the dimensions of your life and relationships. These are the channels by which your well being intertwines with and reinforces the well being of the important people in your life and the well being of your community and world. In Session 2, we'll look closely at what healthy or health-nurturing love and spirituality mean.

Wellness is a popular term today for good reasons. Although I'll use it often, the word does have one limitation. Many people develop a high degree of well being in spite of, or perhaps because of, their lacking robust health. Perhaps someone you know has multiple health problems, disabilities, or an age-related decline in wellness. Yet this person expresses lots of healing love and spirituality in the way he or she lives. Such folks make it clear that well being isn't the absence of health problems or brokenness.

Well being is what you choose, at the center of your life, to do with these frustrating conditions.

Many people with major health problems have impressive degrees of mental, spiritual, and relationship well being. So don't let health limitations rob you of reality-based hope about increasing your well being in many areas of your life. Healthy love and spirituality at the core of your being are powerful resources for learning how to use brokenness as a stimulus for enhancing your life and lifestyle.[4]

Biblical Roots

As you learn how to enhance your wellness as a Christian, it's helpful to know that the roots of concern for healing and wholeness are deep in our rich religious heritage. The main themes of love-centered wellness are embedded in the Bible's wisdom. From this heritage you can derive time-tested insights and resources for use in today's high-tech world.

**Pause now and jot down in the spaces below two or three biblical verses or stories that emphasize themes such as healing, wholeness, and the remarkable capacities of us humans to develop new strengths throughout our lives. /

_____

_____

_____

_____

_____

_____

_____

_____

_____

_____

_____

_____

_____

Now, if you're working with a partner or group, together list all the passages on newsprint. / Use the following biblical insights and stories to compare with and supplement your list. In this way, you'll strengthen your biblical understanding of the nature of Christian lifestyles that foster healing and wellness.

Biblical insights emphasize again and again the remarkable God-given potentialities we human beings have. Jesus' Bible, the Hebrew Scriptures, offers a clear vision of the incredible potentialities of humans and the challenge to develop these as fully as possible. For example, the first creation story in Genesis pictures our species as being created in God's image (Gen.1:27). This is a ringing affirmation of humans' creative gifts and self-transcending possibilities.

In the same vein, the psalmist affirms that humans are created "a little lower than God" (Ps. 8:5). Discovering and developing the divine image by actualizing more of the hidden riches of our full personhood is the task of well being. Jesus' parable of the talents (Matt. 25:14-30) highlights the importance of discovering, developing, and using in responsible and socially constructive ways a person's God-given capacities and talents.

Paul's challenge to the young Timothy was "to stir into flame the gift of God which is within you. . . . For the spirit that God gave us is . . . one to inspire strength, love, and self-discipline" (2 Tim. 1:6-7, NEB). J. B. Phillips' paraphrase of Romans 8:19 communicates the conviction that the power of the spiritual universe is on the side of our fulfilling our potentialities for wholeness: "The whole creation is on tiptoe to see the wonderful sight of the sons [and daughters] of God coming into their own."

The whole-person nature of well being, which involves all dimensions of our lives, is grounded in biblical wisdom. Jesus fed the hungry, encouraged people with powerful teaching stories, quieted people's fears, and challenged the greedy exploiters who were cheating people by demanding exorbitant prices for what they needed for worship. Jesus' healing was holistic in that he healed persons suffering from all types of illnesses—physical, mental, emotional, and interpersonal, as well as spiritual. In these ways he expressed God's intentions in practice, showing that the divine purpose is that healing and health are the birthrights of all God's family.

But Jesus did much more than bring healing to broken people and teach and preach life in all its fullness. He *lived* life in all its fullness, thus embodying well being in who he was. His life demonstrates the incredible potentialities of humans empowered by God. In him one meets a person who is love-filled and growing—a fully alive person who makes visible God's dream of wholeness for all human beings. Jesus' transforming, healing aliveness somehow transcends the centuries. Paul Tillich described this transforming presence as the "new being." Christians who participate in this new being find power and direction for their life journey toward "the full stature of Christ" (Eph. 4:13, NEB). They discover how to develop life in all its fullness.

The Bible understands well being as a growth process. A good person "is like a tree planted by streams of water, that yields its fruit in its season" (Ps. 1:3, RSV). The process toward wholeness is nurtured in relationships where tough, healing love and acceptance are integrated with honest, caring confrontation. As Ephesians states this: "Let us speak the truth in love; so shall we fully grow up into Christ" (4:15, NEB).

The Bible is also clear that well being involves self-investment in the healing and wholeness of others: "For those who would want to save their life will lose it, and those who lose their life for my sake will find it" (Matt. 16:25). Translated into modern terms, if you narcissistically horde the wholeness you have developed, it will atrophy. If you invest yourself in sharing your wholeness with others in need of caring and healing, your own wholeness will blossom.

The biblical view of people is much more reality-based than that of the so-called "positive thinkers" in the fields of religion and psychology. Biblical wisdom is aware both of our profound brokenness and propensity for destructiveness, and of our remarkable capacity for life in all its fullness. We have a deep need for developing the image of God within us, yet we often ingeniously resist and sabotage our own growth and that of others. We possess incredible skills in sabotaging our own wellness and resist doing the things that we know are healthy for us. Conflicts in our deeper minds often paralyze our conscious intentions to live in healthy ways.

Paul wrote to the Christians in Rome: "For even though the desire to do good is in me, I am not able to do it. . . . instead, I do the evil that I do not want to do" (Rom. 7:18-19, TEV). The story of the "fall" from the innocence of the garden of Eden (Genesis 3) is a symbolic way of recognizing that we are estranged from our potential wholeness and alienated from life in all its fullness, from God's creation, and from our intimate bonding with God.

Sin is the traditional religious word for describing this. Whether we call resistance to well being sin, sickness, brokenness, or alienation doesn't really matter. What *does* matter is that any effective approach to human healing and wellness *must* take brokenness and evil seriously. Superficial optimism undercuts well being by ignoring the power, complexity, and omnipresence of the things in us and our world that block our well being.

In the thought world of the Bible, sin and brokenness are forces in individuals, family systems, and society. Those of us who work therapeutically with families often see how patterns of brokenness are transmitted in family systems from one generation to the next. This awareness was anticipated in the biblical understanding that the "sins of the fathers" (and mothers) continue to impact their children's and grandchildren's wholeness.

The biblical writers were keenly aware that our estrangement from ourselves and other people is rooted in our estrangement from God's life-giving love, and that healing comes from reconnecting with that love. They also knew that while the potential for wholeness is a gift of God, it often takes lots of hard work, discipline, and sacrifice to develop and receive this gift fully. This reality-based understanding of sin, evil, and brokenness is communicated by biblical images of taking up one's cross (Matt. 16:24), dying and being born again (John 3:3), and the weeds in the wheat field (Matt. 13:24-30).

New Testament images of rebirth and resurrection are joyful affirmations of the possibility of conversion or radical transformation in human life. As most of us know from experience, the journey toward new life often feels like a series of painful deaths and rebirths. The rebirth to life in all its fullness opens people to new dimensions of themselves, other people, and God. But this resurrection often takes place only after painful realities produce a surrendering of the grandiose self-centeredness that shuts people off from others, life, and God.

Still, Jesus expresses the struggle and

eventual joy of the process in this birthing image: "You will be sorrowful, but your sorrow will turn to joy. When a woman is in travail she has sorrow . . . ; but when she is delivered of the child, she no longer remembers the anguish, for joy that a child is born into the world" (John 16:20-21, RSV).[5] Easter affirms the joyous possibility and power of spiritual transformation.

Transformations in humans occur when persons experience two qualities in relationships—honest confrontation and accepting love. When someone cares enough to "speak the truth in love," to use the apostle Paul's words (Eph. 4:15), we humans may experience a self-confrontation that causes us to take a step toward greater well being. In such times, the incredible resources for growth in people transcend the human resistances to growing toward wholeness. Brokenness is transformed by the healing power of God's grace, often experienced through a transforming human relationship. Despair is transformed by a deeper hope, sin by healing reconciliation, and judgment by God's love and grace.

Healing of human brokenness is a dominant theme in the four Gospels. The terms *salvation* and *healing* are interlaced throughout the Bible, salvation being understood as a kind of ultimate healing that takes place in the transformed age of wholeness already beginning to dawn within and among us. The growth parables of Jesus—the mustard seed's growth (Matt. 13:31-32), the women's putting yeast in bread dough (Matt. 13:33), the farmer' sowing seeds (Matt. 13:3-8)—describe the process by which the new age is coming.

The good news is that all of us human beings are invited to take part as cocreators in the process by which the new age is coming "on earth as it is in heaven" (Matt. 6:10). Fortunately Hebrew-Christian heritages maintain a persistent emphasis, in spite of recurring religious exclusiveness, that we all are members of one family—the human family—with one divine Parent (see Acts 17:25).

The vision of God's new age is of whole persons in loving communities on a whole planet. In this time of concern about planet-wide violence and ecological holocaust, such a spiritually empowered vision of personal and global healing can help us work together for a healthy planet!

The understanding of the good life in the well being approach is in harmony with the Bible's view that wellness involves both intentionality and action. Jesus' statements to those seeking healing frequently includes action imperatives such as "Pick up your bed and walk!" "Get into the pool!" "Go and sin no more." Even though wellness is a gift of God's loving grace, it requires committed effort and self-discipline on our part in order for the closed doors in ourselves to open so that we can receive the gift. New Testament images that point to this reality include taking up one's cross (Matt. 16:24) and the narrow gate and straight road that leads to the new age of God's justice, compassion, caring, and community.

Healing often is the first essential step on the journey toward increased well being. Here too our Christian roots go deep: "Jesus went throughout Galilee, teaching in their synagogues and proclaiming the good news of the kingdom and curing every disease and every sickness among the people" (Matt. 4:23). The New Testament Greek word for salvation (*sozo*) also means "to heal" and "to make whole" (see Matt. 9:20-22). Nearly 20 percent of the Gospels are stories of Jesus' healing miracles. His critics believed that he spent too much time with the sick, the burdened, and the socially rejected. But his allocation of time to such people and his story of the one lost sheep (Matt. 18:12-14) made his priorities quite clear. So did these words to his critics: "Those who are well have no need of a physician, but those who are sick" (Mark 2:17).

Jesus sent his followers out to heal and to teach, as well as baptize, giving them this amazing promise: "I tell you, the one who believes in me will also do the works I do and, in fact, will do greater works than these" (John 14:12).

The New Testament envisions the church as a center for healing, liberation, growth, and the equipping of Christians for their mission in the world. The church is the *people of God* (2 Cor. 6:16), a caring community united by a covenant with God. It is the *body of Christ* (Rom. 12:4-5; 1 Cor. 10:17), a dynamic spiritual organism in which each member has unique gifts to be used for ministering to the world. The church also is the *community of the Holy Spirit* (Acts 10:44-47), a healing redemptive community through which the living Spirit can work in a very needy world.[6] By developing innovative, spiritually centered well being programs, congregations, religious schools, and organizations can respond to the healing and growth needs of countless people. By so doing, they will renew the New Testament's vision of the church as a place where people discover new dimensions of life in all its fullness at each stage and circumstance of life.

 **Awareness Exercise: Pause and reflect on your experiences in your church. When was it most healing and wholeness-nurturing for you? When could it have fulfilled this mission more effectively in your experience? How could it respond more fully to the present needs of people for healing and growth? Jot your responses in the space below.

———————————————————————

———————————————————————

———————————————————————

———————————————————————

———————————————————————

———————————————————————

———————————————————————

———————————————————————

———————————————————————

———————————————————————

———————————————————————

Two Images of Spiritually Centered Well Being

We humans are wondrously complex creatures with multidimensional lives. Every aspect of human life influences all the others in both sickness and in health. If you and I are to increase our present level of health on an ongoing basis, we need to understand the major dimensions of everyone's life, to see how each area influences all the others, and how they together create the pattern of living that is our lifestyle.

The holistic well being approach identifies seven dimensions that need intentional self-care for optimal healing and wholeness. These are spirit, mind, body, relationships, work, play, and the earth. "Earth" refers both to the social world of the community and society in which we live as well as the natural world that is in us as we are in it. The well being of each of these life dimensions is of particular importance to Christians because concern for all of them is rooted in our faith's biblical understanding of the good life. More about these biblical roots appears in the next session.

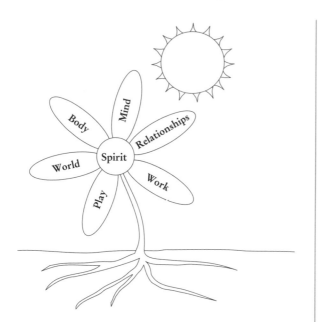

Like a flower, your well being is a living, growing, ever-changing organic process that involves all aspects of your life and your social and natural environments. Healthy, loving spirituality is the integrating center of the flower. Such spirituality holds together all the well being "petals" and gives them organic unity and life. The flower's center provides the channels by which all the petals are nourished. It's also where the flower's gifts to the future grow—the seeds of a new generation of flowers. The flower's roots go deep, drawing nutrients from the soil of our shared humanity. Life-giving oxygen is produced by the flower's leaves.

Above the flower is the sun, a symbol of God's ever-present love that Christians experience in Jesus the Christ. Like all life, well being is totally solar-powered. This love is the energy of healing and wholeness. It empowers the flower to grow, stay beautiful and healthy, and, in due time, produce seeds. Like the flower, well being has its seasons and its cycles of birth, life, death, and rebirth. In the ongoing cycle of continuing creation, there are times of seed-planting and germination, blossoming and seed-making,

withering and dying, and returning to enrich the earth in preparation for the next generation.

I'm grateful to Nelle Morton, pioneer feminist theologian, educator, and friend for suggesting another image. After a spirited discussion of the flower image of wholeness, Nelle sketched this symbol for me.

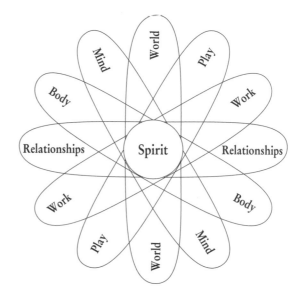

I find lots of energy in her image of well being. She also sent these insightful comments that reflect her personal philosophy and her wisdom as an educator: "Wholeness is never static, always in ferment and growth. Since we live in a global community and are rapidly emerging into a cosmic mind, could we not think of spirit as that flow of energy that brings us and the other six aspects of wholeness into dynamic relationship with one another and with the whole—ever in movement, in tension, interactive, interconnected and interdependent, yet powerfully present?"[7]

In her drawing, as in real life, every dimension of people's lives and health, or lack of health, touches all the others. Rather than being just another aspect of life, spirituality is the unifying center formed by the convergence of the other dimensions, the unifying connection of all the mundane, often grubby aspects of everyday life. Try now to envision the drawing in three dimensions. See the spiritual core as the axle of a wheel on which the whole meaning of one's life turns.

Does Nelle's image remind you of a drawing of an atom in an old physics book? This seems appropriate. Although atoms collectively constitute what appears to be "solid" matter, they're actually dynamic energy fields. They are constantly moving power in dynamic interaction with other energy fields. What an apt image for us human beings with all our powerful possibilities and God-given potentials for aliveness and wholeness!

 **Exercise: So that you will have a visual motif of the seven dimensions of well being, make a sizable copy of Nelle Morton's sketch or draw a sketch on a three-by-five card. You can put your sketch on your mirror so that you will see it as you walk the sevenfold path of well being.

An Idea Whose Time Has Come

The flowering interest in whole-person health is part of a growing groundswell in contemporary society. It represents the beginning of profound changes in many of the sciences, including subatomic physics and biology, the psychosocial sciences, and the healing disciplines, including many psychotherapies. These changes move away from a compartmentalized, highly individualistic view of persons. They affirm a systems-oriented, ecological understanding that all things are interrelated, within and among human beings and their total human, cultural, and natural environments.

This holistic approach provides a new perspective for understanding our experiences of sickness and health as functions of the interaction of all aspects of our lives. The seven dimensions, symbolized by the two images on page 24, are not really separate. They are interdependent facets of whole persons in all their relationships and in their particular social, natural, and historical settings.

A Preview of the Seven Dimensions

Well being is enhanced by balancing better self-care in all dimensions of life and health. The following summary describes these crucial areas of everyone's life. You'll have opportunities to explore each of these facets in more depth in subsequent sessions.

1. *Spiritual Well Being:* This dimension is at the heart of all well being in the Christian view of wholeness. The meanings that give your life some purpose in the midst of loss, the values that guide your choices a thousand times each day, the quality of your relationship with God—all these have a subtle but pervasive influence on all other dimensions of your well being. Healthy religious beliefs, practices, values, and institutions energize and enrich all aspects of our lives. Unhealthy religious beliefs, practices, values, and institutions do precisely the opposite. Spiritual well being is at the core of the Bible's understanding of the good life.

2. *Mental Well Being:* The more psychologists learn about the brain and the mind, the clearer it becomes that most people develop only a small part of their intellectual, problem-solving, creative, and productive capacities, as well as their potential for serving others. In our high-tech information age of mind-boggling social change, lifelong learning, growing, and creativity are increasingly important keys to mental well being. Your mind and your body are profoundly interdependent in both health and sickness. How you use your mind can help keep you well or make you more vulnerable

to illness. Jesus said: "You will know the truth, and the truth will make you free" (John 8:32). Learning liberating truth about life and God is what enables people to live life in all its fullness with deeper understanding.

3. *Physical Well Being:* A healthy physical body is energized, effective in its functioning, sensually alive and satisfying, relatively pain-free, and supportive of mental and spiritual well being. Self-care that nurtures physical well being provides a firm foundation on which to build a Christian wellness lifestyle. The New Testament makes it clear that the well being of our bodies cannot be separated from that of our minds and spirits, although many people develop spiritual depth by transcending physical sicknesses and disabilities. Jesus demonstrated his concern for physical well being when he fed the hungry crowd and served as a healing channel for God's love in the lives of people suffering from a wide variety of bodily illness and disabilities.

4. *Relationship Well Being:* No other factor is more important to our healing and general wellness than the quality of our mutual network of caring people found in families and friends. Because we humans by our genetic endowment are a species characterized by interpersonal bonding, our well being is inescapably rooted in the quality of our relationships. Christianity, like Judaism and Islam, is a relationship-oriented religion. It is not surprising, therefore, that well being in relationships is a dominant motif throughout the Bible.

Wholeness is understood as being nurtured in spiritually empowered communities of mutual love. Both the Hebrew word *shalom* and the New Testament Greek word for the Christian church *koinonia* describe interpersonal communities of love, healing, and wholeness. When giving and receiving healthy love is in short supply in people's lives, their total well being suffers. This is

why, as noted above, healthy self-care is always self-other care.

5. *Work Well Being:* Your work can be like a spring of cool, pure water on a hot, humid day. It can help satisfy the universal human thirst for self-worth, accomplishment, and sense of purpose in life. But work also can be like water from a polluted cistern of conflict, boredom, stress, and frustration. To drink that water regularly poisons one's lifestyle. What is the Christian's key to fostering well being in work and preventing burnout? Traditional religious language describes it as having a sense of vocation, an awareness that your work fulfills some purpose in God's intentions for you, your family, and your community. The religious significance of worthwhile work is underlined by these words from the wisdom literature of the Bible: "Commit your work to the LORD, and your plans will be established" (Prov. 16:3).

6. *Play Well Being:* Work and play are linked because both involve the self-investment of your most precious and limited resource: time. Learning how to balance and blend productive work with revitalizing recreation can increase the well being of both working and playing. The healing, health-giving energy of laughter and playfulness has been recognized since ancient times. Consider this bit of healthy wisdom from the Hebrew Scriptures: "A cheerful heart is a good medicine, but a downcast spirit dries up the bones" (Prov. 17:22). Current psychological and medical research confirms the validity of this ancient saying. Laughing at ourselves and with one another is good for our well being.

7. *Well Being of Our World:* This crucial aspect of a Christian lifestyle includes two interrelated subdimensions. The first is to make our lifestyles more earth-caring, thus protecting the health of God's continuing creation around us. Our personal health and that of those we love is profoundly dependent on the wellness of the natural environment in

which we live, day by day. Life in all its fullness will be possible in the future only if we understand that Christian wellness must include protecting the wellness of God's earth. The healing of the biosphere, that amazing network of life upon which our well being ultimately depends, is an inescapable responsibility for you and me as Christians. It is also an unprecedented Christian opportunity, undergirded by the Bible's view that humans have a sacred responsibility to care for all of God's creation.

The second essential part of caring for our world's well being is to do all that we can as Christians to ensure that the impact of our society's institutions on people leads to greater well being for all. Our work settings, churches, health care institutions, labor unions, social and service agencies, and the political and economic structures of our society shape our level of wellness every day in countless ways for better or, as is often the case, for worse. God calls us as Christians to challenge and help change these institutions.

The Bible's wisdom undergirds the concern for the health of society and its institutions. The Hebrew prophets of the eighth century B.C. proclaimed a passionate caring for the prevention and healing of the massive brokenness produced by oppressive institutions. Their teachings powerfully influenced Jesus' spiritual heritage. Christian concern for well being must start with individuals. But if it stops there, it quits much too soon—even for the ultimate well being of individuals.

 **Awareness/Personal Reflection Exercise: In light of what you have read up to this point, take a few minutes to note in the space below your personal questions and insights about how the seven dimensions relate to your life as a Christian. If you are working with a wellness partner or group, share your insights with one another.

_____

_____

_____

_____

_____

_____

_____

_____

What Is a Christian Well Being Lifestyle?

To understand the goal toward which these sessions can help you move, here is an overview of some characteristics of a Christian well being lifestyle. I suggest that you make notes in the margins about each characteristic.

• A Christian well being lifestyle involves choosing to live intentionally, guided by a New Testament-based understanding of what is good, true, and important in life. Intentionality means choosing to step into the future in a constructive manner as this is illuminated by Christian ethics. Christianity is much more than a way of believing. It is also a way of being and doing, a way of taking action to move into the immediate future in a way that fosters life in all its fullness for yourself, others, and your community and world.[8]

• A well being lifestyle is love-motivated and love-powered. Loving is not only the path to greater wellness but also the power to walk that path! Well being is having a love affair with life—your own sometimes crummy and sometimes joyful life in this little bit of eternity in which you're living, your life with its strange mixture of turmoil and peace, agony and ecstasy. Well being also is having a love affair with God, the Source of all life with its countless good gifts. Thomas Merton, the Trappist mystic, once used this apt phrase: "the wholeness of love."[9] Love is the heart of wholeness; it is the moving power of a healthy lifestyle. Without love, there can be no well being. The hallmark of a well being lifestyle is the reciprocal giving and receiving of love in relationships.

• A well being lifestyle involves actively doing things that will help prevent illness and nurture good health. This requires an investment of time each day in caring for yourself in one or more of the seven dimensions of your life that have been shortchanged healthwise. It's terribly tempting, of course, to take good health for granted—as long as it stays that way.

I remember hearing of a sign on a rural road: "When this sign is under water, the road is impassable"! Would you agree that self-care often is like that? It's difficult to appreciate what a treasure good health is or to get motivated to take care of ourselves until we hit a health crisis such as a heart attack. Treating the consequences of prolonged self-neglect usually has a high cost in lost time, lost vitality, frustration, and pain, as well as money. Regular preventive health maintenance is much better and smarter, as well as cheaper. So why not increase your self-care before you catch a cold or have a heart attack?

• A well being lifestyle must involve learning strategies to cope with pain and frustration, illness and brokenness, which are parts of everyone's life sooner or later. Walking the Christian way involves many ups but also downs. It's a rocky road at times. It winds through the strange lands of each new, unexplored life stage. Sometimes there are dangerous detours and dead ends that produce suffering and fresh wounds and brokenness. At other times the road leads through quiet countrysides and to places where breathtaking vistas of new possibilities come into view.

In our very imperfect world inhabited by very imperfect people like you and I, there are days of agony as well as ecstasy in most people's lives. At times tragedies shatter our well being for a while. The well being perspective views these painful experiences as something like the thorns on roses. Rather than complaining that roses have thorns, as someone has said, it's better to rejoice that some thorns have roses! There are rich resources in our Christian faith that can help us survive and cope with these unwelcome experiences, perhaps even grow a bit spiritually and in our ability to cope.

• A well being lifestyle involves caring outreach to people in need and pain. From a Christian viewpoint, self-caring and caring for others are always linked. Self-care becomes self-other caring. This involves nurturing wholeness in those whose lives touch ours. It also includes joining hands with other people of good will, whatever their faith, to work at healing the injustices that cause large-scale brokenness in our communities and world, perhaps even in our personal lives. A life-in-all-its-fullness lifestyle involves action aimed at helping others to have the best opportunities to develop their God-given potentialities.

It may surprise you to know that *caring outreach is one of the most important things you can do to increase your own well being.* It's encouraging to note that outreach to others as an essential expression of self-caring is a psychologically valid principle, quite apart from the fact that it also is a firm part of our faith's understanding of the good life. Wholeness for individuals grows best in covenants of mutual growth made in relationships. Your own wellness program will be much more likely to succeed if you have a wellness partner to share the experience and give each other support and encouragement.

• A well being lifestyle is a continuing journey, not an arrival. Staying healthy at each life stage involves different challenges and possibilities. There is some continuity, of course, but there also are different pains and gains in each stage. Middle adulthood, for example, has different losses and assets than young adulthood, both of which differ greatly from those of the so-called retirement years. The life journey is a series of bad news–good news scenarios. The bad news is that each life stage, from birth to death, offers you a new set of frustrations, losses, and what we euphemistically call "challenges." But don't ignore the good news—that each age and stage also bring new assets, strengths, and possibilities that you didn't have before.

The strategy for coping constructively with the new pains and problems of your present life stage is to discover and develop its new gains and possibilities. You may be thinking, "Easier said than done." True. But it *is* possible, using well being principles and methods.

Christian well being is walking in a direction that enables us to say "Yes!" to life and to God in spite of stumbling, failures, and backsliding in which we say "No!" to ourselves and the crises and losses that sometimes say a deafening "No!" to us. The Christian lifestyle of well being seeks to travel on today's path with thanksgiving for *this* day in spite of the "downers," aware with inner quietness that *this* is the day the Lord has made (Ps. 118:24). If we live in this way, even part of the time, we increase the likelihood that future days may have increased quality, perhaps even quantity.

• A well being lifestyle involves accepting a fact that is tempting to ignore: that the responsibility for our health care ultimately rests with us. It does not rest with our sickness-care professionals, as seductive as it is to misperceive those important persons as healing gods who will rescue us from years of sloppy or neglected self-care. Well being involves exercising our risky freedom many times each day by choosing those options that

have the most likelihood of enhancing our own wellness as well as the wellness of others and society. Because life is an unfolding journey into an unknown future, it takes courage—the courage to *be* but also the courage to *become* as fit as possible in our present life stage. The decisions often are mundane but seldom simple. They have to do with the healthfulness of the "little things" (that really aren't that little), such as diet, exercise, play, prayer, work, close relations, serving others, and how one cares about and for the natural environment.

• Well being involves the awareness that our wellness is influenced profoundly by the health of the biosphere, the wonderful web of living things of which we all are small parts. As mentioned above, we are in the environment but it is also in us, for better, but often for worse. Making our lifestyle more compatible with care for the earth is a natural for Christians. We cannot care fully for our own wellness and that of our loved ones unless we also care for God's living creation with more understanding and loving concern. We have a rich, largely underused tradition of creation spirituality. It is a splendid source of spiritual energy for caring for both the earth and people in our homes and workplaces and in the places where we worship the Creator.

• Christian well being is very personal but also profoundly social. We humans are "members one of another," as the New Testament puts it (Rom. 12:5). Like brokenness, health is contagious. We catch either illness or health and give them reciprocally in our close relationships as well as in the wider society. Your degree of illness and health is intertwined with the illness and health of your family, community, and society.

• A well being lifestyle involves learning strategies to outwit our ingenious resistance and clever sabotaging of all our wonderfully healthful intentions. Most of us have a collection of unfulfilled resolutions (at New Year's and other times)—promises to ourselves to do healthier things such as lose weight, exercise regularly, relax more, eat less junk food, stop smoking, meditate and pray, live in more earth-friendly ways, and so on. These intentions never made it from talking the talk to walking the walk of wellness. A strategy for outwitting such fruitless intentions will be offered later (see Session 4, pp. 81–83).

• A Christian well being lifestyle claims and celebrates the irreducible worth of every person, beginning with yourself, as made in the likeness of the Creator God. Loving yourself as a child of God gives you a sturdy spiritual foundation for your self-esteem. Equally important, this self-love empowers you to relate with more accepting love to other people as children of the one divine Spirit. Spiritually energized Christian well being involves loving the lovable. That's easy. The difficult part is that it also involves loving the unlovable—in yourself and, by so doing, in other people.

• A well being lifestyle involves cherishing some "impossible dream" in your mind and heart—a dream of a more whole future for yourself and your world. It also involves working to give that dream reality by using your hands, your feet, your voice, your money, and the power of prayer. The New Testament image of God's kingdom provides such a dream for countless Christians. Holding fast to a guiding vision of peace, justice, and ecological health can bring surprising energy. It can help discouraged Christians "keep on keeping on," as they continue to work against odds to increase the well being of themselves; of their family, church, and community; and of the world. Remarkable "can-do" energy is available in an action-producing commitment to a God-inspired dream.

Hope and Wholeness in a Broken but Birthing World

As the daily news reports remind us all too often, epidemics of violence and brokenness flourish throughout our frantic, fragmenting society. The crises and violence around us complicate our personal crises tremendously and make their healing more difficult. I enjoyed a recent cartoon that showed a distraught-looking fellow watching TV. His thoughts are in the bubble over his head: "I need a V chip that blocks out World News Tonight."

The personal and social contexts in which most of us struggle for some degree of well being is at best a mixed bag. No approach to well being dares ignore either the brokenness our world brings or that which we cause ourselves by our foibles and failures, our sins and stupidity.

We all need some small rays of hope in the midst of this brokenness and despair. We need glimmers of hope that may reveal that our broken world is also a birthing world. Awareness of such harbingers of hope are important to our psychological and spiritual well being. In the space below jot down some notes about promising, hope-awakening developments in your world.[10] / (If you have trouble listing several hopeful developments, be sure to see note #10.)

_____

_____

_____

_____

_____

_____

_____

_____

_____

Such promising developments indeed may suggest that some of today's chaotic happenings are the birth struggles of a more wholeness-generating society and world. Obviously the darkness is still very deep for many people and groups. The dawning of a new stage of well being in our world is at best only a faint but promising possibility. The birthing of such a new world depends on the daily decisions that people of good will make in the months and years just ahead. By making decisions that support wellness, we may help to midwife the birth of greater well being in our families, our churches, our communities, and our world.

The good news is that to respond to the challenge of a violent world with informed Christian passion and hope-filled spiritual commitment can enhance our own well being in unexpected ways, whatever the impact on the larger world.

Introduction to Guided Meditations

You will find several awareness exercises or guided meditations in the sessions of this workbook. Their purpose is to help you bring alive in your own experience the holistic wellness ideas you encounter. Such guided meditations combine full-body relaxation and active imaging. They are a fruitful way to use one of your many creative abilities, your imagination, to enliven your body, mind, and spirit.

In my teaching and psychotherapeutic practice, I make frequent use of this approach. This helps people learn how to intentionally use the pictures they form in their minds for healing, growth, and self-care. Like many healing and teaching professionals, I have been impressed repeatedly by the healing and the stimulation toward growth that people often experience when they utilize this simple method.

Guidelines for Using Guided Meditations

1. Prepare yourself for gaining the most benefits by taking time to relax your whole body-mind-spirit organism as fully as possible, using the instructions below, until you are both very relaxed and very alert.

2. Remember that there is no "right" or "correct" way to use a guided meditation. Try to stay open to learning whatever the meditation may have the potential to teach you while at the same time enjoying your freedom to use it in whatever way you choose. If a particular symbol or suggestion or an entire meditation feels threatening to you, change it or simply think about something else. If you decide not to do a part or all of a meditation, I recommend that you examine this decision to see if you can learn something valuable about your inner life. The same is true if you discover that you have taken a siesta during a meditation read by someone in your group.

3. After a meditation, be sure to allow adequate time to reflect on what you have experienced and learned; if you are doing the meditation with someone else, talk together about your experiences. This reflection and dialogue can increase greatly the learning value of the experience.

4. In the event that you get in touch with painful feelings such as grief or anger, it is important to find a trusted person with whom you can talk through these feelings and thus perhaps experience healing and learning.[11]

Experiencing the Seven Dimensions

This guided meditation has three beneficial purposes: (1) to provide an opportunity to start learning how to use guided meditations; (2) to enable you to experience the seven dimensions of healing and well being; (3) to use creative imaging to enrich your well being a little in one or more of the seven dimensions. Pause now to experience the meditation.

Instructions: You can do a meditative imaging exercise alone or with others. If you're alone, simply read the instructions until you come to this signal /, then close your eyes while you do what has been described. If you are working with someone else, one of you can read the meditation aloud, pausing where indicated, while the other does what is suggested. Some people like to read through a meditation, then do what they remember. Let yourself learn all you can about the wellness of your lifestyle in each of the dimensions. If you can't do all seven steps at once, splitting the exercise between two or more sessions is fine. Just remember to repeat the preliminary body-relaxation step each time you do one or more of the steps to prepare yourself to use the exercise most productively.

1. *Enhancing Your Body's Well Being:* Sit in a comfortable position with your spine in a vertical alignment and your feet flat on the floor to encourage the flow of your body's energy. / Close your eyes and focus on how your total body-mind-spirit feels—for example, tense, anxious, tired, uncomfortable or energized, strong, sensuousness, alive. Just experience fully how you feel for a minute or so. / Now, take several deep breaths, letting these raise the energy level throughout your body. / Hunch and wiggle your shoulders and neck; reach up and stretch your upper body. Then, as you continue to breathe deeply, tense and release the muscles all over your body several times, especially in the areas in which you tend to carry tension. Do this until you experience your whole body vividly, very relaxed and very alert. / Do whatever else you need to do to feel more aliveness throughout your body. /

Now, experience the pleasurable flow of energy revitalizing your body, especially the parts that felt discomfort or tension. Just enjoy being in your enlivened body for a few minutes. / Reflect on what you experienced, perhaps asking yourself, "Would my overall lifestyle be healthier if I enlivened my body this way more often?"

2. *Enhancing Your Mind's Well Being:* Staying in touch with your body, picture your consciousness as a room within yourself. / Be alone in that room now. Look around the room, becoming aware of its size, colors, furnishings, smells, sounds, and temperature. Notice how you feel right now in this room of your consciousness. / Do whatever you need to do, in your imagination, to make your room safer and more comfortable, so that it is a good place to be with yourself. For example, if it feels cramped, push back the walls and raise the ceiling, giving yourself more inner space. It's your room, so do whatever you want to make it a warm, love-filled place to be with yourself—for example, clean up the clutter, change the decor, or add more comfortable furniture, a fireplace, music, flowers and growing plants, or perhaps a picture window. / Now just enjoy your loving inner space in a quieting, renewing way for a little while. /

Reflect on this part of the exercise. How are things at your center? Is it a good place to be at home with yourself? If you discovered that you could make it a better place, do you need to do this often? How does your experience at your center, from which you reach out to others, influence the quality of your relationships and the wellness of your lifestyle? Plan what you will do regularly to enhance your consciousness.

3. *Enhancing the Well Being of Your Relationships:* Staying connected with your body and the inner room of your consciousness, think of the person or persons you would most enjoy being close to right now. Picture that person(s) clearly and vividly, letting yourself relate in warm, loving ways to each other in your imagination. / Be aware of how your feelings have changed, compared to when you were alone in your inner room. /

If you're with another person or persons, join hands, keeping your eyes closed so that you can focus on what you're experiencing. / Be aware of the person with whom you're connected, in your imagination or through your hands. This person experiences a range of feelings—hopes, loves, fears, joys, pains—many of these like yours. Be aware that this person, like yourself, is a loved child of God, a precious member of one family. In spite of your differences, let yourself experience your oneness as sisters or brothers in Christ and in the human family. Experience the flow of the loving, healing energy of caring to and from you and the other person or persons. /

Now release hands and reflect on this part of the exercise. What did you learn about your network of nurturing relationships? Were you able to deepen your sense of connectedness? Plan what you will do to enhance your lifestyle by keeping your caring ties of relatedness alive, loving, and mutually nurturing.

4. *Enhancing the Well Being of Your Work:* Staying in touch with the areas of your life you have experienced, now form a vivid picture in your imagination of your workplace. (If you are retired, picture your "workplace" as where you carry on your daily activities.) / Be in that place for a little while, being aware of how you feel when you're there. Is it a nurturing and esteem-fostering place, or is it depleting and toxic? Is your work satisfying and purposeful? / For a few minutes, be in that part of your work environment and relationships where you feel most alive, esteemed, and whole. /

Now move into the part of the job and work relationships where you feel least alive and most vulnerable, depressed, unappreciated, or hurt. / Move back and forth between the two places several times, comparing your aliveness level in each place. / Now think about what you can do to spend more time in the wholeness place or to bring some healing energy from there to make the deadening place more enlivening and conducive to wellness. / Be aware that by focusing on your work setting you have become more aware of one of the key institutions that affects your life by its health or sickness. Later you might try this part of the exercise using the other important institutions that influence your life.

5. *Enhancing the Well Being of Your Play:* Picture a place where your inner child is relaxed and playful. Be there for a little while in your imagination, letting yourself enjoy a minivacation of laughing and playing. Be aware of how your body and mind feel as you let yourself savor life playfully. / Return to where you are sitting and reflect on this dimension of your experience. Perhaps ask yourself questions such as "Is my work well balanced by my play? Would letting myself be playful more often enrich the well being of my lifestyle?"

6. *Enhancing the Well Being of Your Natural Environment:* Staying in touch with the dimensions of your life you have experienced, become aware of the place you are in. / If you're inside, let your body experience being grounded, supported by the chair, the floor, the building's foundation, the earth that undergirds the building and your whole self. / Enlarge your awareness to include the world outside the building—the wind, trees, plants, animals and birds, people, and so on. /

Now form a picture of the place in nature you most enjoy. / Go there now in your imagination. Be there enjoying the beautiful place for a few minutes. Feel the energy exchange to and from the network of living things with your whole body, mind, and spirit. / Return to the place you're sitting and think about this part of the exercise. What did you learn? What will you do to enliven your lifestyle by reconnecting more regularly with God's wonderful living world?

*7. **Enhancing Your Spiritual Well Being:*** To bring this meditation together, become aware of the divine Spirit of life and love and liberation who is very present in this very moment and place. / Open the windows of your life and let the renewing energy of God's love flow in like a clear, warm, healing light. / Beginning with your body, go through the other dimensions, surrounding each with the healing light of this divine love. In this way welcome the divine Spirit into your body, consciousness, relationships, work, play, organizations, and into your experiencing of nature. /

Finish the exercise in whatever way you wish to give it a sense of completion. / Before opening your eyes, reflect for a few minutes on how your experience of God's presence might enrich other dimensions of your lifestyle. /

Now think about your whole seven-dimensional experience. What did you teach yourself about how you intentionally can continue to increase the well being of any of these facets of your life? /

Now gently open your eyes and take a short time to jot down some notes in the space below about insights you received regarding your self-care in one or more dimensions of your well being. / If someone else did this guided meditation with you, learn from each other's experiences by taking a short time to share highlights of this exercise. /

If you enhanced your wellness even a little or found this meditation meaningful in other ways, repeat it several times in the next few days. With practice, many people discover that such awareness exercises become increasingly helpful. Repeating it also gives you a sense of your gradual growth in one or more of the seven dimensions. As you begin each of the upcoming sessions, do the full body-mind relaxation and then repeat the particular steps that correspond to that session's topic, thus helping you get into the topic experientially.

_____

_____

_____

_____

_____

_____

Questions for Reflection

1. What new ideas did you discover or what ideas were confirmed or changed in this session?

2. What issues did you find problematic or challenging?

3. What will you do different as a result of this session?

Beginning Your Self-Care Plan

In light of what you have learned in this session, list some of your well being needs, wants, and hopes—the things you desire from the sessions ahead in each of the seven dimensions of your Christian lifestyle. Use the spaces provided below plus extra sheets of paper, if you need additional room. Under each dimension, list at least one thing that needs changing to increase your well being in that area. (Some of the dimensions are split into two parts in the list below.)

Body:

_____

_____

_____

Mind:

_____

_____

_____

Spirit:

_____

_____

_____

Relationships:

_____

_____

_____

Work:

_____

_____

_____

Play:

_____

_____

_____

The Earth:

_____

_____

_____

Society and Its Institutions:

_____

_____

_____

Look over your list of wellness needs and select one or two that have high priority for you and on which you are able to take some action. Mark these as key places to begin enhancing your self-care. / In the space below, write out a brief workable plan for starting to take action on the goal or goals your picked, between now and the next

session. If you're doing these sessions by yourself, discuss your plan as soon as possible with someone who will give you honest and caring feedback. This will help to strengthen your strategy. / It's important to start implementing your plan soon so as to gain some momentum in self-change. Congratulate yourself on taking these first crucial steps in making your Christian lifestyle healthier. You'll be encouraged to add, week by week, to this preliminary self-care plan.

_____

_____

_____

_____

_____

_____

_____

_____

_____

_____

_____

_____

_____

_____

_____

_____

_____

Closing Song, Prayer, and Evaluation

 Close this session with a brief period of quiet meditation and prayer, celebrating the new insights that came to you during your study. You might sing a hymn, spiritual, or folk song that expresses your commitment to pursuing a path toward well being. Also commit yourself in God's presence to implementation of your self-care plan.

As a way of doing a minievaluation of this session, think about useful insights you have gained. Did your interest increase in developing self-care methods that promise you more healing and wholeness? What would increase the value of the next session for you? If you're working with a partner or group, take two or three minutes to share your evaluations of this session and pool your suggestions for improving the next one.

Continuing Your Self-Care

 The following activities will encourage continuing your self-care for well being between sessions.

• To catch up, read chapters 1 and 2 both in this workbook and in *Well Being*.

• Get a running start on the next session by jotting down issues in your religious life that seem problematic and with which you want to wrestle or discuss in the group.

• Take the do-it-yourself Spiritual Well Being Checkup at the beginning of the next session in this workbook. Follow the instructions to identify parts of your religious life that are strong and those that need strengthening.

• Begin implementing your self-care plan between sessions, keeping track of your progress. If you fail to implement some parts of the plan, don't waste time punishing yourself. It is better to focus on making those parts more workable and attractive and to make sure that these are things you really want to do. The blank space at the close of each session in this workbook may serve as a place for self-care journaling. Remember, your self-care plan is a key to successfully enhancing your well being.

Enriching and Empowering Your Spiritual Life: The Key to Christian Well Being

God loves you—and I'm trying.
—A theologically astute
bumper sticker

For the mystery of human life is not only in living, but in knowing why one lives. Without a clear idea of what to live for, [humanity] will not consent to live and will rather destroy [itself] than remain on the earth, though . . . surrounded by loaves of bread.
—Response by the accused to the Grand Inquisitor in *The Brothers Karamazov*, by Fyodor Dostoyevsky[1]

A Spiritual Well Being Checkup

 If you haven't done so, begin this session by completing the following Spiritual Well Being Checkup. Using and scoring this checkup can enhance your spiritual self-care in two interrelated ways:

First, as a self-discovery instrument, it can give you a quick checkup of your spiritual and ethical health. It can help you identify areas in which your spiritual life is flourishing and those in which you need to cultivate your spiritual growth. In this sense, checkups like this are comparable to the regular checkups you have with your doctor, or, even more, like those you may do on your own when you check your weight, blood pressure, or blood glucose levels.

Second, the items in this checkup are a list of practical suggestions for enhancing your spiritual and ethical wellness. They're a smorgasbord of options from which to choose in nourishing your spiritual hungers more fully.[2] Feel free to shorten the checkup by ignoring items that do not apply to you.

Instructions: Mark each statement in one of three ways:

E = "I'm doing *excellently* in this area of my spiritual life." (If you're being honest with yourself, give yourself a pat on the back. You deserve it.)

OK = "I'm doing *acceptably* in this, but there's room for improvement."

NS = "This is an area where I definitely *need strengthening*." (Commend yourself for identifying places where spiritual growth is both needed and possible.)

____ I have a personal, growing relationship with the living God, the divine Spirit of love and justice.

____ I experience God most fully in the life, teachings, and aliveness of Jesus the Christ.

____ My Christian life increases my ability to love myself, other people (including enemies and people I find unlovely or weird), nature, and God.

_____ My faith enables me to know that I am at home in the universe—that I really *do* belong.

_____ It's easier to accept the unlovely aspects of myself and others, because I know that I am accepted unconditionally by the loving God revealed in Jesus.

_____ My religious and ethical beliefs strengthen my sense of being forgiven and my acceptance of the gift of God's loving grace, rather than causing me to take unproductive guilt trips.

_____ My beliefs increase my hope and inner peace, along with my zest for living and my desire to serve others.

_____ My beliefs help me affirm rather than put down my body and my sexuality.

_____ My spiritual beliefs and everyday spiritual experiences help me cope constructively with my losses.

_____ I have evaluated the beliefs and values I learned in my childhood, reaffirming and retaining only those that still ring true to me in my adult mind and heart.

_____ I have learned to honor my honest doubts, viewing them as healthy growing edges of my faith even when they disturb my nostalgic need for a spiritual security blanket.

_____ The ethical values that guide my life usually are in some harmony with my understanding of love, justice, and wholeness for all people everywhere. My real priorities, as reflected in my use of my time, are in line with the values and causes that are most important to me.

_____ My Christian beliefs and values tend to build bridges, not barriers, between myself and those with very different understandings of God and the good life.

_____ I usually practice some spiritual self-care each day, spending time in such activities as meditation, prayer, serious study, and journal writing on religious issues that affect my life.

_____ My experiences of God's love and forgiveness help me reach out with caring to others, including those wounded by personal tragedies and put down by society.

_____ I am a good friend with my soul, the spiritual self that reflects the divine light within me. I'm seeking new ways to make this more the unifying center of my life.

_____ I often experience a sense of wonder, joy, serenity, and gratitude for God's good gift of life.

_____ I am seeking to align my life with the purposes of God for me as I understand them.

_____ I regularly experience spiritual highs or moments of transcendence through a variety of nonchemical means such as prayer, music, loving, worship, nature, and reflection on inspiring ideas.

_____ I sometimes catch glimpses of everyday miracles in mundane happenings and in ordinary people in whom I sense extraordinary gifts.

_____ I participate in a caring community of shared faith, such as a congregation, that provides meaningful festivals, rituals, celebrations, and honest but caring support that nurtures my continued religious and ethical growth.

_____ I enjoy both the emotional, nurturing, mystical, and receptive (right-brain) side of my spiritual life and the rational, ethical, action- and service-oriented (left-brain) side.

____ I often experience God's presence in the beauty and awe-awakening wonder of God's creation, the natural world. I see nature as God's handiwork, and I seek to live a Christian lifestyle that protects its amazing diversity and aliveness.

____ I affirm that all humans, with our many conflicts and differences, are daughters or sons of the loving Spirit, and each one of us is of unique, irreducible value.

____ I rejoice that I feel called by God to help in small ways to birth a new future—an age of caring and compassion, of justice and community—that will make greater wholeness possible for all people on a healthy earth.

____ I seek to face my feelings about death in the context of a vital faith, so that they become sources of energy to live with more zest and creativity in whatever time I have left on earth.

____ My religious beliefs and experiences foster love, hope, trust, self-esteem, joy, responsibility, inner freedom, and the acceptance of my body and its pleasures. They also help me constructively resolve destructive feelings such as fear, guilt, prejudice, despair, hate, childish dependency, rejection of my body, and feelings of being inwardly trapped.

____ I have learned how to use spiritual approaches that enable me to move from painful alienation from myself, others, and God to healing reconciliation with myself, others, and God.

____ My religious life helps me keep in contact with the creative resources of my deeper mind through living symbols, meaningful rituals and stories, and vital festivals that celebrate anxiety-generating life transitions such as birth, aging, and death.

____ With all the answers available in religious studies, I continue to be aware of the ultimate questions—the mystery and wonder, not only about God, but about the amazing miracle of life itself.

Using Your Findings to Enhance Your Spiritual Well Being

Take the following steps to help you use the results of this checkup in developing your spiritual and ethical self-care plan:

1. Tally your responses and write down the totals below. This will give you an overview of your spiritual well being. / Give yourself a pat on the back for the things you honestly scored "E."

E: ____ __

OK: _____

NS: _____

2. Go through the list and put a star beside those OK and NS items that seem either urgent or especially important to you.

3. What is your overall "feel" concerning the general wellness of your spiritual and ethical life? In the space below, jot down your overall evaluation of the strengths and weaknesses of your spiritual-ethical health.

_____

_____

_____

_____

_____

_____

4. Beside the starred items, make notes about how you could begin to strengthen your spiritual wellness. / You will be encouraged to come back to these items and to elaborate on your ideas as you develop a workable spiritual self-care plan.

Learning Exercise: Look over your tally of the checkup and the notes you made afterward. Keep these issues in mind during this session. Remember—

• the NS and OK spiritual well being items that you checked as seeming particularly important or urgent for you;

• your initial thoughts about what you might do to strengthen your spiritual well being.

A Biblical Perspective

 During his imprisonment in Rome, Paul wrote a pastoral letter to the church at Ephesus, on the coast of the Aegean Sea in what is now Turkey. He expressed what undoubtedly had been both his own experience of the Christian life and his hope for the early Christians there. He put his hope this way: that in Christ their roots might "go down deep into the soil of God's marvelous love" (Eph. 3:17, TLB). The purpose of this session is to help you experience what Paul prayed those early Christians might experience: your spiritual roots' going down deep into the nurturing reality of God's marvelous love—love for yourself, for others, and for God's other marvelous living creatures.

Major Objectives and Themes

 In each session you may choose the learning objectives that are particularly important to you. Simply put a check mark in front of the items below that express your primary interests and concerns as you seek to improve the well being of your spiritual life. In this session you will have opportunities to learn the following:

❑ Reasons healthy Christian spirituality is crucially important to all dimensions of your well being.

❑ Fresh ways to enhance spiritual well being and to gain a new understanding of how spirituality is at the heart of a Christian well being lifestyle.

❑ How to satisfy your spiritual hungers in health-enhancing ways and thus open yourself more fully to the divine Spirit's continuing invitation to wellness for yourself and others.

❑ Resources to enliven your spiritual life.

❑ Spiritual empowerment exercises to assist you in this ongoing process.

❑ How to use the spiritual well being checkup to increase your religious and ethical health.

❑ How to improve your spiritual self-care plan.

**Sharing Stories: Religious Faith Empowers Healthy Living

To personalize the vital importance of people's spirituality for their overall well being, pause and picture in your mind someone you know whose religious faith enables him or her to live a constructive and caring lifestyle in spite of difficult circumstances and losses. This may be yourself, someone in your family, a friend, or a person in your congregation or community who embodies (or embodied, if he or she is no longer on this earth) a transforming Christian faith. / Reflect on what about the religious life of this person enables her or him to maintain hope, strength, and love in her or his heart, despite a situation that otherwise would have produced only bitterness and despair.[3] / Jot down what you learned about wholeness-giving spirituality from your experience in knowing this person.

Building on Discoveries from Your Checkup

If you took and tallied the Spiritual Well Being Checkup, you already know a variety of things you can do to enhance your religious and ethical health. Commend yourself because you have a running start on this session. This session will provide insights and resources for using what you discovered in shaping your spiritual and ethical self-care plan.

Why Healthy Spirituality Is Important to Your Well Being

We humans are inherently spiritual beings, and our most basic wholeness need is to develop our spiritual powers and possibilities. Whether or not we are related to any organized religion, we are spiritual creatures. We live by our hopes and beliefs about what is ultimately important to ourselves and the world. These hopes and beliefs and the religious practices that seek to express them generate some sense of meaning in our turbulent lives. Without at least a minimal sense of meaning and purpose, we cannot stay well.

For this reason, spiritual health is the heart of all other dimensions of wholeness. The aliveness and health of our relationship with God affects the aliveness and health of all our other relationships—with ourselves, with other people, with God's wonderful creation, and with the important institutions in our life. Both sickness-causing and health-enhancing religion reflect and also reinforce sickness or health in the other dimensions of our lives. A healthy, growing relationship with the living God, constructive values to guide our many choices, and Christian meanings that help give our lives purpose— these dynamic aspects of our spirituality influence everything else in our lives.

If our religious and ethical life is impov-erished or vacuous, it will diminish our wholeness in other areas. If our religious and ethical life is a growth-nurturing garden, it will help our whole self to flower by opening us to receive the water of life and the sunlight of God's loving Spirit.

Our spiritual life has to do with all the things that most clearly define us as human beings. These include our spiritual selves (or souls); our need for meaning, purpose, and guiding values; our need for times of spiritual communion with the divine Spirit; our needs for freedom and for self-transcending caring; and, most of all, our profound hunger for an ongoing relationship with God. How well these needs are satisfied determines the quality of our spirituality, which in turn shapes our whole lives. Our spirituality strengthens or weakens our identity, our sense of self worth and inner strength, and our capacity to be loving, caring persons.

Biblical Roots

 **Learning Exercise: Before you read the paragraphs below, take a few minutes to jot down in the space provided a scripture passage or two that emphasize the importance of spirituality in a Christian lifestyle. /

_____

_____

_____

_____

_____

_____

_____

_____

Like the lovely carpet of multicolored wild flowers in a spring meadow, our holy scriptures are adorned with insights and images for spiritual self-care to enhance our overall wellness. Here are a few of many biblical blossoms:

This line from Paul's first letter to the church in Corinth affirms the view that developing greater wholeness is a growth process that ultimately is a gift of God: "I planted, Apollos watered, but God gave the growth" (1 Cor. 3:6).

In both the Hebrew Scriptures and the New Testament, the concepts of salvation and healing are intimately intertwined. A Christian theme that helped launch the freedom revolution of the Protestant movement describes salvation as occurring by "grace through faith" (see Romans 3:21-31). The same spiritual principle also applies to healing and growth in wellness. This means that all these transformations are gifts of God that we can receive only when we open the windows of our lives by responding with trust and faith.

The meaning-rich Hebrew word *shalom*, like the parallel Arabic word *salaam*, is usually translated "peace." But both these words also mean health or wholeness in community. To greet another with "shalom" really says, as a student from the Middle East puts it: "May that which is good within you richly abound and flow out to those around you."[4] Shalom appears over 350 times in the Hebrew Scriptures and is understood as a gift from God. This gift is received best in a spiritual community or congregation united by a bond of mutual caring. Mutual caring encourages each of us to discover and develop more of our God-given possibilities.

 Learning Exercise: Stop reading for a few moments and think about where you find shalom in relationships and community. / If you don't have such a wellness-nurturing network, doing whatever it takes to discover or develop such a community of mutual caring will be more than worth the effort required. Make notes on your thoughts on this topic.

_____

_____

_____

_____

_____

_____

Does Your Spirituality Heal or Hurt?

Let me share a story about a person who has helped shape my spiritual life. Some years ago I unexpectedly began a precious friendship with Erma Pixley, a delightfully alive Christian who had then recently retired as a creative educator and counselor. Erma phoned me to talk about how she could continue helping people find more health in their Christianity, and how churches could be encouraged to become better centers for healing and wholeness. Our friendship grew around our shared passion for these concerns. The dream that we developed together around this concern led to the creation of a program to foster spiritually centered wellness: The Institute of Religion and Wholeness at the School of Theology in Claremont, California, where I was teaching.[5]

Only after our friendship and trust deepened did Erma share the story of her crushing loss in her midyears, the most awful tragedy a parent can know. Her only child, a promising young adult son who was well along in a university graduate program, killed himself while in a deep abyss of depression.

Shortly before her unexpected death in her mid-eighties, Erma shared a powerful image with me that continues to influence my life: "Religion can either be a set of wings for our souls to fly or a lead weight around our necks!" The triumphant faith and loving celebration of life that were Erma's spiritual wings when I got to know her had come in the most difficult of ways. Her inspiring dream had been born as she used her awful loss as a challenge to grow spiritually and interpersonally. Erma was a vibrant embodiment of a Christian spirituality that gave her wings—a liberating spirituality produced by her dark journey through a dismal valley of despair and death. [6]

 Learning Exercise: Pause and think about your own experiences of religion in light of Erma's statement. Have you experienced religion that made it hard for your spirit to fly toward enhanced wholeness? Does your faith provide wings for you? I hope that you have such health-giving spirituality. What a superb gift and blessing! / When you are ready, jot down in the margins of this book or in your journal ideas or memories that have dawned on your mind and heart during this exercise—things you wish to remember and on which you may want to reflect as you seek new ways to deepen your inner pool of life-sustaining spirituality.

The very idea may seem strange that some distortions of the Christian good news make it bad news to people's wholeness. But my personal religious studies and struggles—and my years as a teacher, pastor, and therapist—convince me that Erma was right on target. I remember people who held to religious beliefs that were crippling to their whole-ness—sources of guilt and shame, fear and self-rejection, a lead weight on their souls. I also recall numerous others whose religious life included truly liberating wings with which their souls could soar.

Tragic news stories from places like Waco and Jonestown and Rancho Santa Fe remind us of the destructiveness of some religious cults that are proliferating in our society. But less extreme groups also offer rigid, authoritarian religious approaches. They foster sickness-causing beliefs and exploit people who are starved for a viable faith and worthwhile values. They operate by manipulating people's fears, guilt feelings, and paranoid suspicions, and by promising "the only true path" to salvation. [7]

Quite apart from such extreme examples of life-damaging belief and value systems, all of us need to examine our spiritual lives to identify areas in which our spirituality may be diminishing life in all its fullness for us or others. The universal human need for spiritual meaning and commitment is so powerful that we are all vulnerable to being seduced by distorted beliefs and values that diminish the wellness in our minds, bodies, souls, and relationships.

On the other hand, abundant evidence shows that healthy religion can be a well-spring of enhanced health and well being. Such religion has enabled countless people throughout the centuries to develop a spirituality-with-wings that not only lets their souls fly but also lets their minds, hearts, bodies, and relationships rise to increased wellness. The action-options in the Spiritual Well Being Checkup are ways of enhancing spiritual and ethical well being in your life. The rest of this session describes further self-care steps that you can implement to nurture this religious well being. Both the checkup and these steps are potential resources for developing your self-care plan.

Spiritual Well Being Means Meeting Spiritual Hungers Creatively

Have you ever wondered why our human species, in all known cultures and throughout the eons of the human story, has developed religious beliefs and ethical codes? I can offer two major reasons.

The first is that, as the Hebrew creation stories in Genesis describe it, we are made from the soil of the earth, yet formed in the image of God. Our spirits are created with the ability and hunger to commune with the divine Spirit. We are self-aware, meaning-seeking creatures who have within us a spark of the divine and a longing for God.

The second reason is that we all are aware, though we usually try to ignore the knowledge, that everyone we care about, including ourselves, will someday die. We know that, like all the other animals, we are enmeshed in nature with its cycles of life and death. Yet our human consciousness also transcends nature in our capacities for aware-ness, choice, spirituality, and rationality.

This painful dilemma causes us to hunger for religious experiences and certainties that we hope will protect us from our vulnera-bility and finitude. It generates profound spiritual hungers for meaning, security, and objects of devotion, so that people all around the planet have developed religious beliefs and worshiped an enormous variety of deities. The many religions on our planet all are efforts to meet these spiritual needs. Our Christian faith and ethics are the most effective ways that millions of us have found to satisfy these spiritual hungers.

That we humans are a blend of dust and destiny, of the stuff of animals and of angels, produces the powerful spiritual hungers present in all human beings, including those most secularized in their thinking and living. These profound hungers can only be satisfied in healthful ways by spiritual or religious food. Just as all humans have basic nutritional needs, we also have basic needs for healthy spiritual nourishment. Spiritual health flowers when these spiritual and ethical hungers are satisfied in loving, esteem-strengthening, life-celebrating, reality-respecting ways. The health of other areas of our lives also then tend to flourish.

Spiritual sicknesses occur when people try to satisfy these needs in authority-cen-tered, idolatrous, magical, reality-denying, or fear- and-guilt generating ways. Because of the power of their spiritual needs, people who do not develop wholeness-enhancing beliefs and values, as well as spiritual practices to satisfy them usually grasp various wholeness-depleting idolatries. They vainly seek to satisfy their spiritual hungers in ways that diminish their spiritual health, thereby reducing the wholeness in all other areas of their lives. They give their devotion to a variety of unworthy gods—success, money, power, prestige, possessions, drugs, alcohol, religion, work, sex, or their family, ethnic group, or nation.

Eventually all such idolatries end in despair, and people "hit bottom" when the deep inadequacy of these seductive objects of devotion is discovered. It is well to remember that the religious life of all of us (except perhaps a genuine saint) is a paradoxical blend of healthy and unhealthy, liberating and limiting ways of satisfying our spiritual needs.

Overview of Spiritual Needs

All of us have certain spiritual needs, even though we may not fill these needs appro-priately or in the same ways. The following sections describe seven universal spiritual hungers or needs and how we can meet them constructively. If you're working with a part-ner or group, take turns reading aloud the description of each need, and then discuss your responses to the two questions that follow each one.

Spiritual Need 1: *To Experience Regularly the Healing, Empowering Love of God*

Spiritual well being from the Christian perspective involves enjoying an intimate, growing relationship with the divine Spirit of love and justice whom we know best in Jesus. To paraphrase Saint Augustine, we humans are made for intimacy with God and we are not only restless but also spiritually unfulfilled until we find our rest and renewal in that relationship. Human love, although incredibly important for our total well being, is always fallible and fractured, even in the most loving relationships. It is therefore essential for our own well being and the well being of those relationships to have a divine Source of unconditional love that transcends our most prized human relationships.

We live today in a society suffering from a devastating spiritual drought. In such a parched, thirsty setting, a growing relationship with God's living Spirit is like a bubbling spring of the healing, enlivening water of life. This living water can nurture healing and growth in the dry, broken places in our lives if we open ourselves to receive it regularly. Learning how to open the windows of our lives to receive this healing, liberating flow of God's always-available love is the key to spiritual growth.

My friend and theologian John B. Cobb Jr. says it well: "Above all, the spiritual life can be healthy only as it is grounded in the assurance of an acceptance that no human being can give, the ultimate acceptance that is God's."[8] How wonderful it is that God's full acceptance and loving care, in Christian experience, has absolutely no strings attached.

 **Self-Care Exercise: Pause briefly and reflect on two questions, noting your responses in the space below. / Then, if you're working with a partner or a group, share your responses to these questions so you will learn from one another.

1. How well does my present lifestyle regularly open me to experiences of God's love?

_____

_____

_____

_____

_____

_____

2. What will I do to cultivate the inner garden where God's love can grow in me?

_____

_____

_____

_____

_____

_____

Practicing one or more of the spiritual disciplines is the time-tested path to enlivening our relationships with God. These disciplines include prayer, meditation, spiritual study, and loving service. Let's look first at prayer.

Physician Larry Dossey, cochair of the Office of Alternative Therapy at the National Institutes for Health, was astonished to discover abundant empirical evidence that prayers can heal. Having reviewed many studies on this, Dossey reports, "The evidence is so impressive that I regard it as one of the best-kept secrets in medical science. . . . In the San Francisco study, for example, cardiologist Randolph Byrd, M.D., found that out of 393 coronary patients, those who were prayed for were five times less likely than the others to require antibiotics and three times less likely to develop pulmonary edema (in which the lungs fill with fluid), a risk of coronary disease." Dossey concludes that praying for wellness in oneself and others also may help prevent illnesses.[9]

Spiritually empowering prayer can be an intimate conversation with God as a deeply trusted friend or simply an ongoing awareness of the divine presence in all experiences, even the most earthy and mundane. If prayer has lost its power to lift you up spiritually, learning how to relax your whole body and then meditate and use self-guided imaging may help. This spiritual discipline has helped many people experience God's healing love afresh, awakening them to the power of prayer. Meditation is simply any method of focusing your awareness and quieting your consciousness by temporarily not attending to the stream of consciousness—the busy flow of thoughts, feelings, images, and sensations in your mind.

 Self-Care Exercise: Pause now, and try this approach to nurturing your spiritual aliveness. Quiet your body, mind, and spirit, perhaps using the exercise for relaxing your body that you learned in Session 1. / Then picture in your mind a spiritual image that is alive and meaningful for you. For example, as a Christian, you might choose your inner picture of Jesus the good shepherd or an inspiring woman in the Bible. / Experience a warm, healing light coming from this image and enveloping your whole being. Feel your body, mind, and spirit bathed in its energy and light. Just relax and enjoy the experience for a few minutes. / When you are ready, complete the experience in whatever way is comfortable for you. / Sit quietly for a few minutes afterward, enjoying the quiet aliveness. /

You might jot down in the margins of this workbook or in your journal some insights you gained from this experience. I hope that this exercise may give your prayer life a shot in the arm, letting you experience the divine love in fresh, energizing ways.

Spiritual Need 2: *To Experience Regularly Renewing Moments of Self-Transcendence*

You probably have spiritually high moments. They are the fleeting times of wonder in our lives, when we rise above the routine of existence and enjoy what could be called a tiny taste of eternity. These highs can be surprisingly stress-reducing. They can help heal our spiritual deadness and the painful alienation that diminishes our well being—that sense of being cut off from other people, from healing energies of nature, and, most importantly, from God.

If you learn how to celebrate such little miracle moments with joy and gratitude, you know that you're standing on holy ground. These moments put us in touch with the healing wisdom of the eternal Light within us. Many people experienced the precious gifts of transcendence and healing when they touched Jesus (even the hem of his garment), when he touched them, or when they heard his message.

Among the healthful, nondrug ways of "getting high" are prayer, meditation, worship, music, vigorous exercise, laughter, loving intimacy with people, and being nurtured by nature. In our addictive society many people try to find "highs" in ways that often become disastrous to health. For example, those who seek highs only via alcohol, drugs, or sex[10] are inviting addictions. For your health as a Christian, you need to discover a broad range of non-addictive and spiritual ways to experience the healthy highs you need for healing and wholeness.

A teenager who, according to her pastor, was heavily into the high school drug scene, joined a Christian wellness group in her congregation. After several months she wrote a note to the pastor in which she expressed heartfelt thanks for the group. She reported that in the group she had "learned how to get high on people, music, books, laughter, religion, and service to those in need!"

**Reliving a Spiritual High: Close your eyes to concentrate on what you are experiencing now. Relax your whole body-mind-spirit self to become most open to the energy of healing and wholeness. / Recall the most meaningful and uplifting spiritual experience you've had recently. If you're in a time of spiritual drought or darkness, go back in memory until you find an energizing mountain peak experience of some kind. / Take a few minutes to relive that experience right now. In your vivid imagination, get back into the setting where it first occurred. Relive that experience and allow it to happen again for you now. For a few minutes, enjoy reexperiencing this spiritual high and the lift it brought you with its love, light, energy, inspiration, and healing. /

When you complete this exercise, think about what you learned from it. To even a small degree, did you reenergize your inner life by drawing on your memory of inspiring experiences? It may be worthwhile to jot down your insights in your journal or this workbook. / If you discovered that reexperiencing and savoring this high-energy memory had some meaning for you, why not give yourself the gift of repeating this occasionally, particularly when you feel "down" or "beside yourself" (off center or fragmented) spiritually? Such techniques usually become richer with practice. /

 Self-Care Exercise: Pause briefly and reflect on the following two questions, noting your responses in the space below. / Then, if you're working with a partner or group, share your responses to these questions so you can learn from each other.

1. How well does my present lifestyle open the doors of my spiritual life to renewing, energizing, uplifting spiritual experiences?

_____

_____

_____

_____

_____

_____

_____

_____

_____

2. In what specific ways will I slow down and cultivate more awareness of magical moments of transcendence in my life?

_____

_____

_____

_____

_____

_____

_____

_____

_____

_____

_____

Spiritual Need 3: *To Develop Vital Beliefs and a Worthy Object of Devotion That Give Our Lives Meaning, Purpose, and Hope*

The following spiritual factors increase the odds, on the one hand, that you will experience healing and a healthier lifestyle or, on the other hand, that you will live in unhealthy ways that retard healing and make you more vulnerable to illnesses:

• what you believe in your heart as well as in your head;

• the real object of your ultimate devotion or worship;

• your passionate commitments for which you are willing to make sacrifices;

• the deep inner conviction that your life has at least some small purpose and worth, despite its limitations, tragedies, frustrations, and failures.

Have you noticed that we humans have remarkable God-given capacities to bear incredible hardships without being wiped out spiritually? If your Christian faith gives you spiritually healthy resources in dark days, you'll probably discover ways to use life's hardships to help you grow, to use what gets dumped on you to fertilize the flowers and fruit trees in your life. Three things are particularly important: a sense of meaning and purpose in life, however tenuous; a little hope with a basis in hard reality; and at least one mutually caring relationship. Expressed in New Testament terms, faith, hope, and love are essential to surviving and sometimes even growing a little in what Herman Melville described in *Moby Dick* as "the damp, drizzly November in my soul."

A key question is this: How can we cope constructively with the awareness that we will someday die? There are no psychotherapeutic answers to this anxiety. The Danish philosopher Søren Kierkegaard pointed to the real answer. Kierkegaard observed that the awareness of our mortality can be transformed into what he called a school, meaning an opportunity for learning and growth. But the only power that will make this transformation happen is a meaningful faith. I would add that creative transformation of our anxiety about death takes place when we have a dynamic spirituality that enables us to risk really coming alive in the here-and-now.

A client in growth-oriented psychotherapy taught her therapist (me) a vital truth. As she completed what she described as a "therapeutic rebirth" into greater aliveness, she declared with great feeling, "I came to you for help because I was afraid of dying, but I discovered I was really afraid of living!" The answer to death is living—living life in all its fullness!

Obsolete religious beliefs, which still lurk in our minds and hearts from childhood, are a major block to our enjoying a growing faith in God and life in all its fullness. Even though we no longer accept these "holdover beliefs" with our adult intellects, they often cling like leeches to our feelings and attitudes. These unbelievable beliefs are like opaque paint thrown on the window of our souls, the window through which we otherwise might experience the light of God's healing love in the here-and-now moment.

Such spiritual blocks were among the excess baggage that was loaded on our hearts and minds by wounding experiences of religion in childhood. We uncritically absorbed, as children do, these distorted beliefs and values of our parents, church, and culture by a kind of psychospiritual osmosis.

It often requires spiritual courage to risk letting go of these security-giving childish beliefs and to risk honoring your honest doubts. It is painful to scrape away the protective but vision-blocking paint from the windows of your soul, but the payoff of doing so can be great. It allows you to claim the beliefs and values from childhood that you find to be self-validating in your adult life. It also enables you to replace holdover beliefs and values with what you really believe and prize in your adult experience. Such a painful process of spiritual maturing can free you to live with more spiritual and ethical aliveness, creativity, and joy.

How can you know if you really have found liberation from archaic beliefs? You'll feel lighter in your soul, though perhaps a bit more vulnerable, having let go of your spiritual security blanket. You'll feel a little more alive and energized because you have reclaimed energy that had been wasted on unresolved inner conflicts as you clung to old issues. Releasing obsolete, life-truncating beliefs can contribute to spiritual growth of the kind that the apostle Paul called putting an end to childish ways (1 Cor. 13:11) and growing up into Christ (Eph. 4:15). This happens when we speak the truth in love to ourselves.

 Self-Care Exercise: Pause briefly and reflect on the following two questions, noting your responses in the space below. If you are working with a partner or group, share your responses with one another.

1. How do my beliefs and the object of my devotion give my life meaning, purpose, and hope?

_____

_____

_____

_____

_____

_____

_____

2. What can I do to grow past any "holdover beliefs" that are blocking the windows of my soul so that I can live with more aliveness and joy?[11]

_____

_____

_____

_____

_____

_____

_____

Spiritual Need 4: *To Develop Values, Priorities, and Life Commitments Centered in Love, Integrity, and Justice That Help Us Live in Ways That Are Caring and Responsible, Both Personally and Socially*

Healthy values provide dependable guidelines to living in ways that are caring and responsible, both personally and socially. Your values, intertwined with your religious beliefs, guide you in making countless decisions each day that determine how healthful or unhealthful your lifestyle is. Distorted, immature, or sinful ethical practices are among the causes of many chronic health problems. Your total well being, including your physical health, will be enhanced by a lifestyle that is guided by Christian values such as these: honesty, justice, beauty, playfulness, sensitivity, compassion, self-esteem, cooperation with others, self-care balanced with caring for others, forgiveness, peacemaking, humility, and the willingness to sacrifice when this is needed for a higher good.

Living by these values is the best protection against the epidemic of spiritual-ethical illnesses in our society. Symptoms of these illnesses are the life-diminishing feelings that produce destructive living. These symptoms include hopelessness, powerlessness, shame, meaninglessness, boredom, fear of death, loss of faith, and loss of a zest for living with purpose, joy, and commitment to life in all its fullness for oneself, others, and society.

It is important to men's spiritual and overall health and that of their families and society, to prize and practice the so-called "soft values" that are prominent in the Christian way. These values include tenderness, compassion, vulnerability, and loving care for others. In this way, men can humanize the falsely labeled "strong values" that most men in our culture have been taught to overdevelop—competition, control, power, aggressiveness, technical mastery, and winning over others.

These "strong values" tend to produce violence against women, children, other men, and God's creation. In the process, men often inflict violence against themselves that shortens their lives. Male and female strength must be redefined to include both "soft" and "strong" values. Studies have showed that both genders tend to be healthier if they develop both sets of values in a balanced way. As more and more Christians do this, their spirituality and their congregations will express greater well being.

The health of our consciences is a primary factor in our spiritual wholeness. Trivial guilt feelings attached to "oughts" and "shoulds" learned in childhood squander today's ethical energies in yesterday's moralisms. Privatized consciences—which ignore the social context of individual ethical problems—together with obsolete moralizing, prevent some Christians from investing their moral influence in important values such as justice, integrity, peacemaking, and concern for God's creation. If people lived by these values, they could substantially improve their own personal lives and chance for survival, and they could help create a world in which children will be able to live a healthy life on a healthy planet.

A Time-Values Inventory: In your journal (or on another sheet of paper), quickly list the ten most important things in your life—people, activities, causes, possessions, achievements, institutions, and so on. / Now beside each of your "top ten" values, note approximately how much time you actually gave to this value in the last week (or the last month). Be alert to places where your time-identified priorities—your *real* priorities—are in serious conflict with your top ten values. / In light of your values and priorities and the lifestyle they produce, answer the following questions as candidly as possible. Pause while you think about each question and then jot down your responses, particularly to those that you want to do something about.

Do my values and priorities and the lifestyle that they shape enable me to:

• Give adequate time to the most important people and values in my life? Remember that "the most important things in life are not things."

• Take good care of my body? my mind? my work? my playfulness? Avoid burnout?

• Do the spiritual self-care that could enhance my total well being?

• Enjoy my most-loved people? nature? my creativity? my sense of humor? my sexuality? the things I love to do most?

• Work with others to help save a livable planet for all the children of the human family, including my own?

• Do the exciting, worthwhile things for myself and others that I really want to do during the unknown amount of time, long or short, I have left on planet earth?

Now, in light of your candid responses to these queries, ask yourself the final question: *What changes must I make to create a lifestyle more consistent with what's really most important to me, including the well being of my life and of my spiritual-ethical health?*

Note tentative plans for change in your journal or in spaces in this workbook. /

As you probably know, changing long-standing values, priorities, and life commitments is not easy. It can be tough even if your present lifestyle is killing you—spiritually, if not physically. Ask yourself, "Why wait for a painful family or medical crisis before I make changes that will help my life be more fulfilling, healthier, Christian, and, who knows, a tad longer?" Obviously, the smart thing to do is to change out-of-kilter priorities today before costly calamities or irreparable breakdowns occur.

 Self-Care Exercise: Pause briefly and reflect on the following two questions, noting your responses in the space below. / Then, if you're working with a partner or group, share your responses so you can learn from each other.

1. How well does my present lifestyle express *healthy* Christian values and priorities?

_____

_____

_____

_____

_____

2. What will I do to revise my values and priorities toward increasing my spiritual-ethical well being? When will I begin?

_____

_____

_____

_____

_____

Spiritual Need 5: *To Discover and Develop the Capacities in Our Souls for Wisdom, Creativity, and Agape Love*[12]

In traditional religious language, the spiritual center of our personality is called the "soul." Well being involves loving your soul and making it the integrating core of your whole life. As this spiritual center becomes a more peaceful, loving place, you may be surprised by how "together" you are, even when the storms within and around you make you feel turbulent and torn in other areas of your life. Your spiritual self can be your open channel to God's love. It is also the place from which you can reach out to other persons and species, aware of your oneness with God and with God's awe-inspiring network of living things!

Knowing how to keep the soul alive and well and developing our soul's potential are important for our total health because our soul channels the divine light within us. Our soul is the channel by which we connect with God's healing spirit. The soul is a potential wellspring of spiritual wisdom and guidance, giving us the power to respond as instruments of the Christ to the needs of others. Revitalizing your spiritual life may well be the key that unlocks the doorway to developing more love-centered well being in all departments of your life. The more we Christians make our spiritual self the integrating center of our lives, the more our whole body-mind-spirit will be energized by God's ever-present love.

Our secular, surface-living society makes it difficult to remain aware of the soul at the deeper center of our lives. It is very easy to feel disconnected from this transpersonal self. Discovering and caring for our spiritual centers can help heal the fragmentation of our lives. When we reconnect with our spiritual self, we will search for ways to express the love we experience by reaching out to others. Our sense of having a Christian vocation, by whatever name we call it, comes into focus as we discover a place where we can invest our talents to make a difference in the lives of other people, our church and community, and the wider world.

It often is appropriate to be skeptical at first when you meet people who believe that they have a special "mission" in life. But few things contribute as much to "getting it together" as a unifying sense of purpose that transcends our own brief life. Discovering such a larger purpose often brings zest to people's life and work and, as it does this, enhances their health.

 Soulful Spiritual Well Being Exercise: Stop reading, close your eyes, and take a few minutes to relax your body, mind, and spirit deeply (without going to sleep), so you are both very alert and very relaxed. / Now, see if you can go to the place deeper in your consciousness where you're "together" and at peace, in spite of any storms on the surface of your life today. If you haven't been in that safe, serene place for a while, it may require some time to find your way there again. /

When you are in that place, let yourself enjoy just being there cleansed and renewed by the gentle healing light of God's love. / When you are ready, look at some problem you're facing currently, viewing it from the perspective of your spiritual self. See what happens to it from this self-transcending viewpoint. / Reflect about your Christian lifestyle. Be aware of insights that may bubble up into your awareness as you stay quietly centered in your spiritual self, open to the divine Spirit within you. /

When you're ready, return in your mind to the place where you are sitting. / I hope that this simple technique for becoming more connected with your spiritual self opened you to some blessings and that the healing environment of that inner sanctuary brought

fresh light on an issue with which you're struggling.

If this self-care exercise was at all helpful, jot down any discoveries you wish to remember, reflect on, and perhaps do something about. Make a note to yourself to repeat this exercise when you find yourself obsessing about a problem and forgetting the possibilities that may be hidden within it.

_____

_____

_____

_____

 Self-Care Exercise: Pause briefly and reflect on the following two questions, noting your responses in the space below. / Then, if you're working with a partner or group, share your responses to these questions and to the exercise above.

1. How well does my present lifestyle let me stay connected with my soul?

_____

_____

_____

_____

_____

2. What will I do to reconnect more regularly with this self-transcending, spiritual self?

_____

_____

_____

_____

Spiritual Need 6: *To Experience Our Deep Connections with Other People and with God's Wonderful Creation, the Natural World*

The quality of our most important relationships does more than anything else to determine the health of our total selves, including our spiritual well being. Human brokenness involves alienation from rejected aspects of ourselves that produces alienation from other people, nature, and God. Our deepest alienation, often hidden from view in our secularized society, is our alienation from our spiritual self. This spiritual alienation is an underlying, though often unrecognized, cause of the other painful alienations that cause people to search for healing.

In our very natures, we humans are relationship creatures. We are created with a spiritual hunger for experiencing mutually nurturing interaction with our network of family and friends and with the wonderful network of other living things. Our healing and wholeness, even our physical survival, depend on interaction with our social and natural environments. Spiritually centered well being grows best in the loving relationships of a small group or community committed to mutual spiritual growth around shared values.

A healthy, caring congregation is like a garden where each person's unique dreams and potentials for spiritual growth are cultivated. In a society suffering from an epidemic of loneliness, such a church is like a welcome oasis in a dry, barren land. It is like an extended family where people's spiritual life and values are shaped by a Christian understanding of life's ultimate meaning.

I remember these words by a lonely young seminarian in a spiritual growth group: "Once before I die I would like to get close enough to another human being to really touch souls." Other members of that group nodded in agreement as he expressed the human longing for *spiritual* intimacy. Pause and ask yourself, *Have I ever longed for this kind of soul-to-soul communion with another person? /*

Experiencing what has been called a "soul friend" can occur in many different relationships—for example, in a creatively close marriage or a deep friendship; in a warm, caring congregation; in a life-saving twelve-step recovery group; in a spiritual caring and sharing group committed to mutual spiritual-ethical discoveries. In such interpersonal environments, caring love, refreshing honesty, and open communication come together to generate healing and wholeness.

Another spiritual relationship need we humans have is to bond with God's creation, the natural world all around as well as within us. John Muir loved the beautiful High Sierras, the towering mountains that form the geological backbone of California. He was aware of what is now called the bottom-line ecological principle—that all things are interconnected and interdependent. Muir knew firsthand the wider interconnectedness that can support our individual and relationship wellness. In one of his journals, he wrote, "When we try to pick out anything by itself, we find it hitched to everything else in the Universe."[13] Such an ecological consciousness, when rooted in an earthy, creation-oriented spirituality, awakens an awareness that we really are at home in the universe. We really do belong!

An ecological consciousness also can produce a sensual spirituality that is rooted in the earth. This spirituality is fed by an awareness that our minds, bodies, spirits, and relationships are integral parts of this interdependent living network. Our wholeness is mutually nurtured by other people and creatures and by the continually creating spirit of the God who is the dynamic source of the human and natural networks that sustain us.

Self-Care Exercise: Pause briefly and reflect on the following two questions, noting your responses in the space below. / If you're working with a partner or group, share your responses to these questions so you can learn from each other.

1. How well does my present lifestyle cause me to enjoy and deepen my connectedness with other people and the biosphere?

_____

_____

_____

_____

2. What will I do to celebrate my deep ecological connections with both human and natural environments?

_____

_____

_____

_____

Spiritual Need 7: *To Develop Spiritual Resources to Enhance Our Trust, Self-Esteem, Hope, and Love of People and Life; and to Develop Spiritual Resources to Help Heal the Wounds of Grief, Guilt, Shame, Resentment, and Self-Rejection*

The most reliable ways to evaluate the health of one's spirituality is to discover the degree to which it nurtures self-esteem and other people-loving attitudes and the degree to which it helps heal the wounds of grief, guilt, shame, resentment, anger, self-rejection, and lack of forgiveness. Spiritual resources are essential for these purposes. Only spiritual resources, for example, will bring healing to experiences of being deeply shattered by grief. The next session will focus especially on this essential spiritual hunger.

How Whole (and Nonsexist) Is Your Spirituality?

The spirituality of each individual needs to reflect the spiritual wisdom of both women and men. Jesus' life wonderfully reflects a liberated man who demonstrated the strength of nonsexist wholeness. As all the Gospels show, Jesus had developed both the nurturing, caring side and the assertive, leadership sides of his personality. His nonsexist response to Mary and Martha went against his society's role expectations of women. Jesus regarded women as precious daughters of God, just as men are precious sons of God. For the mental, physical, and spiritual health of ourselves and our relationships, we would be wise to emulate Jesus.

We should remember and follow the liberating words of Paul when he says that in Christ "there is no longer male and female" (Gal. 3:28). The important thing in God's sight is not our gender but our humanity.

Unfortunately, some of the statements about women attributed to Paul—for example, their being speechless in church and submissive to husbands—reflect the sexism of his first-century culture and have been used to constrict women in ways that have prevented their using many of their gifts from God. The male-dominated beliefs and images of our faith have hurt deeply the spiritual well being not only of women but also of men.

Fortunately, many women in churches are joining hands with one another and with enlightened men to change this so that Christian women will have full opportunities to use their rich resources for the healing and wholeness of themselves, their families, and their churches and communities.

Ours is an exciting as well as a chaotic time for Christian spirituality as it becomes enriched and healthier by integrating the spiritual wisdom of women with that of men. Women spiritual pioneers like Nelle Morton,

Rosemary Radford Ruether, and Catherine Keller are helping Christian women and men recover the spiritual wisdom of women through the centuries, wisdom that was often ignored or suppressed by male church leaders. Nelle's statement is on target: "A whole theology is possible only when the whole people become part of its process, and that includes women."[14]

Creative Coping with the Human Family's Spiritual Crisis

Satisfying our spiritual hungers in healthy ways is a difficult challenge today because of humankind's global spiritual-ethical crisis. The mind-boggling speed of social and technological change has produced a massive breakdown of traditional belief and value systems. Millions of people are flatly rejecting old authority-centered ways of defining what is really good or ultimately true. Experiencing spiritual transcendence as a vital force has largely disappeared from the lives of millions of people in Western societies. Old ways of believing and valuing are no longer acceptable to them, but many have not yet developed new ways that work for them. Vacuums in meaning and values proliferate, rooted in our profoundly materialistic, thing-worshiping lifestyles.

This spiritual crisis in our culture leaves us terribly vulnerable to the ego-chill of the fear of death. When people are terribly frightened, they may sacrifice their freedom to think and believe as they seek the fragile security of authoritarian religion or other "solutions." People often retreat into rigid, fundamentalist expressions of faith with spiritual gurus who claim to have the only truth about religious issues. This is a destructive defense against the ego-chill.

But the spiritual crisis also is an unprecedented opportunity to grow up spiritually and ethically. It is spiritually healthy that so many people, despite their anxieties, are no longer giving away their spiritual power to authoritarian religious leaders and institutions. In his great hymn to love in 1 Corinthians, the Apostle Paul says that he has "put an end to childish ways" in the area of faith (1 Cor. 13:11).

This is our challenging opportunity today. As never before in human history, we are challenged to use our new spiritual freedom to relinquish childish ways and to replace them with beliefs and values that we can affirm wholeheartedly and live by with zest, love, and joy. We must recognize that our own spiritual health and general well being is inextricably interdependent with the spiritual health and general well being of our sisters and brothers in the human family all around the planet. To undergird the health of our world, our beliefs and values must emphasize interfaith solidarity based on justice and mutual respect. They must aim at saving a healthy planet for all future generations. They must incorporate the incredibly rich but often ignored spiritual heritage of women as well as men.

Developing such liberating beliefs and values promises to be an exciting spiritual journey that demands great courage. It is a journey to which God in Christ calls us today.

 Spiritual Renewal/Self-Care Exercise: Pause now and try this guided healing and energizing exercise.

Sit in a comfortable position with your spine erect and both feet on the floor so that you feel firmly grounded and facilitate the flow of energy in your whole body. / Become aware of your body, especially any areas in which you are holding tension. Tense the muscles of those parts of your body even tighter, holding this for a few seconds and then releasing the tension. Repeat this several times, until you feel those areas relaxing. / As you exhale, feel the stress flow out with each breath. Then, as you inhale, visualize the fresh oxygen going throughout your whole body, bringing energy to every cell in it. Do this several times until your body and mind are in a very alert but deeply relaxed state. /

Now with your eyes closed to concentrate on what you are experiencing, place your two cupped hands together to form a bowl in front of you. / Become aware of the burdensome feelings you'd like to get rid of. Place them in your bowl, one at a time—fears, angers, resentments, guilt feelings, shame, worries, old hurts, pet peeves—the feelings that feel heavy as you become aware of them. / Be aware of the weight in your cupped hands. / When you are ready, turn your hands over and empty the bowl, releasing the heavy feelings. Turn them over to the Lord. / If you feel a little lighter now, you know that you truly have let go of these burdens on your mind and heart.

Now put your cupped hands together again to form another bowl in front of you. / This time, let the bowl be a receptacle to receive the healing, cleansing, renewing, forgiving energy of God's loving spirit. This love is always present if we open our awareness to receive the gift. / As your bowl fills with this amazing divine grace, let the spiritual energy flow through your arms into your whole body, bathing it with healing, relaxed aliveness. Experience the divine energy bathing your brain and your mind in this vitality and joy. /

For Christians and other caring people, the healing love we receive is to be shared. If you are with others, join hands now, keeping your eyes closed to concentrate on what you are experiencing. / Let this spiritual energy flow both ways through your linked hands, giving and receiving God's love with each other. Be aware of how the experience of God's love is changed by this sharing. / When you are ready, finish the exercise in whatever way you choose to give it a sense of completion. /

Whether you have done this exercise alone or with someone else, sit quietly with eyes closed, reflecting on what you experienced and what this may teach you about spiritual self-care, healing, and wholeness. / Open your eyes and take a few minutes to make notes on your experience. / If you've done this exercise with someone else, take a few minutes now to share your experiences, particularly what you learned that may be valuable to your health in even a small way. Be sure to share anything you intend to do with what you learned. /

If you've done the exercise solo, decide with whom you wish to share what you have learned at the first opportunity. (Sharing with others increases mutual learning. It also reinforces each individual's own insights and increases the likelihood that these will be remembered and used in constructive ways.)

Questions for Reflection

1. Does it make sense in your experience to understand spiritual well being as the result of learning to satisfy your basic spiritual needs in healthier ways? Do you have spiritual needs in addition to the seven listed?

2. How well are your spiritual and ethical needs being met by yourself and your congregation?

3. Do you agree that everything a church does in its wellness program should be spiritually centered, understanding "spiritual" to include all dimensions of a religious lifestyle?

4. What can you do to enable your congregation to become more effective as a spiritual wholeness center for yourself and others?

Strengthening Your Self-Care Plan

Summarize what you have learned in this session by writing out a tentative spiritual self-care plan for yourself in this work-book or in your journal. Be sure to include the NS and OK items in your spiritual checkup that you really wanted to strengthen. Add insights concerning how you could satisfy your seven basic spiritual needs more fully.[15] (Note: Be sure to read this note for suggestions about making your plan work for you.)

Closing Song, Prayer, and Evaluation

Whether you are studying Christian well being alone or with a wellness partner or in a group, close this session by doing the following things:

• Sing a hymn, spiritual, or folk song that expresses your understanding of the importance of healthy spirituality as the heart of Christian wholeness in all dimensions of life.

• Celebrate the new understandings you have gained by spending some time in prayer expressing joy and thanksgiving for such insights. Commit yourself in passionate prayer to the implemention of any new plans you have made during this session.

• Do a brief evaluation of the session, aimed at increasing the benefits to well being of future sessions.

Continuing Your Self-Care

The following actions will help you continue your wellness work between sessions. Whether you are doing these sessions alone or with a wellness partner or group, these things will also prepare you to use the next session to gain maximal benefits for your mental well being.

• Spend at least ten minutes each day implementing the high priority item or items you included in your spiritual self-care plan; in your journal keep track of how your spiritual wellness is affected by this invest-ment of time in enriching your religious and ethical life.

• Read Session 3 in this workbook, underlining or highlighting the things that seem especially relevant to your mental and emotional self-care. If you have time, also scan Chapter 3 in the other text, *Well Being*. Before the next session, complete the Mental Well Being Checkup at the beginning of Session 3 in this workbook. This will enable you to identify aspects of your mental life that are strong and those that need strengthening. Make two lists for future reference — one of key items you marked OK (acceptable but room for improvement), the other for items you marked NS (definitely need strengthening). As you do this, you may think of things you want to do to enhance this crucial aspect of your overall wellness.

• In your mind picture yourself sur-rounded with the light of your caring and with God's healing love. If you are studying with a wellness partner or group, do the same for your partner or other group members. This form of imaging intercessory prayer is an energizing way to express your care for others. Many people have discovered its effectiveness. Repeat this exercise several times between sessions.

Session 3

Empowering Your Mind for Healing, Creativity, and Loving Outreach to Others

We are commanded to love God with all our minds, as well as with all our hearts, and we commit a great sin if we forbid or prevent that cultivation of the mind in others which would enable them to perform this duty.

—Angelina Grimke (1805–79), American feminist and abolitionist, in "Appeal to the Christian Women of the South," 1836[1]

God grant me the serenity to accept the things I cannot change, courage to change the things I can, and the wisdom to know the difference.

—Reinhold Niebuhr, "Serenity Prayer," widely used in Twelve-Step recovery programs

A Mental Well Being Checkup

 Prepare to gain the greatest benefits for your mental well being from this session by taking and scoring this checkup first. It can give you practical help in enhancing your mental self-care. By using it, you can quickly identify the areas where your mental well being is robust and those areas that need increased self-care. The checkup items are like a rich smorgasbord of things you can do to enjoy and empower your mind by releasing its creativity, using it to nurture your wellness and reaching out to people you love and care about. Most of the suggestions for increasing mental wellness in the session that follows are previewed in the checkup.[2]

Instructions: Mark each statement in one of three ways:

E = "I'm doing *excellently* in this area of my mental life." (If you're being honest with yourself, give yourself a pat on the back. You deserve it.)

OK = "I'm doing *acceptably* in this, but there's room for improvement."

NS = "This is an area where I definitely *need strengthening*." (Commend yourself for identifying places where spiritual growth is both needed and possible.)

____ I often enjoy God's good gift of being alive and aware in the fleeting, here-and-now moments, even though this makes me more vulnerable to life's painful side.

____ I recharge my mental, spiritual, and physical batteries by giving myself regular quiet times for relaxed meditation, inspirational reading, and prayer. I also find renewal through laughter and playful mental frolicking at appropriate times.

____ Self-care of my mind by regular study, reading, and reflection on tough issues is an important part of my lifestyle. I know that this is how I can "love God with my mind" (as the Apostle Paul writes), thus developing more of my mind's assets and using them to increase the well being of myself and others.

____ I use my mind to help heal and enliven my body, mind, and relationships.

____ I enjoy using my mind to learn new things and to "spark" new ideas by spirited dialogue and debate with other people, including those who disagree with my viewpoints.

____ I balance my rational, analytical, verbal, quantitative, "left-brain" activities with frequent intuitive, playful, nonanalytical, "right-brain" activities—such as music, drawing, gardening, joking, meditative prayer, storytelling.

____ I intermingle intellectual activities with physical and people-centered activities.

____ I have a solid sense of worth as a unique person and child of God. My self-esteem is not derived from collecting either achievements or the approval of others.

____ I usually resolve constructively my "negative" feelings and impulses such as guilt, jealousy, lack of forgiveness, shame, resentment, loneliness, despair, and chronic anger and fear, so that they will not diminish the well being of myself or others.

____ I cultivate "positive" feelings such as love, caring, hope, trust, celebration, playfulness, happiness, serenity, joy, and connectedness with other people and nature, so that these feelings nurture my total well being.

____ I practice the art of forgiving myself, thus becoming better able to forgive others and life for their imperfections. I usually avoid wasting creative energy on useless remorse about the past or unrealistic fears about the future. I avoid depressing myself by not turning anger inward on myself and putting myself down.

____ When serious problems, crises, and failures hit me, I mobilize my coping resources, turn to caring people, and try to be open to learning from the pain, thus using the problems as opportunities for mental, spiritual, and interpersonal growth.

____ I can confront the pain, evil, injustice, and tragedies in society and in my own life without losing touch with life's goodness, beauty, love, and fun.

____ I check out my perceptions of people and events with those I trust, thus anchoring my understanding in the real situations I face. I usually have sufficient awareness of myself to avoid responding to threatening situations in inappropriate, self-defeating ways.

____ I usually avoid obsessing about personal problems, and I balance these concerns by wrestling with important issues outside my own private world.

____ I like my God-given sensual and sexual feelings, and I use them constructively to bring sparkle and passion to my life.

____ I know and befriend my less attractive hidden or "shadow" side, thus avoiding projecting this onto others and fighting or fearing in them what really is in me.

____ I practice body-mind-spirit stress reduction or deep relaxation methods at least once a day to renew myself and increase my openness to the still small voice of the loving God.

____ I often use methods for healing painful memories, thus making peace with my past and avoiding wasting today's energy on yesterday's mistakes and tragedies.

____ When I experience ongoing inner conflicts or unresolved problems, I find courage to seek help from a competent, caring friend, family member, pastor, counselor, or psychotherapist.

____ I organize and prioritize the clamoring claims on my time to avoid "hurry-itis," thus enabling myself to accomplish reasonable objectives, rather than frustrating myself by unrealistic, perfectionistic goals.

____ I keep track of and befriend my night dreams and daydreams, using them to stay in touch with the wisdom of my deeper, unconscious mind.

____ I usually keep the responsible adult side of my personality in the driver's seat of my mind but balance this by encouraging my inner child to enjoy playing and by nurturing my inner parent to be caring of others.

____ I am aware of the profound interconnectedness of my head, heart, spirit, and body, as well as their connections with other people, nature, and the divine Spirit.

____ I often join things of the head and the heart because I know that truth-linked-with-love is what heals people and nurtures wholeness in myself and others.

____ I find satisfaction and personal enrichment in using my head, heart, and hands to help other people and my community with the complex problems we all face.

____ I prefer to live with unanswered questions rather than escape into simplistic or authority-given "answers" to life's complex issues, paradoxes, and dilemmas.

____ I have a healthy dislike for long checklists like this, even though I'm open to discovering if they might provide some insights that are useful for my wellness.

Using Your Findings to Enhance Your Mental Well Being

Take the following steps to help you use the results of this checkup in developing your mental self-care plan:

1. Tally your responses and write down the totals below. This will provide you with an overview of your mental well being. / Give yourself a pat on the back for the things you honestly scored "E."

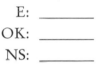

> E: _____
> OK: _____
> NS: _____

2. Go through the list and put a star beside those OK and NS items that seem either urgent or especially important to you. /

3. What is your overall "feel" concerning your general mental wellness? In the space below, jot down your overall evaluation of the strengths and weaknesses of your mental well being.

_____

_____

_____

_____

_____

_____

_____

4. Beside the starred items, make notes about how you could strengthen your mind's wellness. / In this session on mental well being, you will be encouraged to come back to these items and elaborate on your ideas as you develop a workable mental self-care plan.

A Biblical Perspective

 The following story sets the tone for this session. It communicates the crucial importance of continuing to discover and develop the many gifts of God in our minds and personalities. In the Gospels of Mark and Matthew, this scene occurs when powerful religious leaders who were threatened by Jesus' message asked him a series of trick questions. They hoped to elicit answers that would give them grounds to arrest him.

One of these leaders asked, "Which commandment is the first of all?" Jesus answered by quoting the two key commandments from Hebrew Scriptures: "You shall love the Lord your God with all your heart, and with all your soul, and with all your mind, and with all your strength. . . . You shall love your neighbor as yourself" (Mark 12:28-31). (In the good news according to Luke, a religious leader tries to test Jesus by asking: "Teacher, what must I do to inherit eternal life?" Jesus wisely turns the question back to him, asking what the Jewish law says. The man quotes the same verses from Leviticus and Deuteronomy and Jesus affirms his answer (Luke 10:25-27).

What in the world does loving God with all our heart, soul, mind, and strength mean when translated into contemporary language? It means loving God by developing all dimensions of our personalities—our emotional, spiritual, and intellectual resources, and our inner strengths—through lifelong, whole-person learning, and then using these gifts to serve the needs of God's

human family and natural world. The purpose of this session is to explore some ways we can love God with our minds in these confusing times.

Reread Angelina Grimke's declaration at the beginning of this session. It was written in the context of her tireless struggles for the liberation of women as well as African American men and women. Her courageous statement remains on target for Christian women and men today, more than 130 years later, because, sad to say, the struggle is unfinished and must continue. The goal today is still the same: to enable both women and African Americans, as well as all people whose growth opportunities are constricted by society's prejudices, to love God fully with their minds!

Major Objectives and Themes

 Put a check mark in front of the objectives and themes below that are personally important to you as you seek to enhance your Christian lifestyle. In this session you'll have opportunities to learn the following:

❑ The profound interrelationship of your mind with your spirit and your body.

❑ The roots of mental well being in the Bible.

❑ How to develop more of your mind's many unused gifts.

❑ New ways to use your mind for both self-healing and self-caring.

❑ Methods for increasing your creativity, inner joy, and problem-solving ability.

❑ Ways to use your mind to reach out with informed caring to others.

❑ Strategies for enhancing your overall mental well being.

The items you checked reflect what you hope to learn in this session. Jot down in the space below notes about these personal objectives.

_____

_____

_____

_____

_____

_____

_____

_____

Biblical Roots

 **Learning Exercise: Before reading the following section, draw on your own knowledge of the Bible. Take a few minutes to jot down some biblical passages that emphasize the importance of truth-seeking and education for Christians.

_____

_____

_____

_____

_____

_____

_____

_____

Let's look at several Bible passages containing truths about the well being of our minds. To understand Jesus' teachings, it helps to keep in mind the first-century world in which he lived and thought and taught. The culture in which his personality and his spiritually centered approach to life were shaped had (and still has today) a profound appreciation for education, for spiritual wisdom, and for those who teach it.

What is called the "wisdom literature" by scholars of Jesus' Bible (the Hebrew Scriptures) includes the book of Proverbs. It reflects a deep respect for the education of children, including their ethical guidance: "Train children in the right way, and when old, they will not stray" (Prov. 22:6). Proverbs also expresses these wise admonitions for anyone seeking enhanced mental well being: "Apply your mind to instruction and your ears to words of knowledge" (Prov. 23:12). "Get wisdom; get insight; . . . love her, and she will guard you" (Prov. 4:5-6). It is noteworthy that the Hebrew term for "wisdom" is a feminine word. The wisdom literature is one of the relatively few places in the Bible that preserves ancient wisdom about healthy, spiritually empowered living. Gems about living that are valuable for both genders are included in this stream of the Bible.

The great respect in which Jesus' disciples held him was expressed in the term they often used to address him: *rabbouni* or *rabbi*, the Hebrew word for "teacher." In light of this, consider these words attributed to Jesus in the most lyrical of the Gospels: "You will know the truth, and the truth will make you free" (John 8:32).

This statement affirms the liberating power of truth, particularly the spiritual truths found in the New Testament about the fullness of life. This passage also highlights the importance for Christians at each stage of their life to seek new understandings of themselves, God, nature, and the abundant life. Loving God with our minds means doing whatever is required to enlarge the horizons of our understanding about and care for all of God's creation.

Jesus recognized, as does modern psychology, that the quality of people's inner lives profoundly shapes their behavior, including their speech. Their patterns of behavior, therefore, often reveal who they really are at their center. In his discussion of recognizing good and bad trees by their fruits, Jesus declared, "For out of the abundance of the heart the mouth speaks. The good person brings good things out of good treasure, and the evil person brings evil things out of evil treasure" (Matt. 12:34-35). Transformation at the center of people's lives is what Christian conversion is all about.

Paul's second letter to the young disciple Timothy reflects a recognition of the gifts of God that are at the roots of mentally healthy attitudes and empowerment. His wise advice includes these words: "Rekindle the gift of God that is within you . . . for God did not give us a spirit of cowardice, but rather a spirit of power and of love and of self-discipline" (2 Tim. 1:6-7). Paul wrote the first-century church in Rome to prepare them for his hoped-for pastoral visit. He challenged the recipients not to be conformists to the secular culture of their world but to be what we might label "countercultural" today. He wrote, "Be transformed by the renewing of your minds" (Rom. 12:2).

We can understand this verse as a call to continued nurture and development of the God-given capacities of the mind. Being "born again" (John 3:3, NIV) is understood as the process of rebirth or transformation. The Christian lifestyle is not a static state but a process of being born again, and again, and again, as our changing life experiences bring new glimpses of truth from God about living life in all its fullness. Loving God by empowering and renewing our minds through new learnings constitutes the path of continuing transformation that is well being.

What Is Mental Well Being?

In these pages, people are understood to be mentally healthy to the degree that their personalities have these interrelated characteristics:

- They have self-acceptance, self-esteem, accurate self-perception, inner serenity, and joy.
- They are continuing to develop their God-given possibilities.
- They have an integrated sense of who they are and what their important values are as these reflect God's intention for them and the world.
- They see the reality of the world and other people accurately, undistorted by their subjective needs.
- They have "emotional intelligence" characterized by empathy, social skills, self-awareness, control of impulses, and motivation to persist with optimism in the face of setbacks.
- They relate to other people and God in constructive ways and are aware of being supported by the divine Spirit.
- They are able to cope with life's miserable downside and yet continue to enjoy loving and working, laughing and playing.

If these criteria seem psychologically heavy, remember that everyone's mental wellness is a matter of degree and also an ongoing process that has its downs as well as ups.

A healthy Christian lifestyle can strengthen mental well being in a variety of ways, including enhancing these essential ingredients: self-esteem, competence, a sense of inner strength, and reality-based hope. All of us humans have an inescapable need for a sense of our inherent worth, for the knowledge and skills to accomplish the things that are important to us, for the inner strength to control and guide our own lives and to influence others in constructive directions, and for hope grounded in reality.

Numerous studies show that people who have a meaningful faith and are involved regularly in the life of a healthy congregation tend to have more stability in their personal lives and family life than those who lack these religious resources.

In our depersonalizing modern society, countless people suffer from the severely depleted self-esteem that Martin Luther King Jr. called "nobody-ness." This prevents them from living constructively and making needed contributions to their community. But those who share the Christian belief that they are precious individuals of irreducible worth in God's sight have a spiritual awareness of their own worth. This helps protect them from the blows they receive to their self-esteem from other people, their work, and their society.

Health-giving Christian faith and caring fellowship also make people aware that their vulnerable strength is undergirded by the everlasting arms of the divine Spirit. This healthy Christian empowerment is not power *over* or power *against* others but mainly power *with* others and sometimes power *for* helping persons in need.

Such empowerment grows when people relate in caring and affirming ways that support one another's importance, competence, and strengths. Persons who crave power over or against others cannot relate to others in such mutually supportive ways because of a painful lack of inner feelings of esteem, competence, and strength.

The Christian good news also brings hope to those in the middle of despair-saturated circumstances. To know that long-term hope for ourselves and our world is grounded in the intention and power of a loving God can sustain hope in otherwise hopeless situations. Such spiritually based hope is an invaluable mental health asset in today's despairing world.

A hope-filled development in contemporary psychology is the identification of "emotional intelligence" (emotional quotient or EQ), defined as having empathy, social skills, self-awareness, impulse control, and motivation to continue optimistically when hit by misfortune.[3] This form of intelligence is at least as important to human well being as the intellectual intelligence measured by standard IQ tests. In fact, for happy marriages, successful careers, and the effectiveness of our immune systems, EQ seems to be much more important than IQ.

Fortunately, parents can help their children develop more emotional intelligence by handling their own feelings and relationships constructively, modeling EQ in their relations with their offspring and coaching them in finding constructive ways to handle their emotions and relationship conflicts. My professional experience suggests that people with a vital faith and a meaningful church family tend to have greater emotional intelligence than those who lack a vital faith and caring congregation.

 Learning Exercise: Pause now and reflect on how effective your Christian faith is in strengthening your mental well being, including your awareness of your inherent value, your competence in living, your sense of healthy empowerment, and your inner joy and peace. / Make notes to yourself about how your religious life is increasing or diminishing these essential ingredients in your mental health. / If you are studying with a wellness partner or group, take turns sharing briefly what you learned in this exercise. /

_____

_____

_____

_____

_____

_____

_____

Your Mind's Well Being Is Crucial to Your Total Wellness

To understand why your mind's health is so important, consider the two interdependent keys that can unlock the door to increasing your well being—the health of your spirit and the health of your mind. We saw in the last session how the health of our spirituality and ethical values influences both our physical and mental health. Focus now on the second key—how your ideas, attitudes, perceptions, memories, feelings, images, beliefs, and future expectations can powerfully impact your general well being. How you care for and use your mind can help keep you well and enable you to heal more quickly, on the one hand, or contribute to sickness, on the other.

Chronic anger, depression, guilt, self-rejection, purposelessness, powerlessness, and pathological religion can contribute to a wide variety of physical, mental, and spiritual illnesses. In contrast, hopefulness, forgiveness (of self and others), self-esteem, purposefulness, feeling in charge of your life, and healthy religion can help keep your body well and facilitate more rapid healing when you have surgery or are ill.

Psychologist Joan Borysenko, former director of the Mind Body Clinic at Harvard Medical School, summarizes the amazing discoveries of contemporary mind-body research for understanding our health and sickness: "We are entering a new level in the scientific understanding of mechanisms by which faith, belief, and imagination can actually unlock the mysteries of healing."[4] This research has revealed a circular mind-body interaction. What people believe and the images they hold in their mind can increase their overall vulnerability to illness or increase the likelihood of their staying well or recovering more quickly. In other words, the mental and spiritual attitudes of persons may help to cause as well as cure illnesses.[5]

A second reason that self-care of our minds is so crucial is that most people use only a small part of the intellectual, interpersonal, problem-solving, and creative potentialities of their minds. Psychologists such as Abraham Maslow estimate this as only 15 to 25 percent. The good news is that most people (including you) have more mental gifts and creativity and more capacity to live joyfully and productively than they have yet discovered. Improving our mental well being is the process of discovering and developing these gifts in ways that enhance our lives and enable us to reach out to those in need more effectively. Our minds are certainly one of God's most precious gifts. The challenge for us as Christians is to learn how to love the Lord more fully with our whole minds.

How can we do this? We do this by using more of our mental possibilities in the lifelong adventures of continuing to learn and of coping with life's challenges. Developing constructive ways to cope with the knotty personal, family, and job problems that most of us face sooner or later frequently depends on using fresh problem-solving strategies.

In addition, Christians who are committed to life in all its fullness must also be concerned with helping to make their communities better places in which to live and learn. They must work to help heal the complex social problems that hurt everyone's wholeness. Joining heads as well as hearts and hands with Christians and people of other faiths to generate cooperative strategies for curing these social malignancies is a way to enable this social healing.

The mind-boggling and accelerating social change in our society offers another crucial reason to take care of our minds. Lifelong learning is necessary to stay in touch with a world being reinvented repeatedly in one's lifetime. The amazing information and communication revolutions today, made possible by computers and the global electronic network, can make continued learning not only easier but also more necessary to our total well being. In an avalanche of easily available information that threatens to bury us, the ability to distinguish information from knowledge and knowledge from real wisdom, is more and more important.

From both spiritual and intellectual perspectives, it is crucial that we learn to prize the relevant and time-tested wisdom of the ages that can guide us in using new knowledge for human well being. We Christians, seeking to follow the footsteps of one who was the great Teacher, should make sure that our congregations are exciting places of lifelong exploration, spiritual research, study, and learning.

Building On Your Discoveries from the Checkup

If you took and tallied the Mental Well Being Checkup before this session, congratulations! You have a running start on using this session to enhance your mind's self-care. (If you haven't done the checkup yet, I suggest that you turn back to it now and take ten or fifteen minutes to do so.)

 Learning Exercise: Look over your tally of the checkup and the notes you made after taking it, keeping these issues in mind:
   • the NS and OK items that you checked as seeming particularly important or urgent;
   • your preliminary thoughts about steps you might take to strengthen your mental well being; and
   • additional resources that may be useful in implementing your tentative plans.

If you are studying with a wellness partner or in a group, take a few minutes now to share what you discovered and plan to do

as a result of taking the checkup. / When you have finished, jot down useful insights you gained in the process of reflecting and sharing. / If you are studying alone, talk about your plans with a person or persons interested in enhancing their own mental well being.

_____
_____
_____
_____
_____
_____
_____
_____
_____

I trust that what you learned from this checkup has suggested a variety of things you can do to increase the well being of your mind and personality. If so, I encourage you to implement these action-options first, giving them priority in your mental fitness program. The strategies for enhancing your mind's fitness discussed below can help you build on what you have decided. They summarize several key steps people have found useful in increasing their mental well being.[6]

Increase Self-Responsibility for Your Lifestyle's Wellness

Self-responsibility means accepting the fact that the buck stops with you for most of the decisions that determine how healthy or unhealthy your lifestyle is. Health care professionals such as physician Bernie Siegel report that the patients who gain the most help from medical expertise and tend to need it less often are those who decide to be active and intentional partners in their own healing and health care. (The approach to pastoral counseling and therapy that I call "growth counseling" also emphasizes self-responsibility.)

Intentionality and choice are motifs running throughout the Bible's ethical insights about how to live a healthy life. In New Testament accounts of Jesus' healing miracles, self-responsibility is a continuing theme, expressed in such words as "stand up, take your bed, and go home" (Mark 2:9, NEB). A Christian lifestyle involves using your mental muscles of self-direction and self-responsibility. Christian self-responsibility means letting go of the comfortable but dangerous assumption that God or some godlike doctor will be able to rescue us from continued neglect of our day-to-day wellness care.

Acting with intentionality is the opposite of playing a passive victim, a role that puts you at the mercy of circumstances. Responsible self-care means using whatever options you have today to choose to take small steps toward a more whole future.

How can you enhance your responsible health care? You're already moving toward more responsible self-care by upgrading your expertise concerning health issues and by using a preventive self-care plan that fits your physical health, age, life situation, and preferences. You are the only person who can walk the road that leads toward a healthier life for you. Having wise guides at critical points on the journey can be extremely important, even lifesaving. So consult caring and competent health professionals, therapists, and teachers as guides when you need their special knowledge and skills.

 Learning Exercise: Pause and think briefly about what you need to do about a particular health issue. / Consider how Christian resources may help you decide among your available action-options on this personal health concern. / Take the step you decide on, and use the resources of your Christian faith to guide and energize your action. / By doing so, you will be practicing Christian intentionality and choice in your self-care.

Love God by Exercising Your Mind— Vigorously and Often

Apply the well-documented "use it and you won't lose it!" principle by stretching and strengthening your mind's mental muscles. This may involve firming up your couch-potato intellectual flabbiness caused by passively watching television for prolonged periods of time, by avoiding reading stimulating books and wrestling with tough, intellectual issues, and by neglecting to use your creative capacities to generate needed innovations in your life.

While writing this section, I'm taking time out to play with our ten-month-old grandson. He's at a fascinating stage where he seems to use nearly every waking moment to learn about his surroundings. He does so by nonstop touching, looking, exploring, or trying to put everything within reach into his mouth. What a pity that many of us grown-ups seldom feel even a momentary urge to enjoy the adventure of using our minds in spontaneous learning and discovery.

Loving God with our minds involves using them to expand our horizons of understanding in a variety of ways that express our love of life, our caring for people, and our passion to discover fresh fragments of truth.

We can increase our capacity to live the Christian life of caring service only by life-long learning. People who have not had a really new idea in a decade, and who probably would be frightened if one came into their consciousness, are neglecting the full use of God's great gift—the blessing of human intelligence.

Reflecting on a Window of Wholeness: Read the vignette about George Washington Carver in *Well Being*, pages 55–56. / I hope that this refreshes your memory about an African-American genius. Carver was a spiritually motivated person who used his brains and inventive creativity, despite enormous odds, to contribute countless benefits to all the people in the region where he lived and did his research. Let me repeat for emphasis what I wrote in *Well Being* about Carver: "His life and work are an inspiring example of loving God, nature, and human beings with one's mind!"

Use Your Mind for Stress Reduction

Chronic stress overload contributes to sickness and low levels of well being. Learning how to regularly reduce the stress you experience is crucially important to self-care. Consider the following good news about the nature of stress. Physiological psychologist Barbara Brown, an expert on stress disorders, concludes from her research that "stress is 90 percent how the mind looks at difficulties in life and relieving stress is 100 percent the way the mind uses its resources to . . . deal with stress without distress."[7]

This means that whatever the external pressures in your life, the stress they produce within you is largely determined by your *perception of and response to them*. Stress is something that happens *in* you, rather than *to* you. This internal function gives you the mental ability to choose how you respond to frustrating situations and irritating people.

You can do so in ways that keep them from getting to you in such stress-producing ways. This is often easier said than done, and some crises produce inescapable stress. But, with practice, you can learn to protect yourself from many external forces that cause stress.

Many folks have found the following guidelines for stress reduction helpful.[8] As you read them now, jot down your ideas about how to apply them successfully in your current life.

• Learn to think of your stresses as challenges and opportunities.

• Learn how to interrupt the vicious cycle of anger, worry, guilt, and anxiety that causes the buildup of body tensions, which in turn produce more distressing feelings.

• Practice some form of meditation or contemplative prayer to quiet your body-mind spirit at least once a day, particularly when inner stresses build up.

• Learn to use simple deep-breathing exercises and body-mind relaxation techniques to release tensions before, during, or after a stress-arousing event or near the end of the day to prepare for deeper sleep.

• Remind yourself during pressure-cooker situations that "this too shall pass."

• Learn to release tensions by letting your inner child play and laugh more—at yourself and with others.

• Pray and apply the Serenity Prayer quoted at the beginning of this session.[9] A psychiatrist I knew once said that if her patients would learn how to practice this simple prayer, they probably would not need her services. Repeat this prayer today when small or large frustrations hit you. I think you'll discover that the attitudes it engenders can reduce your stress.

• If self-help methods don't suffice, make an excellent investment in your overall wellness by consulting a competent pastoral psychotherapist or other counselor for a few sessions to learn techniques for reducing stress.

Learn Methods to Resolve Destructive Feelings

The feelings that have the power to diminish overall wellness include chronic anger, resentment, fear, guilt, shame, depression, and lack of forgiveness. When these negative feelings remain unresolved for extended periods, they devour and waste the mind's energies and creativity. Some misunderstandings of the Christian faith tend to block the healing of such distressing feelings. They offer repressive "answers" based on the false belief that if people have enough faith and pray hard enough, these "bad" feelings will disappear.

Certain New Testament statements about anger and fear have been misused in ways that cause people either to suffer painful guilt or to suppress these feelings as being "un-Christian." Actually, feelings themselves are not bad or good. What determines if they are destructive or constructive is how they are handled and expressed in behavior.

Consider guilt feelings, for example. It is important to distinguish between appropriate and inappropriate or neurotic guilt. The Christian church has many centuries of experience in helping sufferers resolve the guilt they *should* feel when they have misused their freedom in ways that hurt themselves or other people. The steps by which people move from appropriate guilt to forgiveness and reconciliation are expressed in what is known now as the "sacrament of reconciliation" in the Roman Catholic Church. The same wise healing process is found in twelve-step recovery programs in the seven steps pertaining to a moral inventory.

Inappropriate guilt feelings do not respond to such approaches. They are often triggered by feelings such as anger or by sexual fantasies about which many people were taught in their early life that they should feel guilty. Unhealthy understandings of the Christian ethical life feed such inappropriate guilt feelings and make neurotic feelings worse. Healing comes by unearthing the roots of such obsolete programming.

Using Methods for Resolving Negative Feelings: If particular negative feelings are of special concern for you, try the methods described in *Well Being*, pages 60–66. Steps for moving from appropriate guilt and unforgiveness to reconciliation with yourself and others are listed on pages 65–66. You'll find suggestions for moving from anger, resentment and fear to inner peace on pages 63–64. If "Moving from Depression to Self-Esteem" is your concern, try the wholeness exercise on pages 60–61. Methods of generating reality-based hope are described on pages 65–66. Pause now and try the approaches that appeal to you.

For comprehensive self-help methods for resolving destructive feelings, I recommend David D. Burns's *Feeling Good: The New Mood Therapy*.[10] In my counseling experience, the methods Burns describes have helped many people interrupt cycles of despair and hopelessness by changing their thinking and perceptions.

Love God with Your Mind by Developing Your Creativity

One of the most rewarding ways that the image of God is expressed in us humans is by exercising our creativity. Jesus' immense creativity was expressed in many facets of his life and work. His skills in carpentry, healing, and teaching, and his unfolding of fresh spiritual truths are some expressions of his God-given creativity. According to the Christian way, we are invited to be co-creators of a better world with the divine Spirit whom Jesus called *Abba* ("Father").

Developing your creative gifts can be an important form of mind-care and health care. By the word *creativity* I don't mean just the so-called "artistic" things. I mean the capacity to produce something worthwhile that enhances people's lives, however unpretentious this may be. The inherent creative urge is expressed in countless ways in the everyday lives of people—in their working, their thinking, their relationships, their hobbies, their playing, and their praying. Gardening, meditating, making music in your own way, loving, enjoying life, or trying new approaches to solving old problems—these are a few examples of everyday creativity.

As is true of intellectual abilities and emotional intelligence, most people have far more creative potential than they have yet discovered or developed. Continuing to do something that expresses your own creativity is one of the secrets of effective aging. Having a creativity break once a day or more can help you avoid burnout.

A wellness-centered congregation challenges and encourages people to use their creativity in a wide variety of ways throughout the life cycle. When people discover how to use their potential creativity, their energy level goes up, as does their sense of self-esteem, competence, and inner strength for living. The programs of education, music, worship, drama, dance, lay caring, life enrichment, social action, and outreach to the community—all these and many more components of congregational life can provide opportunities for people to develop and enjoy their creativity.

 Learning Exercise: I encourage you to pause now, or later when you have time, and try moving through the four stages of the process of creativity enhancement described in *Well Being*, pages 57–59. Each stage—preparation, incubation, illumination, and verification-implementation—has been demonstrated to contribute to energizing the creative process. Learning to use this four-stage approach may help you enhance your creativity in ways that are both satisfying and surprising.

Learn Methods of Meditation, Guided Imaging, and Befriending Dreams

These approaches can help you connect the resources of your deeper mind with your surface-level consciousness. Many of the stories, images, myths, and festivals of the Bible, of our Christian tradition and other religions have the power to help us keep in touch with the riches of our unconscious minds. Long before modern depth psychology, dreams were taken very seriously in the Bible as potential channels for gaining spiritual truths. Contemporary methods of befriending and learning from your dreams can make the wisdom and resources of your deeper mind available to enrich your conscious life.

Two books that provide valuable insights about dreams as sources for spiritual enrichment are John A. Sanford's *Dreams: God's Forgotten Language* (San Francisco: HarperSan Francisco, 1989) and Morton Kelsey's *Dreams: A Way to Listen to God* (New York: Paulist Press, 1978).

Reach Out to Find and Give Support When Mental Problems Hit

While congregations are focusing innovative energies on nurturing mental well being in all their members, they should also provide acceptance and support for families who are struggling to cope with mentally ill family members. Former U.S. First Lady Rosalynn Carter, a courageous advocate for the mentally ill and their families, describes the stigma that unfortunately still clings to this widespread problem: "It refers to a feeling that, if somebody is mentally ill, they're dangerous, they're different, they're people to be avoided, they're not like us. . . . It's a pervasive feeling, not only within our communities but within our churches. . . . There are many families in our churches taking care of someone mentally ill at home. To be able to go to church and have that family member accepted is rare."

She continues, emphasizing the church's opportunity to provide continuing support and education about mental illness to the "forgotten caregivers" in the home who have exhausting, nonstop responsibilities. She adds, "One role for churches and all faith groups is to become advocates for our mentally ill citizens."[11] If one adds the families who care for the frail elderly and physically ill, it is estimated that 25 million Americans carry this load, often with little help.

Develop a New Mind for a New Century, Millennium, and World

Human beings today face an urgent need to make radical changes in thinking about our collective problems. Robert Ornstein, a research psychologist, and Paul Ehrlich, a population and ecology expert, observe that human minds have been conditioned through many eons to patterns of thought that are increasingly obsolete, even dangerous, in our radically changed new world. Traditionally humankind has thought in we-versus-they terms, has focused on immediate information rather than on long-term consequences, and has judged everything by surface-level appearances. These "old-think" patterns had survival value for our species in the old world.

Now, however, that traditional world is ceasing to exist. Lightning-fast social change, the global electronic village, the population explosion, and a planet-wide deteriorating environment make it essential that we

humans develop a "new-mindedness" that fits the radically changed world in which we now live.

In *New World, New Mind: Moving toward Conscious Evolution*,[12] Ornstein and Ehrlich show how education is needed to equip humankind with the knowledge to guide rapid social change; to be concerned about the well being of all humanity and the global environment; to integrate modern understandings from the human sciences with the best in the world's great religions; to recognize that violence, especially war, is obsolete and to develop constructive alternatives to war; to understand the long-range consequences of today's social practices to change those practices that are destructive to the human family.

This spiritually centered way of thinking and acting is the best path to both whole-person well being and to a healthy planet. For us Christians, our time-tested ethical and spiritual heritage affirms as very old these "new" ways of thinking and understanding. Christians today should take the lead in helping develop these new-old ways of understanding and behaving. People of all ages should learn these truths that are so necessary for our survival in their churches. Our Christian lifestyles should apply these principles to all dimensions of our living.

Discover Your Hidden Treasures

Here is a true story that has become for me a guiding image of how people can discover their hidden gifts. A number of years ago, my long-time partner and I were sitting on a beautiful beach in Hawaii. We were relaxing after enjoying one of our most fun activities—snorkeling in an undersea wonderland of tropical fish and coral, certainly one of God's most gorgeous creations. We noticed a man walking toward us slowly, holding an electronic gadget just above the sand.

Periodically he would pause and dig in the sand. When he came near, I asked him what he was doing. He smiled and replied, "This is a treasure finder [an electronic metal detector]. I'm hunting for coins, wristwatches, and other valuable things people like you have lost in the sand."

Consider a "treasure-finder" as an image of one way we can increase wellness in our lives. The personal experience of countless Christians shows that the life and teachings of Jesus can put in our hands such a treasure-finder for spirit-centered wellness.

Perhaps this image calls to mind Jesus' parable about the kingdom of God being like a treasure discovered in a field. You remember that the finder regarded it as so precious that to acquire the treasure, "in his joy he goes and sells all that he has and buys that field" (Matt. 13:44). The kingdom is the coming, spirit-empowered community of caring, conscience, and compassion. In a real sense, being a Christian is to live in that community now and thus to help it develop more fully. Life in all its fullness is best nurtured in such a learning community. A congregation that emphasizes growing in wholeness is one such community.

Increasing the wellness of your lifestyle often begins when the awareness dawns that you're capable of lots more living and loving than you are doing at the moment. The brilliant psychologist-philosopher William James was a major pioneer in developing my academic discipline—the psychology of religion. He once used a striking image to depict people's neglect of their minds' gifts: "Most people live, whether physically, intellectually, or morally, in a very restricted circle of their potential being. They make use of a very small portion of their possible consciousness, and of their soul's resources in general, much like a man who, out of his whole bodily organism, should get into a habit of using and moving only his little finger. Great emergencies and crises show us how much greater our vital resources are than we had supposed."[13]

A Guided Meditation for Discovery

 I invite you to experience a meditation whose purpose is to encourage the discovery of more of the gifts of God within you. Remember that a slash mark (/) means to pause while you do what has been described.

Stretch all your muscles tightly and then relax them like limp rubber bands. Repeat this several times until your body is energized and your mind alert, but both are relaxed and receptive to new experiences. / Now, create a picture of a beautiful, spring meadow in your imagination. / Be *in* the meadow, letting yourself enjoy being nurtured by nature in this lovely, alive, peaceful place. /

Become aware that this meadow is a very special place with valuable and beautiful things to be found. Wander playfully in the meadow now, like a child on an exciting treasure hunt, exploring it to find out what is there. Remember that this is *your* meadow. You created it. Its treasures are yours—a part of your creative inner life. They are talents and dreams, personal gifts and possibilities waiting to be discovered and used if you choose. / Continue to explore the meadow, asking yourself what each treasure you find represents and how you might use it in your everyday world. /

Be aware that there's a very special treasure in one part of the meadow to which you now feel drawn. Move toward where that treasure is and uncover it. / Walk around it, examining it from all sides. / Be aware that it's a gift from your Creator, a precious resource that you perhaps need to develop to make your life more whole for yourself and more effective in reaching out with love to others. / When you're ready, think about how you might develop, use, and enjoy this special treasure you have discovered within yourself.

Decide what you will do to claim and use this gift. /

Become aware of the energy of the divine Spirit of love and light and liberation, the source of this gift, surrounding you at this very moment. Open the windows of your soul, letting this empowering love flow in now, giving you the strength and courage to use the treasures for the well being of yourself and those whose lives touch yours. / Create a movie screen in your mind as you are there in your meadow. On the screen watch yourself using this treasure you've discovered to enliven your lifestyle, making it more joyful and loving and purposefully whole. / Now complete this meditation in whatever way you choose to give it a sense of completion. /

Jot down in the margins of this workbook or in your journal whatever you taught yourself in this awareness exercise—discoveries you made and plans you are formulating to use one of your gifts more fully. / With someone you trust, share the significant discoveries you've made and invite their feedback about your discoveries and plans. / If this exercise has been meaningful to you, I encourage you to commit yourself to following through on the plans that are emerging, developing and implementing them to benefit your own well being and perhaps that of your family, congregation, and community. / Later you may wish to explore other treasures that you found in the meadow of your inner life. /

If the meditation had little or no meaning for you, I suggest you try it again later. Many people find this a new way to use their creative mind, a way that improves with practice.

People who are open to fresh options, particularly if they know they are neglecting some of their major interests and skills, can use this exercise to move into what can become a land of new possibilities.

Years ago, after a workshop in New England where I had led a large group on this treasure hunt, I received an unexpected but very welcome note from a woman who had been there. I felt joy when I read her words saying that she had used this exercise to produce what she called "a significant turning point in my life." She said that it had begun a process that helped her gain the courage to move beyond the devastating loss of her life partner. As a result of the way she used this meditation, she had decided to begin the further education she needed for a challenging, though scary, new chapter in her work that she had been wanting to enter since her major loss.

Numerous treasures are waiting to be developed in most people's lives, including yours. Some of these treasures are related to living life in more of its potential fullness and, to use a French phrase, *joie de vivre*—learning the joy of living. Other treasures may be the development of interpersonal empathy, love, and imagination and the productive use of emotional intelligence and skills in responding to the needs of lonely, burdened, oppressed people. May God give you a time of surprising and exciting discovery as you explore your meadow of hidden treasures!

Questions for Reflection

 1. Do the ways of "loving God with your mind" described in this chapter make sense to you as a searching Christian?

2. How do you understand the connection between and interdependence of spiritual and mental well being?

3. What action-options do you need to implement to enhance the well being of your mind and personality?

4. Does the view make sense that a church needs to become a center of more effective lifelong learning? If so, how can you help this happen in your congregational family?

Strengthening Your Self-Care Plan

 Now, firm up your self-care plan, adding mental self-care to the spiritual self-care plan developed in the last session. Review key insights and action plans you made as you tallied the checkup and read this session. Write out a *realistic* plan for developing the unused capacities of your mind and personality and for using your mind to nurture both the wellness of your body-mind-spirit and the wellness of others about whom you care as a Christian.

Be sure to make your plan love-motivated, playful, and energized by your spiritual resources. / Pick one or two attractive but also achievable objectives and begin moving toward them in the next day or two. Remember, momentum and hope from small successes can help overcome your resistance to self-change. /

Closing Song, Prayer, and Evaluation

 Whether you are studying well being alone or with a wellness partner or in a group, it is important to close this session by doing the following things:

• Sing a hymn that expresses the awareness that education is a central task of persons seeking to live a Christian lifestyle. One example is the hymn that begins "Open my eyes, that I may see glimpses of truth thou hast for me."14

• Celebrate any new understandings that have come by spending some time in prayer expressing joy and thanksgiving for these insights.

• Do a brief evaluation of the session aimed at increasing the benefits to well being of future sessions.

Continuing Your Self-Care

 Here are some suggestions for continuing your wellness work between sessions. These suggestions will prepare you to gain the most benefits from the next session.

• Spend a brief time each day implementing the high-priority items you included in your spiritual and mental self-care plans. Doing between-sessions wellness work can enhance the self-care of your mind in the ways for which you are hoping. In this workbook or in your journal, keep track of how your mental life is affected by increased self-care.

• Write out on cards the key ideas and actions in your self-care plan, and put these in places where you'll see them as reminders during your busy days.

• Read Session 4, underlining or highlighting the things that seem especially relevant to your body's self-care. If physical health is of special concern to you, take or make time to also read or at least scan *Well Being*, Chapter 4.

• Take and tally the Physical Well Being Checkup at the beginning of the next session in this workbook, making two lists for future use of the items you mark either OK or NS. As you do this, think of which things you want to include in your physical health-care plan.

• Picture yourself in your mind for a short time, surrounded by the light of your caring and by God's truth-awakening love. If you are studying with a wellness partner or group, do the same for this person or persons. Also do this for other people you love, particularly those about whom you are especially concerned. Repeat this intercessory imaging exercise several times between sessions.

Loving and Empowering Your Body for Fitness, Pleasure, and Service

God put me on earth to accomplish a certain number of things. Right now I am so far behind, I probably will never die.

—Lapel button worn by frantic person with a sense of humor

"Relax—As Hard As You Can!"

—Bumper Sticker

The act of putting into your mouth what the earth has grown is perhaps your most direct interaction with the earth.

—Frances Moore Lappé, *Diet for a Small Planet*[1]

A Physical Well Being Checkup

 To help you gain the greatest benefits from this session, take and score this checkup first. Keep in mind that it is not a test but a tool to increase your body's physical well being. It will give you a quick evaluation of areas in which your physical self-care is relatively strong and those that need more regular attention. The items in the checkup are a list of things you can do to increase the fitness, strength, health, and pleasure of your body.

Instructions: Mark each statement in one of three ways:

   E = "I'm doing *excellently* in this."

OK = "I'm doing *acceptably*, but there's room for improvement."

NS = "This is an area where I definitely *need strengthening*."

____ I know that good self-care of my body is an essential expression of my Christian lifestyle, an important spiritual discipline.

____ I have discovered that my spiritual and mental life are energized and enriched by good physical self-care and vice versa.

____ I like my body (in spite of its limitations) and treat it respectfully with regular, loving care as a temple of the divine Spirit.

____ I'm reasonably self-disciplined about doing physical fitness activities that enhance my overall well being. I spend some time each day giving my body loving care to increase its aliveness; its attractiveness (especially to myself); and its power to function with energy, strength, and effectiveness.

____ I listen to my body and learn from what it tells me, such as, "Slow down!" "Play and rest more!" "Relax!"

____ I'm cultivating my body's awareness and sensuality, letting myself discover and enjoy its wonderful God-given potential to give and receive pleasure.

____ I do not use Christian beliefs about self-sacrifice as a rationalization for neglecting or mistreating my body.

____ When I have to neglect self-care for a short while because of caring for loved ones and other things I must do, I usually make up for this neglect by extra self-care later.

____ I have one or more forms of big muscle exercise appropriate to my age and level of health, which I enjoy doing three or four times a week for a minimum of thirty minutes—things such as brisk walking, biking, jogging, swimming, aerobics, or vigorous sports. If I cannot do thirty minutes at one time, I do several shorter aerobic workouts.

____ I practice the basic principles of health-giving nutrition by consuming a balanced diet with lots of vegetables, fruits, and whole grains, and cutting back on my consumption of junk food, refined sugars, fats (especially animal fats), salt, caffeine, alcohol, nicotine, and other drugs.

____ I balance my calories and my exercise so as to maintain my weight within ten pounds of the optimum for my age, height, and gender.

____ By not smoking, I avoid many lethal health hazards while increasing the quality and probably the length of my life.

____ I practice some form of deep relaxation at least once a day to reduce the stress load I carry in my body.

____ I sleep seven or eight hours (more or less, depending on what my body and mind require for full renewal), at least four nights a week.

____ When I neglect the "sabbath principle" of a day off on the weekend, I often take a renewing Sabbath by resting and playing on another day.

____ I take a vacation that is genuinely renewing each year.

____ I satisfy my sensual needs or "skin hunger" regularly, in ways that contribute to my wellness as well as that of my partner.

____ I remember that cars can be lethal, so I wear a seatbelt whenever I'm in a vehicle, drive carefully when I'm at the wheel, and don't drink and then drive.

____ I regularly keep my knowledge of physical fitness updated.

____ I usually don't waste creative energy by self-flagellation if I backslide temporarily or take an occasional "holiday" from positive health practices.

Using Your Findings to Enhance Your Body's Well Being

Take the following steps to help you use the results of this checkup in developing your physical self-care plan:

1. Tally your responses and write down the totals below. This will provide you with an overview of your physical well being. / Give yourself a pat on the back for the things you honestly scored "E."

E: _____

OK: _____

NS: _____

2. Go through the list and put a star beside those OK and NS items that seem either urgent or especially important to you. /

3. What is your overall "feel" concerning your general physical wellness? In the space below, jot down your evaluation of the strengths and weaknesses of your physical self-care. /

4. Beside the starred items, make notes about how you could strengthen your body's wellness. / Later in this session, you will be encouraged to come back to these items and elaborate on your ideas as you develop a workable physical self-care plan.

A Biblical Perspective

According to the Apostle Paul, Christians are called to love God by caring for their bodies with respect. In his first letter to the church in the Greek city of Corinth, Paul discusses the special responsibilities of Christians living in a world with other faith traditions. He describes the human body as a temple of the Holy Spirit, a gift of God. He challenges those struggling Corinthian Christians to "glorify God in your body" (1 Cor. 6:19-20). What does it mean today for us as Christians to treat our bodies as temples of the Spirit? What is involved in glorifying God in our bodies?

This session seeks to throw helpful light on these issues. It proposes that we glorify God in our bodies when we love and respect them in ways that enable us to maximize our fitness at our present life stage. Profound spiritual benefits can come from learning to befriend our bodies more lovingly as marvelous temples of the divine Spirit within us.

Stories of "Otherwise-Abled" People

I must have been in my early teens when Glenn Cunningham came to speak at our hometown YMCA in Springfield, Illinois. He then held the world's record for the fastest mile. His inspiring story was a much-needed gift to a tall, awkward, pimply-faced lad whose self-esteem was depleted by feeling that his body fell far short of the body images of male sports heroes who were my role models. As I remember Cunningham's story, he told how his legs had been so severely burned in a fire when he was a boy that doctors predicted that he would never be able to walk normally.

Cunningham refused to accept the doctors' prognosis. With an indomitable spirit of determination, he forced himself to walk again, despite the scar tissue and pain in his legs. He did this by holding on to the back of a horse-drawn wagon in which his father delivered groceries. With agonizing slowness, his leg muscles learned how to walk again. He continued walking, a little faster and then a little faster still, until he was at last able to begin to run. He continued running until he eventually ran that record-breaking fastest mile.[2]

Our culture's tendency to glorify youthful, "perfect" bodies leads to widespread rejection of and guilt about bodies in our culture. Before focusing on the importance of physical fitness, to keep matters in perspective let's remember that millions of people learn to live remarkably satisfying, productive, and creative lives, despite major bodily limitations. Like Glenn Cunningham, they illustrate the remarkable ability of "otherwise-abled" people to transcend huge physical problems. They use their handicaps as incentives to develop high degrees of mental, spiritual, and interpersonal well being, and often bodily fitness, against huge odds. Certainly they glorify God in their far-from-perfect bodies.

As one who has had to learn to live with a disability, I enjoy remembering true stories about Thomas Edison, the incredibly creative inventor. When he applied for life insurance, he initially was turned down because of his diabetes and other health problems (probably including his deafness). He found another company that agreed to insure him but with the exclusion of "death by electrocution." A company employee noted on his application, "This man fools around with something called electricity."

Learning Exercise: To personalize all this, I invite you to picture in your mind someone you know who transcends physical limitations or the physical decline of aging by regular exercise, healthy nutrition, and adequate rest. This may be yourself or a person in your family, your circle of friends, or your congregation or community. If you have not known such a person, re-read the Windows of Wholeness in *Well Being* that highlight the lives of star Olympic runner Wilma "Skeeter" Rudolph (p. 80), clergyman Harold Wilke, born without arms (p. 229), and my former parishioner, Frank Jones (p. 90). / Be aware of how such persons maintain well being while transcending huge disabilities because their spiritual vitality and self-care help them maintain healthy mental attitudes about their disabilities. /

If you have a minor or major physical limitation, as most people do, try to view it in the context of stories like these. / If you're studying with a wellness partner or group, take a few minutes now to learn from each other's stories and reflections. / Make notes to yourself of any insights you wish to remember from this exercise.

Major Objectives and Themes

Put a check mark in front of those objectives and themes listed below that are important to you as you seek to enhance your Christian lifestyle. They are your personal objectives for this session. In this session, you will have opportunities to learn the following:

❑ Resources for enhancing the loving self-care of your body.

❑ Biblical guidelines and resources for your body's well being.

❑ Ways to use the findings of your physical well being checkup.

❑ Several basic physical wellness exercises.

❑ How to broaden your overall self-care plan by adding exercises for physical well being.

❑ Some ways to outwit inner resistance and roadblocks to physical health.

Biblical Roots

Learning Exercise: Take a few minutes to jot down Bible passages that support care of our bodies as a part of God's plan for living. These passages can help provide a biblical foundation for this session.

_____

_____

_____

_____

_____

_____

_____

_____

_____

The ancient Hebrews held to a unified understanding of persons and their health and salvation. This understanding is what is called "holistic" today. Health and sickness are understood to occur in a unified, inclusive, interrelated world encompassing body, mind, spirit, and community. Such a holistic view is found throughout the Hebrew Scriptures and is in harmony with contemporary views that reject a divided understanding of our humanity. This is a view that Jesus undoubtedly learned as a boy in his religious instruction.

The religious laws and rituals of the Jews regarding eating, drinking, and resting reflect a belief that God's activity and concern are involved in the everyday well being of people's bodies. Their dietary laws are based in part on beliefs about healthy living. They also reflect a theological view that food is a good gift of God and that eating is a life-sustaining activity that has spiritual as well as interpersonal significance. The psalmist declares: "You cause the grass to grow for the cattle, and plants for people to use, to bring forth food from the earth, and wine to gladden the human heart, . . . and bread to strengthen the human heart" (Ps. 104:14-15). God is seen as one "who gives food to all flesh, for his steadfast love endures forever" (Ps. 136:25).

The sabbath principle of a regular day of rest has its roots in the first creation story in which God rested on the seventh day after completing the work of creation: "So God blessed the seventh day and hallowed it" (Gen. 2:3). This understanding illuminates why devout Jews respect the Sabbath as a day of rest.

Jesus' ministry, reflecting the Hebrew, nondualistic view, was very down to earth. He obviously attended to his own bodily needs as well as to those of others around him. Numerous illustrations of this are found in the Gospels. They include his feeding the five thousand hungry people who had some of their soul hungers satisfied by his message. Jesus healed people of a wide variety of illnesses, and he used his miraculous powers to provide good wine for a wedding party. He honored his own need for rest by taking a nap on the boat during a storm. By leading his closest followers to a wilderness place for rest and renewal, Jesus respected his own needs and those of his disciples for quiet and for seeking spiritual renewal away from the needs of the crowds.

The Christian belief in the incarnation of God's spirit in Jesus has profound implications concerning the human body. In Jesus "the Word became flesh and dwelt among us, full of grace and truth" (John 1:14, RSV). This speaks volumes about the interrelationships of spirit, mind, and body in us humans. The very idea that the divine Spirit would express itself in a human body and mind affirms the view that there is no separation between body and mind and spirit. Thinking that divides body and mind or body and spirit does not reflect the best in biblical understanding. The glorification taken in mortifying the body, which has happened at times in the church's history, reflects a basic misunderstanding of incarnational biblical theology.[3]

Physical Self-Care and a Christian Lifestyle

In light of these biblical understandings, we Christians are on target when we recognize that taking care of our bodies is an essential part of a Christian lifestyle. Doing this is really a spiritual discipline with both multiple mental and physical benefits but also spiritual benefits. The flowering of our minds and the blossoming of our spirits needs to be supported by keeping our bodies as alive and fit as possible. According to one Gallup poll, people who work out regularly are over twice as likely to be happy as a group of couch potatoes. Regular exercisers also reported feeling more self-esteem, a greater ability to relax, healthier eating habits, and greater control over their health; they also were more likely to have lost weight.

And in case you are having trouble with the idea that body-care is an important spiritual discipline, consider the most surprising finding of this poll: Those working out regularly reported *being more open to spiritual experiences* than the people who did not exercise.[4]

I'm glad to report that current psychosomatic medical research confirms these fascinating findings. They make it clear that whatever affects our bodies also influences our minds, and vice versa. In addition, whatever affects the quality of our spiritual lives influences both our minds and bodies. The opposite is also true—whatever affects our bodies and minds has a significant influence on our spiritual lives.

On a personal level, when I neglect my early-morning, vigorous aerobic walks for several days or have a junk food relapse, my mind loses sharpness and my spirit feels as though it is covered by a thin layer of dust. Conversely, when I get too busy to attend to my spiritual nurture for a while, my motivation to give my body needed self-care is diminished. Have you had similar experiences?

Another potential benefit of befriending your body with enhanced self-care is that this may help your spirituality become more sensual. Pioneer body therapist Alexander Lowen reports that people who have long neglected their bodies often reclaim their "forsaken body with all the fervor of the lost child finding its loving mother."[5] Such an awakening can be described as a welcome rediscovery of what creation theologian Matthew Fox calls "sensual spirituality." This means spirituality that is not detached or "up in the air" but is empowered by being rooted in the rich energies and sensual capacities of our bodies.

Christians should view their lives as a precious gift of God to be used well for as long as possible. Consider an additional reason that good self-care of your body is a potentially valuable spiritual discipline: The evidence from the science of aging (gerontology) increasingly supports the view that the physical aging process can be slowed or accelerated by how well or poorly we treat our bodies. And in terms of the quality of life, even if self-care does not add many years to our lives, it certainly will add pleasure and productiveness to our years.

You may wonder why the title of this session includes "Loving Your Body." It points to yet another reason why healthy body-caring is a must for Christians. Love is the most indispensable ingredient in a good life or a good relationship, according to the New Testament (1 Cor. 13:13).

What is the most powerful motivation to replace unhealthy habits like smoking, overeating, or excessive consumption of toxins like junk food, nicotine, drugs, and alcohol? In one sentence, it is to learn to love your whole body-mind-spirit self more.

Learning to love your body is the often-hidden key for which many folks are searching. Loving our bodies and knowing that God loves our whole selves, including our bodies, is the key both to cutting down on body-hurting behaviors and to increasing our loving body self-care. This has been confirmed repeatedly in both my personal and professional experiences of working with people struggling to control "bad habits" that are damaging their health.

 Awareness Exercise: Take a few minutes to close your eyes while you ask yourself and respond to two questions: How would I treat my body differently if I believed more deeply that it is really loved by God as a precious temple of the Spirit? How can I welcome God's love and grace more holistically by loving my whole body-mind-spirit self and treating myself with more grace? / Following this inner conversation note things to remember or to share with others. If you are studying with a wellness partner or group, discuss together what you each learned from this exercise. /

To summarize, by keeping your body as fit and healthy as possible, you give yourself a valuable gift: a firm foundation on which to develop a spiritually centered well being lifestyle. Regardless of your physical limitations, improving your body self-care will tend to make it more energized, functionally fit, pain-free, and supportive of your spiritually centered well being. I like to think of caring for my body as if I were a loving mother or father, remembering the biblical image of God as loving parent.

If you do this, you move away from an I-It and toward an I-Thou treatment of your body, to use philosopher Martin Buber's familiar terms. This is an expression of that embodied, sensual spirituality that is crucial for living life in all its fullness as a Christian.

What Does Body Fitness Care Involve?

Perhaps like many people, you are fed up with nonstop, changing, often contradictory advice about what's healthy and what's unhealthy in terms of nutrition and exercise. If so, I hope that you'll find this succinct overview of the basic ingredients of a healthy lifestyle useful. The focus of discussions like this often is on avoiding grossly health-sabotaging behavior such as compulsive eating, "pigging out" on junk food, exercise aversion, smoking, chronic sleep deprivation, television addiction, or excessive use of alcohol or drugs.

The good news is that a Christian wellness lifestyle should begin at a different place than just saying "No!" to such health-damaging habits. It is far more effective to begin just by saying "Yes!" to God. This means saying a resounding "Yes!" to life as a good gift of God. People who savor the satisfactions of saying "Yes" to life usually discover that the occasions when they need to say "No" to seductive, life-diminishing patterns occur much less often. Furthermore, saying "No" becomes easier when it's necessary.

How can we say such a "Yes"? By choosing to develop a healthier lifestyle in five crucial areas of self-care. Taken together, these constitute a well-rounded fitness program:

1. Do vigorous exercising you enjoy several times a week for half an hour or so. For optimal fitness, you should include three different types of exercises: those that increase aerobic fitness, flexibility, and strength.

2. Eat a nutritious and balanced diet, and limit your calories to those that will be burned for energy by the amount of exercise you do.

3. Get adequate sleep to renew your body-mind-spirit at least five or six nights each week and use regular stress-reducing methods such as full-body relaxation, deep breathing, stretching, meditating, or just "vegetating" for brief periods several times daily, especially during high-tension times.

4. Eliminate or drastically limit your consumption of hazardous, consciousness-changing chemicals such as alcohol, nicotine, and drugs, and avoid seeking your highs through sugar and fat binges.

5. Give your body noncaloric sensual satisfactions regularly by enjoying such things as soaking in a warm bath, a self-massage, or a mutual couple massage.

Whatever your present physical condition—particularly if you're a junk food addict or an inert couch potato—you can increase the health, strength, and pleasure of your body-mind-spirit by giving yourself the good gifts of regular self-care in these five areas. For most busy folks, it is most time-effective to work these in briefly throughout their daily schedules. When people try to fit lengthy times for health care into already overloaded days, they usually don't find the time. What follows are brief window-openers into each of these areas.

Type One Exercise—For Aerobic Fitness

Be aware that there are three different types of exercising, and each type has value for your body's well being. The three types are big-muscle aerobic exercises, exercises to maintain or enhance your strength, and stretching exercises to sustain healthy flexibility in your body, especially your joints. Each type has unique health benefits that make it more than worth the time invested.

Aerobic exercise is the most vital in maintaining high levels of wellness and increasing your probable life expectancy. Like engine tune-ups, aerobic exercises help keep the cardiovascular system throughout your whole body functioning more efficiently and effectively. It enables your heart, lungs, and blood-delivery system to increase the fresh oxygen and energy that they transport to all your body's cells, while cleansing the cells of the waste products. Other potential benefits

include increased stamina, decreased fat storage in your body, and improved utilization of the food you eat.

Furthermore, studies show that people who exercise aerobically tend to experience some decreased craving for junk food and other frustration-relieving chemicals such as refined sugar, fat, salt, alcohol, nicotine, and other drugs. Unfortunately, more than half of all Americans say that they are "too tired, too lazy, or too busy" to exercise, in spite of spending an average of three hours per day glued to the television, often munching junk food. (Suggestions for dealing with rationalizations and resistance to doing what we know would be good for our health are discussed below.)

What are some popular forms of aerobic exercising? Fast walking, jogging, bike riding, swimming laps, vigorous dancing, skating (roller or ice), cross-country skiing (on a machine or outdoors), and even doing housework or gardening vigorously may qualify. They do so only if they raise and sustain your pulse rate to an optimal level during the exercise times. If you are over thirty or have a personal or family history of heart problems, be sure to have a full checkup by a qualified health professional before you launch into a vigorous exercise program.

The safest, most low-cost, and effective lifetime aerobic exercise is brisk walking. In the Gospels, it is clear that Jesus did a lot of walking. Again and again, the Gospel writers tell of his walking considerable distances to teach and heal and feed the spiritual hungers of the people. Before Jesus began his ambulatory ministry, he must have had lots of healthy exercise in the carpenter shop and in the course of business and family activities. In our society where we are "wedded to the automobile," most people must take time to intentionally incorporate regular walking into their wellness programs.

In the last few years, to reduce wear and

tear on my knees, I gradually have replaced jogging by fast walking outdoors, four or five days a week for twenty to thirty minutes. I carry light weights in each hand to increase upper body exercise while I walk. My personal experience leads me to affirm physician Andrew Weil's enthusiastic endorsement of walking. In his book *Spontaneous Healing*, he writes, "Human beings are meant to walk. We are bipedal, upright organisms with bodies designed for locomotion. . . . So I am going to pare my advice and comments on exercise down to one word: Walk! In my opinion, walking is the most healthful form of physical activity, the one that has the greatest capacity to keep the healing system in good working order and increase the likelihood of spontaneous healing in case of illness." [6]

Weil points out that walking has many advantages over other exercise as well as numerous health benefits beyond its aerobic effects. You don't have to learn how to do it, and you can do it anywhere—even indoors in a shopping mall during stormy weather. It costs nothing except time and requires no special equipment except suitable shoes. Compared with running and competitive sports, injuries seldom occur. Walking outdoors lets you enjoy the aliveness of the natural world around you. Walking outdoors is far more stimulating than using treadmills or stationary bicycles. And walking and talking with a family member or friend can be fun.

Experience has made me aware of several additional advantages of walking. It is an almost ideal exercise for many of us in the older years. A recent study found that older people who walk one mile at least four days a week cut in half the likelihood that they will develop a disability that limits both walking and other activities.[7] At any age, walking is a therapeutic way of releasing tension and draining off frustration-caused anger and aggression. For me and many others, walking tends to stimulate the flow of creative juices in the mind. And in terms of my spiritual life, walking often helps me reconnect with my spiritual center and enjoy awareness of the creator God's healing, energizing presence.

You can make your walking more health-enhancing simply by doing three things: One, buy a good pair of walking shoes and have them fitted by someone with expertise in footwear. This is a good investment that won't cost much per year if spread over the lifetime of good-quality shoes. Two, walk briskly and swing your arms vigorously. And three, build more walking into your everyday activities, for example by taking short walks in place of using your car, parking several blocks from a destination, or using the stairs and avoiding elevators whenever feasible.

Remember that participating in your favorite sport is fun but it probably won't do much to increase your aerobic capacity. Taking an active part in sports may, of course, be very good for your mental and emotional health by reducing chronic stress and draining off pent-up frustrations in harmless and fun ways.

Type Two Exercise—For Flexibility

Flexibility exercises are valuable for your lifelong body-mind-spirit wellness because they may help keep your joints more flexible, stretch your muscles, make your posture more comfortable and your body movements more graceful. They tend to keep your body flexible and energized, helping to slow down the body's aging processes. Any gentle, full-body stretching and moving that you enjoy and do regularly can bring you these benefits.

Some exercising, such as vigorous dancing or aerobic workouts, can give both aerobic and flexibility benefits. You can devise a home-grown approach to type two exercises to make that combination. For example, adapt one of the centuries-old body movement approaches such as yoga or tai chi, a gentle flowing dance that evolved from Taoism. You can use these methods without necessarily adopting their Eastern philosophical assumptions. Personally, at some periods of my life, I have found hatha yoga helpful as a gentle, tension-reducing, and body-energizing form of movement. Some of its beneficial movements can be done fully clothed while at home, at the office, or on an airplane.[8]

 Body-Energizing Exercise: Pause for a few minutes, stand up and gently move your upper body. Begin by stretching the muscles of your face and head and neck, breathing more intentionally and deeply as you move. / If possible, put some favorite music on a CD or tape player, and then enjoy moving freely around the room. Simply allow your body to flow with the music as you stretch and move gently in whatever directions are comfortable. Be aware of how your energy level and spirits change as you move.

Type Three Exercise—For Strength

The obvious benefit of weight-resisting exercises is that they keep your muscles strong, in good shape, and toned-up. Lifting weights and doing calisthenics such as pull-ups, push-ups, and sit-ups are easily available forms of this type of exercise. The weight machines in health clubs, as well as in some homes, are other forms. Remember that strength-increasing exercises do not take the place of the other two essential types. In the past, strength-increasing exercises have been used mainly by those preparing for athletic competition and by men desiring to impress women or intimidate other men. Because of the latter, it has received some bad press.

Recent studies have demonstrated that such exercises have wide benefits for many people. They have been used to help older adults, even residents in nursing homes. When older people exercise with light weights and increase their muscle strength, they are able to use their bodies more effectively and to move about with less danger of falling. Often their depression lifts as their mental alertness and sense of having more control in their lives increase. Many women have discovered that they benefit by strength-enhancement exercising with weights. Having a stronger body tends to strengthen their self-confidence and esteem. It may also lessen excessive fears of male violence in our society where women must unfortunately always be on guard.

If you want to energize your body-mind-spirit by doing one or more of these types of exercises regularly, develop a non-complicated routine that is realistic for your schedule. Choose forms of exercise that you really enjoy. The dropout rate from expensive commercial exercise programs is very high, as it also is from complicated, time-gobbling programs at home with costly equipment. This is particularly true when the main motivation is "I *ought* to be exercising more," and when the "no pain, no gain" philosophy dominates people's minds. So be sure to keep experimenting until you find exercises that give you as much personal satisfaction and pleasure as possible.

It's also crucial to listen to your body carefully to avoid straining or injuring it. Effective exercise programs certainly do require some investment of time, self-discipline, and hard work; but they can also be fun, especially if done with friends.

Eating for Body-Mind-Spirit Well Being

A healthy diet is the second essential component of high-level physical wellness. Eating and drinking the things that will enhance our wellness show respect for our bodies as temples of the Spirit. Following the health-giving principles listed below can help sustain our body's remarkable self-protecting immune system; improve the odds that we will enjoy a long, productive, and satisfying life; and give us the energy to make a contribution to a better world for ourselves and our children.

• Eat a balanced diet that includes only appropriate amounts of the six types of food elements needed for your body's health: proteins, carbohydrates, fats, water, vitamins, and minerals. To be on the safe side, take a multivitamin and mineral supplement pill each day. It is wise to obtain guidance on such supplements from an accredited nutritionist or other health professional trained in nutrition.

• Reduce drastically your intake of all types of fat, especially those derived from animals. Many Americans could be labeled "fat-aholics" since over 30 percent of their daily calories comes from the fat they eat. Medical evidence confirms that if we did only one thing to make our diets healthier, cutting fat consumption in half would be it. Cutting our fat intake would reduce our risk of contracting many serious illnesses and would help us keep our weight at healthy levels.

• Reduce the amount and raise the healthfulness of the protein you eat. Do this by reducing drastically your consumption of red meat, substituting some seafood, white turkey or chicken meat, or, even better, vegetable proteins such as are found in grains, tofu, and beans. Tofu is an especially healthful protein. The average American overdoses on far more total protein than the body needs for health.

• Increase the complex carbohydrates and fiber in your diet by eating whole grains, beans, and fresh fruits and vegetables, and drastically reduce the amount of processed carbohydrates such as refined sugar, ice cream, alcohol, sodas, and most packaged cereals. Highly refined carbohydrates con-

tribute to obesity and provide mainly "empty calories" because they have few vitamins, fiber, and minerals. Reduce your consumption of fast foods, which are loaded with unhealthy amounts of refined sugar, fat, and salt. High-fiber diets aid healthy digestion and elimination, lower cholesterol and blood sugar, and may also reduce the incidence of certain cancers.

• Eat at least three helpings of fresh fruit and five helpings of uncooked or steamed vegetables each day. These sources of valuable food elements strengthen the immune system and enable the body to protect itself from infections and cancers. Whenever possible, use food grown organically without hazardous pesticides and fertilizers, the long-term toxic effects of which are seldom known. These chemicals probably hurt your health, and they seriously harm the low-paid workers—who have no medical insurance—who plant, cultivate, and harvest your food.

• Get in touch with and resolve emotional hungers that you may be trying unsuccessfully to satisfy by unhealthy and excessive eating. In his book *Comfort Me with Apples*, Peter DeVries writes: "Gluttony is an emotional escape, a sign something is eating us."[9] Even when your emotional life and relationships are working relatively well, spiritual and emotional hungers can fuel cravings for quick oral satisfaction that unfortunately fails to satisfy for more than the moment.

• Become aware of the social and spiritual significance of eating and drinking that make these activities much more than just ways of satisfying biological hungers pleasurably. Such awareness can help make our patterns of consumption healthier. Sacramental meals such as the Lord's Supper in Christianity, the Hebrew Passover in Judaism, and ritual meals in other religions point to an awareness of the mystery of eating and particularly of eating together. The same could be said for the feasts in many cultures associated with grief about endings and joy mixed with anxiety about new beginnings. Perhaps we are subconsciously aware of the physiological miracle that transforms what we eat and drink into thoughts and feelings, words and wit, poetry and prayers, sexuality, music, and loving. Perhaps this is why so many of us are moved to join hands and express ritual thanks before eating together.

I have had a continuing struggle trying to alter gratifying but destructive eating patterns learned in childhood. (Changing such patterns is like letting go of the dangerous old belief that suntans are healthy and recognizing that there is no such thing as a healthy tan.) But health researchers have discovered that changing such destructive eating patterns at almost any point in life can enhance one's health and thus make life in all its fullness more possible.

Eating as a Christian in a Hungry World

As caring religious people, you and I should care about the well being of all God's children. It is important to our spiritual health, therefore, to view all facets of our lifestyles, including what we eat and drink, in their global context. Think about the fact that one out of every three Americans is overweight, that the percentage is increasing, and that three out of four of us say that we have been or are planning to go on a diet. Reflect on this in light of another fact—that at least one-third of God's children went to bed hungry or malnourished last night.

I hope this will not just put a guilt trip on you but will help you understand that how we eat and waste food is far more than a major physical health problem for caring Christians. In a world with the capacity to feed everyone adequately, it is a profound and urgent global spiritual and ethical problem.

What is a Christian's spiritual approach to eating and drinking in such a world? Eating lower on the food chain is not just better for our health; it is also a small but worthwhile way to implement our Christian commitment to help end hunger, both at home and abroad. The production of red meat so affluent people can enjoy a juicy steak uses enormous amounts of grain that otherwise could be made available to feed many more hungry people. Pictures of starving children should motivate us as human beings, and even more so as Christians, to join hands with other people of goodwill to help create a just world economy where hunger is obsolete.

God intends for all our sisters and brothers on planet earth, including millions of homeless people in wealthy countries like the United States, to have enough nutritious food to sustain their well being. The one who fed the five thousand calls us to be partners with God and work together for the coming of a world where this is a reality. Practical strategies of a Christian response to world hunger are spelled out in Owen D. Owens's insightful book *Stones into Bread? What Does the Bible Say about Feeding the Hungry Today?*[10]

Renewing Your Body-Mind-Spirit with Rest

Giving yourself adequate rest and relaxation to replenish your inner springs of life energy is an essential, oft-neglected part of Christian self-care. In our high-pressure society, insufficient relaxation and deprivation of restorative sleep are widespread problems that dull the creative edge of life. Chronic, severe sleep deprivation increases vulnerability to physical, mental, emotional, and relationship problems.

Since I am an inveterate "to do list" devotee, columnist Ellen Goodman touched me deeply in one column. She began by mentioning that the lilacs were gone from beside her back door for another year and expressing her regret that she had not taken time to enjoy fully their wonderful fragrance. Then she used a painfully apt image— "channel surfing through life"—that she described in this way: "Work, click, kids, click, parents, click, errands, click. With split-second timing it was possible to cover everything—but only if we stay on the surface. What happens when life becomes a list . . . When even the pleasurable things become items to be checked off?"

Goodman identifies a subtle but significant loss we experience when we allow ourselves to get so busy that we do not slow down long enough to really see and enjoy the beauty that often is below the surface of life. What we miss by rushing along on the surface is the fragrance of all the now-departed lilacs in our super-busy living.[11]

Jesus' respect of his own need for rest and renewal in the midst of pressures from many needy people was mentioned earlier. He practiced the healthful "Sabbath principle" of taking regular times of rest and renewal. When we Christians become overinvolved in nonstop living and have a wall-to-wall list of things we "have to do," emulating Jesus would certainly increase our total well being.

 Well Being Exercises: Take a few minutes to reflect on any problems you have regarding adequate rest, relaxation, and sleep. / If you are plagued by frequent insomnia or run yourself ragged by "hurry-itis," I recommend that you turn to *Well Being* and try one or more of these self-help approaches:

1. If insomnia is your problem, follow the suggestions for slowing down and increasing the probability of falling asleep, page 99.

2. If self-stressing is your concern, try the method of deep, full-body relaxation described on page 101.

One way to help yourself learn to relax is to give yourself two or three minivacations of five to fifteen minutes each day. For example, right now, stop and go outside for a minivacation. Walk briskly around the block, breathing the fresh air and feeling the wind on your face. Or look briefly at something beautiful—*really* look so that you experience it at the center of your life. Even just stretching and breathing deeply for a minute or two will help reenergize and relax you.

If all else fails, try laughing at yourself, especially at the absurd expectations you sometimes put on yourself. I say more about this in the discussion of playfulness and laughter in Session 6.

Protect Your Body-Mind-Spirit by Reducing Toxins

There is more than a tad of truth in identifying the mouth as the most dangerous orifice of our bodies, both in terms of what we send out of it and what we put into it. The words that we send out can wound other people and ourselves deeply. The substances we put into our bodies via our mouths can wound them severely, even fatally. You can give your body-mind-spirit a welcome wellness gift by learning effective ways to reduce drastically or eliminate the things you consume through your mouth that diminish your health.

Giving yourself this gift involves finding other, healthy ways to satisfy the nagging needs that these toxins may meet temporarily. Comforting, consciousness-changing chemicals such as refined sugar, junk food, caffeine, alcohol, nicotine, and many drugs (both prescription and street drugs) are very popular self-medications. They may bring short-term comfort or what feels like blessed escape. People take them in an attempt to cope with their many painful feelings. These include stress, depression, boredom, anxiety, emotional conflict, low self-esteem, sexual frustration, loneliness, and emotional poison or starvation caused by dysfunctional or toxic relationships.

These self-medications often work at least temporarily. Unfortunately, most of these substances lend themselves to our becoming increasingly dependent on them. When people become hooked, what was originally a "solution" becomes a major problem because it increases the very emotional pain and problems it had temporarily relieved. Our Christian compassion may grow if we simply remember that many people eat or drink too much because they hurt so much. But eventually their pain-masking medication causes them to suffer much, much more.

We may have a better understanding of personal and family problems caused by addiction to chemical comforters if we bear in mind that our society encourages us to overuse as well as misuse these substances. Alcohol has been humankind's all-time favorite, domesticated, mood-changing drug. Many centuries ago, the psalmist thanked God for the fruit of the vine, "wine to gladden the human heart" (Ps. 104:15). Today the majority of Americans, including many Christians, regard alcohol as a pleasant way to take a minivacation from their burdens and responsibilities and perhaps a way to activate their playful inner child so they can have some relaxed fun.

For many decades in the last century and the early decades of this one, several mainline Protestant denominations devoted intense efforts to this issue. They attempted to diminish the widespread human pain caused by the misuse of alcohol. They did this through education aimed at abstinence and by supporting the prohibition movement. In more recent years, for a variety of historical reasons including disillusionment about prohibition, many Christians and their churches have relaxed their concern about alcohol.

In the meantime, alcohol abuse and addiction has continued to soar, together with multiple addictions to nicotine and other drugs. Instead of using wine to make their hearts glad, many people have used them to put their souls to sleep. Nicotine addictions caused by smoking and other uses of tobacco have also skyrocketed, causing more deaths, in all probability, than all other drug addictions combined—including alcoholism. All this has become enormously costly to the health and well being of the individuals, their families, and their communities.

In most congregations, some people who appear to function normally are on the road to full-blown addiction to one or more of the following drugs: alcohol, nicotine, tranquilizers, sedatives, antidepressants, barbiturates, amphetamines (pep pills), diet pills, and street drugs such as cocaine or pot. Unfortunately, physicians often prescribe psychoactive drugs such as tranquilizers for ordinary life stresses and losses. This is especially true for women patients, and unrecognized addictions to prescribed drugs have become a near epidemic among women.

The addiction process is usually gradual. It sneaks up on people, and they become hooked long before they are aware that they have lost control of their use of these substances. Their body chemistry has adapted to the presence of the drug so that they must take increasing doses to get the same sought-after effects. Heavy drinking and drug use produce a tremendous variety of physical, mental, and spiritual illnesses.

Without returning to the failed strategy of the past, the time has come for caring, concerned Christians and their congregations to become involved in innovative ways. We can be major participants in our society's efforts to help victims find healing and to develop programs of prevention focusing on all mind-altering chemicals. Individual Christians and churches have the potential to contribute in significant ways to helping prevent the disastrous impact of these substances on the well being of millions of people. Such programs should involve strategies such as the following:

• Help individual Christians learn how to evaluate their own use of any hazardous but attractive chemicals so as to identify less-than-responsible patterns that interfere with living life in all its fullness and should be changed.

• If you smoke, give yourself what probably will be your most important wellness gift ever. Do whatever it takes to stop! This addiction is tough to break, but half the people who have ever smoked in the United States have succeeded in quitting. They report that their payoff in enhanced health and longevity is more than worth the struggle. Remember, it has been estimated that as many people die from smoking in each three-year period as lost their lives in all the wars in U.S. history! Worldwide, smoking by 1.1 billion people is a ticking time bomb, healthwise. Currently the deaths of three million people are linked with smoking, but it is estimated that this could rise to ten million by early in the next century.[12]

• Teach our children and youth, by example and by accurate information, how to live as a responsible, creative Christian in our psychochemical addictive society.

• Make a variety of wellness programs widely available as one part of a congregation's education program. Do this because you know that learning nonchemical ways to cope with discomfort and losses and finding the lift of healthy spirituality are among the most effective ways to prevent abuse of and addictions to these substances.

• Give robust support to the effective programs of education, prevention, and treatment that now exist in most communities. This includes encouraging people who may need them to go to treatment programs, including twelve-step recovery programs like AA (Alcoholics Anonymous), NA (Narcotics Anonymous), GA (Gamblers Anonymous), and OA (Overeaters Anonymous). It also includes welcoming recovering persons with open arms into the supportive circle of mutual caring that is a healthy congregation.

• Welcome recovering persons with open arms into spiritual study and growth groups. Such groups can help them integrate the resources of a particular religious tradition with the spirituality that often is reborn in twelve-step groups.

 **Well Being Exercise: Answer the short list of questions in the "Pre-Addiction Checklist," pages 97–98 in *Well Being*. This can be useful, even if you are sure that you have no problems in this area. It is a quick way to learn to recognize some of the early warning symptoms of addictions. Remember that in most if not all congregations, there are hidden alcoholics and people dependent on prescription drugs who have not yet recognized the nature of their problem. / Consider how you could activate interest in your congregation in developing innovative preventive programs.[13]

Increasing Sensual Satisfactions

I did not originally think of sensual satisfaction as an important component of body well being. But I have become increasingly aware of how important sensual satisfaction is to our physical, mental, and spiritual well being. Anxiety about pleasure is a common symptom among church people who were raised to believe that their spiritual and sensual needs are somehow contradictory rather than potentially complementary. They have not made the enlivening discovery that our sensuality and body pleasures are good gifts of God to be used both responsibly and joyfully.

The Gospels make it clear that Jesus enjoyed fellowship. He ate with all kinds of people. The religious leaders who associated being "really religious" with denying their sensuality and repressing their capacity for enjoying pleasure compared Jesus unfavorably with the ascetic John the Baptist. They could not understand a young man of such spiritual depth who also was so in love with life that he celebrated both people and the God-given satisfactions of life.

As Christians, affirming the God-given pleasure potentials of our bodies is a way of celebrating this gift in our total self-care program. Elaboration of how to fulfill this need is explored in the context of discovering the healing possibilities of playfulness and laughter (see Session 6).

Overcoming Inner Roadblocks to Self-Care

Most people seem to know a lot more about healthy self-care than they put into practice. In my own experience, inner resistance and rationalizations often get in the way of exercising and other body self-care that I know I should do. This is especially true when my life is particularly hectic. This is not a new dilemma. The Apostle Paul described his self-sabotage in this way: "For I do not do the good I want, but the evil I do not want is what I do" (Rom. 7:19).

If you resist doing the self-care things you know you *ought* to do and perhaps even *want* to do, let me review some strategies that may help:

1. Find yourself a wellness partner[14] and do things together that you'll both find enjoyable and good for your bodies. When either of you backslides in your self-care, you may help to motivate each other. Sustaining healthy practices is usually easier if you don't try to go it alone.

2. Start small. For example, instead of trying to find time for a long walk on a busy day, start with a short brisk walk. Plans that will require large time commitments often fall victim to backsliding.

3. Whenever possible, do things that have immediate, built-in rewards. For example, if you're trying to resist the high-fat, sugar, and caffeine-laden snacks that are available at work or the fast-food lunch, take some healthy snacks to share or make a healthy lunch that is also delicious. It's difficult to forgo immediate oral gratification if you have only long-range, hoped-for rewards such as making your body feel more alive and trim.

4. If your spirituality is a source of motivation in your life, make sure that you keep your self-care rooted in your spirituality. It is well documented that people who have a meaningful religious life tend to be healthier than those who do not have that spiritual sustenance. The benefits reported include being better adjusted in marriage and personally happier, as well as experiencing greater longevity and faster recovery after life-threatening illnesses and heart surgery.

5. It's important to make body self-care an integral part of your lifestyle in addition to whatever times you specifically set aside for it. For example, when you walk, stride fast enough to get some aerobic benefits rather than just meandering. The latter is fine and healthful when you want to reflect, meditate, or connect more intimately with the world around you as you walk. If you keep your physical self-care wants and needs in the back of your mind, you can gradually build small opportunities for physical self-care into your day until they become a natural part of your lifestyle. For example, briefly doing simple stretching exercises several times during each day can help keep your body more relaxed, energized, and flexible.

6. Don't give up if your first efforts to change unhealthy behavior patterns fail. Such

change is a process. Most people who succeed do so only after several relapses. One report is that 85 percent of those who succeed in the difficult task of quitting smoking had several relapses before they quit.[15]

Looking Back—Looking Ahead

Is the active involvement of Christians and churches in physical health care, for which there will be an increasing need in the world of the twenty-first century, an unprecedented development? It has new aspects, but it also is deeply rooted in our centuries-old Christian heritage. From the time of Christ, religious groups have pioneered in responding to the healing and health-care needs that were unmet by the society at large. Church organizations established the first hospitals, for example.

A striking expression of this heritage occurred in the mid-eighteenth century. In 1747, a landmark book entitled *Primitive Physic: or An Easy and Natural Method of Curing Most Diseases*[16] was published in England. It became the "standard home doctor book" for almost one hundred years and was used widely in both England and America. The author was John Wesley, an Anglican clergyman and cofounder of the Methodist movement. He also had practiced New Testament modes of healing and had established dispensaries where impoverished people in the slums of London could obtain sorely needed medicines. He wrote the book so that the common people could learn how to prevent many illnesses and find inexpensive and safe remedies for the countless medical problems that he discussed.

Wesley had a philosophy and theology of natural good health and understood that God, the "Author of Nature," brings healing through many channels, including good self-care and various natural substances. Some of his advice seems quaint or erroneous and even humorous today. But much of it is still valid as guidance for preventive self-care. Consider these gems from his "Plain Easy Rules":

> The air we breathe is of great consequence to our health. . . . Every one that would preserve health should be as clean and sweet as possible in their homes, clothes, and furniture. . . . Water is the wholesomest of all drinks; quickens the appetite and strengthens the digestion the most. . . . A due degree of exercise is indispensably necessary to health and long life. Walking is the best exercise for those who are able to bear it. . . . The open air, when the weather is fair, contributes much to the benefit of exercise. We may strengthen any weak part of the body by constant exercise. . . . The passions [emotions] have a greater influence upon health than most people are aware of. . . . The love of God, as it is the sovereign remedy of all miseries, so in particular it effectively prevents all the bodily disorders the passions introduce, by keeping the passions within due bounds. And by the unspeakable joy, and perfect calm, serenity, and tranquillity it gives the mind, it becomes the most powerful of all the means of health and long life.[17]

In uncommon or persistent problems, Wesley advised "every [one] without delay to apply to a physician that fears God."

Questions for Reflection

1. What are the most important things you need to change or do to treat your body with more respect and care?

2. Does the view that giving your body care is a spiritual as well as a physical discipline make sense in the context of your religious faith?

3. How can Christians treat our bodies as temples of the Spirit but avoid what seems like body-worship in some health-fad circles?

4. What is the best strategy for encouraging your congregation to include Christian approaches to exercise, healthy nutrition, rest, reducing toxins, and celebrating sensuality and healthy sexuality in its education programs?

Using Checkup Findings to Strengthen Your Self-Care Plan

 If you took and tallied the Physical Well Being Checkup before this session, I trust that it primed the pump for you to use this session productively. You came to the session with an overview of the issues and some awareness of things you need to do to improve your physical self-care. You undoubtedly have acquired other body-care ideas during this session. (If for any reason you haven't done the checkup yet, turn back to it now and take a few minutes to learn what it can teach you.) Now is the time to strengthen and enrich your self-care plan by taking the following steps:

1. Look over your tally of the checkup and any notes you made after taking it, paying particular attention to NS and OK items that you checked as particularly important or urgent for taking action. Also review your initial thoughts about what you can and should do to implement these action-options. /

2. Review other options to which you were attracted during this session as important to your physical self-care. /

3. Now, using these ideas from the checkup and session, enhance your self-care plan by adding a section listing the most important items of physical self-care. / Spell out the specific objectives you want to achieve, practical plans for moving toward these, a time line, and rewards you'll give yourself as you take each step.

4. Select one or two high-priority items that are both attractive and achievable, and make concrete plans for implementing them within the next day or two. Be sure to pick options that are relatively easy to implement so that you can enjoy the rewards of improved physical self-care in the short-term as well as the long-term. Trying to change long-standing, unhealthy lifestyle patterns is not easy and probably is not the best place to begin. Remember that in self-change struggles, nothing succeeds like success. Go for it!

Closing Song, Prayer, and Evaluation

 Whether you are studying alone or with a wellness partner or in a group, close this session by doing the following:

• Sing a hymn, spiritual, or folk song that celebrates the wonders of our bodies or gives thanks to God for the gifts of our bodies.

• Celebrate new understandings that have dawned during this session by first listing these and then by praying with passion and thanksgiving.

• Do a brief evaluation of the strengths and weaknesses of the session, aiming at increasing the wellness benefits of future sessions.

Continuing Your Self-Care

 If you're doing these sessions alone or with others, the following activities will help you continue your wellness process between study sessions.

• Each day, spend at least a brief time in imaging prayer for the healing and wellness of your body and the bodies of others you care about. Visualize yourself and them enveloped in the warm healing light of God's love. Ask for insights and guidance about new ways to glorify God in your body and to respect both your own body and those of others as temples of the divine Spirit.

• Read chapter 5 in both textbooks. And, at least scan the two other chapters in *Well Being* that are directly related to relationship issues. These are Chapter 11, "Challenges to Your Well Being as a Woman or Man," and Chapter 10, "Sex and Well Being: 10 Ways to Enjoy Sensual Love." Highlight or underline the things that seem particularly important for enhancing your care of your close relationships.

• Take and score the Relationship Well Being Checkup before the next session.

• Each day, implement several of the spiritual, mental, and physical action-options now included in your overall self-care plan. You'll receive the wellness payoff gradually as you put these plans into action.

• Consider how you will encourage those who plan your congregation's education and holistic wellness programs to include more physical self-care offerings.

Session 5

Nurturing Loving Well Being
in Your Intimate Relationships

*The animals are getting along fine.
It's the intelligent life I'm having
problems with.*

—Cartoon showing a worried Noah
on the deck of the ark

A Relationship Well Being Checkup

 To help you gain the greatest benefits to your well being in relationships from this session, take and score this checkup first. If you are married or in another committed relationship, invite your partner to take and score the checkup independently. In either case you will find guidelines in this session for using what you learn to enrich your relationships.

If you are in a lonely place on your life journey, this inventory and the chapter may be painful. But they also can be useful as you search for ways to find and nurture love in your relationships. Keep in mind that it is not a test but a tool to increase the mutual care and well being of intimate relationships. It will provide a quick evaluation of areas in which your relationships are strong and growing, as well as those areas that need more mutual care. The items in the checkup provide a list of things you can do to nurture mutual love in relationships.

The checkup is worded in terms of a two-person relationship such as marriage or any

close friendship. But the same relationship-enriching principles apply to families. If you are using this checkup with your nuclear or extended family, simply change the wording to fit relationships of more than two persons. If you are presently not in a close relationship, change the "We" to "I" in the checkup statements.

Instructions: Mark each statement in one of three ways:

E = "I'm doing *excellently* in this."

OK = "I'm doing *acceptably*, but there's room for improvement."

NS = "This is an area where I definitely *need strengthening*."

_____ Knowing that love continues to grow when people nurture their relationships intentionally, we invest some time, almost every day, in communicating about issues and concerns that really matter to each of us. In this way we often clear the air of little hurts and irritants that occur in our day-by-day living.

_____ The relationship agreement or covenant between us regarding the rights and responsibilities of each person is fair, explicit, and open to renegotiation whenever circumstances change or conflicts signal that this is needed.

_____ In our relationship, we give each other respect, pleasure, loving care, freedom, and encouragement to grow by developing more of our gifts and possibilities.

_____ The give and take in our relationship is generally fairly balanced in both directions. But we are willing to do more giving than taking for a time, when one of us is under heavy pressures, sick, or facing grief, such as the loss of a job.

_____ When our individual needs or wants are very different and therefore in conflict, we try to negotiate fair, win-win compromises so that each person's needs and wants are met as fully as possible.

_____ If our self-help efforts do not resolve serious differences in a reasonable time, we both are willing to seek help from a competent pastoral counselor or marriage and family therapist.

_____ Opportunities for job satisfactions, further education, travel, recreation, self-care, and time alone are fairly divided between us.

_____ Responsibilities for the care of others (children or aging parents, for example), house and yard work, and other necessary chores also are divided fairly.

_____ We often are playful in our relationship. We have regular times set aside for having fun together. We frequently laugh at ourselves and with each other about our shared foibles and vicissitudes.

_____ We give each other the touching, hugging, and physical closeness we each want or need.

_____ When crises and losses strike, we respond with empathy, caring support, loving touching, and responsive listening.

_____ Our relationship has the ongoing support of a caring circle of friends and extended family members.

_____ Our togetherness is balanced by times of being apart, whether by ourselves or with others. We enjoy meaningful relationships with other couples, families, and singles, and with persons of different ages.

_____ We frequently give each other affirmation and appreciation, warm support, forgiveness, and constructive criticism that focuses on issues and does not attack each other's self-esteem or integrity.

_____ We usually communicate openly, expressing our real feelings and discussing complex problems honestly with each other. We ask openly for what we need and say what we believe in an honest but noncombative manner, even when it is difficult to do so.

_____ We have accepted (however reluctantly) the futility of trying to re-make each other to be like ourselves, like the parent we wanted and did not have as children, or like some idealized image of a partner.

_____ We try to show respect for each other's differences and deal with conflicts and frustrations openly and regularly rather than letting them grind on without resolution, thereby causing coldness, anger, and alienation between us.

_____ When we become distant because we have hurt each other, we try to correct the underlying causes of the pain rather than fall into a vicious and futile pattern of attacking and counterattacking.

_____ We often learn from the painful conflicts, griefs, life transitions, and ongoing problems in our relationship.

_____ We try to avoid manipulative games aimed at keeping peace at any price in our relationship, knowing that such peace is neither genuine nor lasting.

_____ Meeting each other's needs often is mutually satisfying because doing so meets our own need to enhance each other's happiness and well being.

_____ We enjoy and affirm each other's successes, accomplishments, and strengths, knowing that appreciation is the language of love.

_____ Our emotional and physical closeness flowers when we are nurturing love, trust, and respect in our relationship.

_____ We both are working to free ourselves from residues of traditional stereotypes of women and men, stereotypes we learned as children in a sexist society. We know that being assertive, analytical, rational, and self-sufficient, on the one hand; or being gentle, vulnerable, sensitive to feelings, and nurturing in relationships, on the other, are complementary capacities that both women and men need to develop in order to be whole persons.

_____ Each of us is aware of the health hazards of both the male "success" treadmill and also the female super-mom, caregiving treadmill. We are seeking to liberate ourselves and our relationship from this sexist programming by embracing mutual empowerment and healthy interdependence.

_____ We have let go of blaming our parents for their faults and for their imperfect modeling of healthy male-female relationships. This frees us to develop our own style of relating that contributes most to our mutual love and growth.

_____ We are in touch with our inner strength and inherent worth as persons so that we don't need to engage in power-trips or compete with each other in order to feel strong or worthwhile.

_____ We are making determined efforts to practice equality and justice in our relationship.

_____ We respect and care for our bodies lovingly rather than treating them either like a macho machine or a female sex object.

_____ We both find healing and power in the spiritual discoveries of women as well as men and in the so-called "feminine" dimension of the divine Spirit.

_____ Our relationship is deepened by shared spirituality and values and by engaging in meditation, prayer, or spiritual study together as we seek God's loving guidance in enhancing both love and justice between us.

_____ We participate regularly in a caring congregation where we have a sense of belonging, meet our deep spiritual hungers, and fulfill our need to reach out with caring to the hungry, lonely, and oppressed.

_____ We share a love of God's living creation. We enjoy being nurtured by beautiful places in nature, by "greening" our home, and by doing earth-caring work to help save a healthy earth for all the children of the human family as well as other species.

_____ Our relationship is enriched by working together for causes much larger than our relationship—causes aimed at helping heal the wounds and enhance the well being of people in our community and around the planet.

_____ Our relationship is very far from perfect, of course, in spite of our best efforts to enhance it. We know that this is because we are imperfect people seeking to create and re-create something that is both complicated and potentially precious—an ongoing, intimate, growing, committed, trustful, loving relationship. We rejoice that in our relationship we both can explore the challenges of "life in all its fullness" for us as Christians who have chosen to journey together.

Using Your Findings to Enhance Your Relationships

Take the following steps to help you use the results of this checkup in developing a plan to increase the well being of your relationships:

1. Tally your responses and write down the totals below. This will give you an overview of your relationship's strengths and weaknesses. / Congratulate yourself on the items you marked "E." If you and your partner both did the checkup, share and compare how you marked various items and what you can learn from these similarities and differences. / Congratulate each other on shared E items and note the OK and NS items, remembering that these are areas where increased self-other care may increase your relationship's health, mutual satisfaction, and love.

Yourself:	Your Partner:
E: _____	E: _____
OK: _____	OK: _____
NS: _____	NS: _____

2. Go through the list and put a star beside those OK and NS items that seem either urgent or especially important to you. / If you and your partner both took the checkup, put double stars beside items that both of you marked OK or NS. Share your tentative thoughts about what you might do together to enhance the flow of love, esteem, sensuality, and communication between you.

3. What is your overall "feel" concerning the general wellness of your relationship? In the space below, jot down your evaluation of the strengths and weaknesses of your relationship.

_____

_____

_____

_____

_____

_____

_____

_____

4. Now, in the space below, make notes about preliminary plans to strengthen your relationship's well being by implementing some of each person's starred options. / In the following session, you will be encouraged to come back and elaborate on your ideas, as you develop a workable self-other care plan.

_____

_____

_____

_____

_____

_____

_____

_____

_____

A Biblical Perspective

 To set the tone for this session, remember one of the most loved chapters in the Bible, often read at Christian wedding services. This is the beautiful hymn to love written by the Apostle Paul in his first letter to the church in Corinth. In the last verse of that stirring passage, after highlighting the characteristics of mature Christian love, Paul identifies three things that are essential for relationships that last and flourish—faith, hope, and love. Then, as a ringing climax, he points to the most important of all three: "the greatest of these is love" (1 Cor. 13:13).

Through my years of doing marriage enrichment and family counseling (as well as in my personal life), one fact has become increasingly clear: This ancient affirmation of the supremacy of love in human relationships is as true in today's society as it was in the first century. Couples and families who know how to cultivate growth-enabling love among themselves can transcend enormous odds and draw closer together. In contrast, couples and families who lack basic love-nurturing abilities often fall apart when they encounter relatively minor crises. The wise scientist-philosopher Pierre Teilhard de Chardin put the truth well: "Love alone is capable of uniting living beings in such a way as to complete and fulfill them, for it alone takes them and joins them by what is deepest in themselves. This is a fact of daily experience."[1]

This session aims at helping you enhance the love-nurturing insights and skills that are crucially important for the well being of any close personal relationship.

Major Objectives and Themes

 Put a check mark in front of those objectives and themes listed below that are important to you as you seek to increase the well being of your relationships. They will be your personal objectives for this session. In this session, you will have opportunities to learn the following:

- ❏ Why the quality of your close relationships is so important to your total well being.
- ❏ Biblical resources that can strengthen shared spirituality in your intimate relationships.
- ❏ Insights about the nature of Christian love.
- ❏ Strategies that help resolve conflicts and nurture the growth of love in intimate relationships.
- ❏ A valuable do-it-yourself communication tool called the Intentional Relationship Method, designed to help couples or families prevent and heal conflicts, and also cultivate their love intentionally.
- ❏ How to strengthen your overall self-care plan by adding steps of caring for others.

Biblical Roots

Before reading the paragraphs below, jot down in the space provided one or two biblical passages that emphasize Christian understandings of love and its importance in relationships. /

_____
_____
_____
_____
_____

Here are some of the many passages in the Hebrew and Christian scriptures that illuminate the role of love in human relationships:

The relational nature of spiritually empowered living is a major theme throughout the Bible. The First Letter of John includes these memorable words about the spiritual roots of love and the need for translating our love into deeds of caring and service: "How does God's love abide in anyone who has the world's goods and sees a brother or sister in need and yet refuses help? Little children, let us love, not in word or speech, but in truth and action" (3:17-18).

Later in First John, the author identifies loving as the bridge to experiencing God and the energy of divine love: "Beloved, let us love one another, because love is from God; everyone who loves is born of God and knows God. Whoever does not love does not know God, for God is love" (4:7-8). The Christian awareness that genuine human love flows from divine love is expressed beautifully in the same chapter, as is the way fear may be healed by love: "God is love, and those who abide in love abide in God, and God abides in them. . . . There is no fear in love, but perfect love casts out fear" (1 John 4:16, 18). (Unfortunately, most human love is far from perfect.)

The book of Ecclesiasticus, dating from the time between the Hebrew and Christian scriptures, includes this gem: "A faithful friend is the medicine of life" (Eccles. 6:16). The Bible reveals many faithful friendships, including Naomi and Ruth, David and Jonathan, Timothy and Paul, and the friendships of Jesus with Mary, Martha, Lazarus, and the disciples. I hope you know the energizing, healing power of real friendship in your personal life.

Quoting from his own Hebrew Scriptures (Lev. 19:18), Jesus emphasized love as the heart of wholeness by encouraging people to love their neighbors as they loved themselves (Mark 12:31). Note that this passage does not put down loving oneself. Rather, it speaks of self-love as a bridge for relating lovingly to others.

What Is Christian Well Being in Relationships?

As a Christian, do you reject or feel uneasy about the view that loving yourself and focusing on self-care are healthy things to do? If so, remember that when Jesus spoke of loving our neighbors as we love ourselves, he was responding to a trick question about the greatest commandment. In his reply, Jesus articulated a fundamental principle of loving that modern psychology has also affirmed. Love of neighbor depends on love of self! These conditions are interdependent, not mutually exclusive.

Loving ourselves in health-giving ways is the opposite of selfishness and egocentricity. Such self-love expresses self-respect, self-acceptance, and self-esteem, and these provide the secret of diminishing unhealthy pride. Self-care is an essential expression of and preparation for really loving ourselves. Those who continually neglect self-care because they are too busy caring for others eventually discover that their ability to serve others is diminished drastically. In their emotional and spiritual exhaustion, they often suffer compassion burnout.

Here is a useful definition of healthy love that I have found helpful to people in marriage, family enrichment, and creative singlehood workshops: *Love is caring about and commitment to one's own and the other's continuing growth, empowerment, and self-esteem.* Translated into religious language, the definition could read, Love is caring about and commitment to doing everything possible to enable oneself and loved persons to discover and develop the many gifts with which God has blessed them.

If you really love someone (including yourself), you will do all you can to encourage that person to become all that God dreams for him or her to be. Well being involves loving and growing in relationships by feeding each other's deepest heart hungers with the warm bread of caring.

**Pause and reflect on this question: "What are the things I most want to receive and give in my close relationships?" Jot these down in the space below.

_____

_____

_____

_____

_____

Compare the following list of hungers of the heart with those you have listed: love, respect, trust, affirmation, comfort, forgiveness, warm closeness and touching, dependable continuity, freedom, and intellectual, emotional, and spiritual sharing. To the degree that people nurture each other's hungers for spiritual and emotional food, they experience healing and growth in their love and relating.

Why Is Well Being in Relationships So Vital?

I recall chuckling at this tongue-in-cheek radio advertisement by a local telephone company: "With us you are more than a name—you're a number!" Because many people today feel as if they are merely numbers in our high-tech society, relationships in which people know our names are crucially important for our well being. In those relationships we hope to be loved by people who know us well, including our weaknesses and warts.

The Christian "good news" concerns the wholeness of our four fundamental relationships—those with ourselves, with other people, with God, and with God's creation. To learn how to live a more Christian lifestyle, therefore, means healing the alienation and enhancing the vitality of love in each of these basic relationships. Many people suffer from loneliness and long for deeper friendships with themselves, other people, nature, and God. Love is the essential bridge that connects us in each of these relationships.

Modern medical science offers increasing evidence that chronic loneliness can damage your health. Physical, mental, and spiritual problems proliferate among persons who are isolated from caring relationships. Increasing your communication and conflict-resolution skills so that you can cause the tender flower of health-giving love to grow in all dimensions of your life is probably the most valuable thing you can do for your overall well being!

Building on Discoveries from Your Checkup

If you took and tallied the Relationship Well Being Checkup before this session, as recommended, you already know some things you need to do to nurture love in those relationships that matter most to you. Commend yourself for having a running start on this session. (If you haven't completed the checkup yet, turn back to it now and take ten or fifteen minutes to do so.)

 Learning Exercise: Look over your tally of the checkup and the notes you made after taking it, keeping these issues in mind:

• the NS and OK relationship-enhancing items that you (and perhaps your partner) checked as seeming particularly important or urgent for taking action;

• your initial thoughts (and those of your partner) about what you might do to strengthen your intimate relationships by implementing these action-options; and

• additional resources that may be useful in implementing any tentative plans.

To learn from your own and each other's findings, take a few minutes now to share with your partner or the group what you discovered and plan to do as a result of taking the checkup. If you are working solo, share your findings soon with a person or persons who are interested in enhancing their own relational well being. / When you have finished doing this, jot down useful insights you gained in the process of sharing.

_____

_____

_____

_____

_____

_____

_____

_____

Strategies to Increase Self-Other Care in Relationships

Here are a baker's dozen strategies that highlight some of the most important relationship-enrichment methods contained in the checkup. I distilled these strategies over the years from countless experiences in family life education, marriage therapy, and enrichment work. More importantly, they come from five-plus decades of on-the-job training in my most challenging and important relationships—those with my spouse and our children and grandchildren. I invite you to use these thirteen strategies as tools to enrich the love in your most important relationships.

**To get the most help from these strategies, pause after reading each one and ask yourself two questions: (1) How well am I (or are we) doing this in our relationship? (2) How might we use this strategy to enrich our relationship? Building on insights you gained from the Relationship Well Being Checkup, jot down ideas for taking concrete steps that come to you as you reflect on these strategies.

If you are sharing this session with a close friend or your spouse (who, I hope, is also a close friend), I suggest that you take turns reading the strategies aloud, pausing after each one for a brief discussion of how you might apply it in your relationship. You could then jot down insights you gained from the discussion.

Love-Nurturing Strategy 1

Set aside some time each day (at least fifteen minutes, preferably more) to communicate about what really matters to each of you. Communication is as vital to your relationships as oxygen is to your body. The hungers of your heart and your basic personality needs, including your all-important need for love, can be met only by caring communication, both verbal and nonverbal. Conflicts can be resolved only by effective communication. The good news is that poor communicators usually are people who can strengthen their basic communication skills by learning to do three things more effectively:

• expressing their ideas, feelings, and needs clearly and honestly;

• listening more carefully to understand what the other person is really trying to say;

• checking out what they heard to make sure they understood the message accurately.

Relationship Caring Exercise: Reflect on the two questions suggested above as they relate to your communication. / Then write down notes about your insights and/or share them with your partner.

Love-Nurturing Strategy 2

Feed each other's heart-hungers regularly and intentionally, particularly the deep hungers for mutual appreciation, respect, touching, warm caring, intimacy, integrity, laughter, and fun. Love flowers when these needs are met. Love withers when mutual needs are neglected or replaced by toxic communication that produces mutual emotional starvation. Later in this chapter you'll learn the Intentional Relationship Method, a valuable tool for increasing your skill in feeding each other's heart hungers.

Relationship Caring Exercise: Reflect on the two questions suggested above as they relate to feeding each other's deep hungers. / Then write notes about your insights and/or share them with your partner.

Love-Nurturing Strategy 3

Continue to grow as individuals by developing your own special interests and talents. As persons in close relationship develop their own unique gifts and enhance their wholeness by becoming more alive and well, they are able to give more to each other and to their children and community. This strategy requires giving up the possessiveness that causes some couples to believe (erroneously) that they own each other. To the degree that they believe this, respect for each other's autonomy and healthy interdependent intimacy are sacrificed.

Balancing times of emotional, physical, and spiritual sharing; time alone for self-care; and time with children and friends is very difficult for couples in our high-pressure society. Finding and balancing time for each of these three important needs is essential for each person's well being and that of the relationship. Negotiating a workable balance of being together and apart is a challenge for many couples, especially two-career couples and those recently retired.

Relationship Caring Exercise: Reflect on the two suggested questions as they relate to your encouraging each other's continuing growth: (1) How well am I (or are we) doing this in our relationship? (2) How might we use this strategy to enrich our relationship? / Then write down notes about your insights and/or share them with your partner.

Love-Nurturing Strategy 4

Affirm each other's gifts, both actual and potential, and sustain equal opportunities for developing these gifts. The hallmark of genuine love in close friendships and marriage is that the partners support the fulfilling of each other's potentialities and dreams. For this to happen best for you, your working agreement or relationship covenant must be as fair and just as you can make it. Without a firm foundation of fairness and justice, the house of love is like the house in Jesus' parable—built on unstable sand so that it cannot survive any storm or flood. In my experience as a counselor, the most complex issue many couples face today is how they can provide equal opportunities for both persons to develop their unused or underused gifts.

Relationship Caring Exercise: Reflect on the two questions suggested at the beginning of these strategies as they relate to the justice and fairness level of your relationship. / Then write down notes about your insights and/or share them with your partner.

Love-Nurturing Strategy 5

Learn effective ways to prevent the cold wall of unhealed conflict, hurt, anger, and resentment from blocking the flow of caring, passion, joy, and love between you. Conflict is a normal part of any vital human relationship. The question is not whether we have conflict but whether we handle it constructively. Perhaps you can feel some empathy, as I can, for Sam Keene's statement: "My wife and I have had a hard fought love affair for over twenty years." The biblical wisdom about not letting the sun go down on our anger (Eph. 4:26) is healthy advice today.

Anger from unhealed, accumulated hurts is a major cause of the loss of vitality in relationships, because it robs them of joy, intimacy, and playful passion. Long-accumulated anger can turn into dangerous rage that may be expressed in tragic explosions of violence as evidenced by the epidemic of domestic violence against women and children. One-fourth of all the murders in the United States are committed by spouses and other live-in partners. Even when physical violence does not occur, emotional and spiritual violence in families deadens joy and love, and it deeply wounds children's self-esteem and security. Learning how to heal the hurt and resolve the conflicts behind the anger is essential if loving wholeness is to grow.

Relationship Caring Exercise: Reflect on the two questions suggested at the beginning of these strategies, as they relate to resolving negative feelings. / Then write notes about your insights and/or share them with your partner.

Love-Nurturing Strategy 6

Keep your friendship lively and growing and continue to have fun together regularly. *Psychology Today* magazine conducted a survey of 351 couples married fifteen years or longer, 300 of whom said they were happily married. The findings were both surprising and encouraging. When asked what had kept their marriages going, the first and second reasons given most frequently by both women and men were, "My spouse is my best friend" and "I like my spouse as a person." Among the top ten reasons given by both sexes were "My spouse has grown more interesting" and "We laugh together."

It is significant that "We agree about our sex life" was only twelfth for men and fourteenth for women among the reasons for their relationship's continuing. Sex is a powerful factor that draws couples together initially. But the best long-term cement for sustaining an intimate relationship and also keeping the fires of romance glowing is liking each other as friends.

Relationship Caring Exercise: Remembering that playfulness and laughing together are enjoyable and low-budget ways to nurture joyful love, pause in your reading now and, with your partner, plan a shared minivacation for today. This simply means having fifteen minutes (more or less) of playful relaxation that you'll both enjoy. / While you're in the mood, take time to plan a fun "date"—an opportunity for intimate mental, physical, and spiritual reconnecting—for later this week. Regular dates are particularly important if you live a high-adrenaline lifestyle or have a two-career relationship. / If your partner isn't available right now, make these joint plans soon at a mutually convenient time.

Love-Nurturing Strategy 7

Open yourselves frequently to shared spiritual highs and other times of enjoying your spiritual lives together. Many years ago, my wife Charlotte and I wrote together about the health-giving power of spiritual intimacy. We pointed out that it not only strengthens relationships but that the spirituality itself can be strengthened by the quality of the relationship: "No single factor does more to give a marriage joy and keep it both a venture and an adventure in mutual fulfillment than shared commitment to spiritual discovery. The life of the spirit is deeply personal, so the moments of sharing on the spiritual level are tender, precious moments in a relationship."[2]

Would you agree that in today's anxious,

alienated world with its epidemic of spiritual emptiness and value vacuums, spiritual intimacy is even more relevant to creative closeness than it was years ago?

Our Christian heritage recognizes that human love is a good gift of the divine Spirit, rooted in and empowered by the love of God. I hope that you have experienced some exciting moments when you have discovered, perhaps unexpectedly, that your finite, fractured human love had become an imperfect but open door through which you could experience the Love of the universe. Here is a paraphrase of a statement about such peak experiences by that wise philosopher of relationships Martin Buber: "When the thou in each of you really meet, you encounter the eternal Thou" (from his book *I and Thou*).

An amazing, down-to-earth miracle occurs when our human love in a marriage or a close friendship becomes a channel for God's healing love to bathe people with cleansing and healing. When this occurs, God's love comes alive in our very human caring, touching, and intimacy. Beyond this, spiritual intimacy often enhances creative closeness in other important areas of our lives.

Relationship Caring Exercise: If you are with your partner, turn back to Session 2 and scan various methods described there for deepening spiritual intimacy between the two of you as well as within each of you as individuals. (Do this later if you are alone.) Choose one or two spiritual enrichment practices that you would both enjoy doing together, such as meditation, prayer, inspirational reading, worship, communion with nature, or helping those in need. / Spend time together sharing one or more of these.

Love-Nurturing Strategy 8

Take good care of your caring community— the close friends and family members who love you and support your relationship in all the ups and downs of the passing years. Studies of healthy families show that they interact a lot with their biological extended family and/or their "friend family," so that they become a mutual support system for one another. Isolated families miss the enrichment that comes from relating with a cluster of caring people in a variety of life stages, ethnic backgrounds, and lifestyles. Lonely nuclear families are especially vulnerable when crises strike.

So I encourage you to do whatever is required to discover or develop your health-nurturing caring community. As you probably know, a warm, family-like congregation is one of the best places to put down roots quickly when you have moved to a new community.

Relationship Caring Exercise: Reflect on the two questions suggested at the beginning of these strategies, as they relate to the strengthening of your support group: (1) How well am I (or are we) doing this in our relationship? (2) How might we use this strategy to enrich our relationship? / Then write notes about your insights and/or share them with your partner.

Love-Nurturing Strategy 9

Discover and enjoy together the special romance, challenges, opportunities, wisdom, and excitements of your present life stage. As most of us are aware, each family life stage, like all individual life stages, has a new set of problems, losses, and griefs. The good news that many folks need to discover is that each individual and family life stage also has a whole new set of possibilities and assets. Learning to savor the changing seasons of your life together with all their shadows and sunlight is an invaluable art in these times of extended life spans.

If you're a couple in the midyears, I hope you have made the welcome discovery that a special deeper romance is possible for you because of all the ups and downs you have shared through the years together. If you're a younger person, I hope you know at least one older couple who demonstrate that the widespread belief that romantic love is only for the young is a fallacy. It is true only if you believe it or if you have neglected cultivating a growing relationship through the years. If so, a couple's enrichment retreat for those in midyears or beyond may provide the growth stimulus you want and need.

Relationship Caring Exercise: Reflect on the two suggested questions as they relate to discovering the gifts of your present life stage. / Then write notes about your insights and/or share them with your partner.

Love-Nurturing Strategy 10

Find at least one important cause for which you enjoy working together. Harry Emerson Fosdick, the prominent pastor-preacher who was an inspiration to me in my early years, once observed that persons wrapped up in themselves make very small packages. The same is true of intimate relationships. Your love for each other will tend to deepen if you express it, among other ways, through working to help make your community and world a little healthier for everyone.

People's circle of concern usually begins with their immediate self-interests, of course. But broadening this circle beyond themselves and their intimate relationships saves people from what could be called family narcissism, an unhealthy malady something like an ingrown toenail. Expanding our horizons of concern also brings increased well being to intimate relationships. Furthermore, investing time, money, intelligence, passion, and hard work in a larger cause, such as hunger, ecology, peace, and justice is an effective expression of a Christian lifestyle. To paraphrase Jesus' words, a person who hordes life will

end up losing it. The key to finding life in all its fullness is to share it with those in need (see Mark 8:35).

Relationship Caring Exercise: The healing-yourself-by-healing-the-planet methods described in Session 8 can be used with your family or friends to respond to this challenge together. Look over these approaches and decide which one you might enjoy sharing as a couple or family. In doing this you probably will enjoy the shared satisfactions of helping, in small but significant ways, to heal a little of the widespread pain and brokenness in your congregation, your community, and your world.

Love-Nurturing Strategy 11

Develop and invest yourselves in implementing an intentional plan of mutual care for your relationship—a covenant of mutual well being! Strategies described in this session and in the checkup can be valuable ingredients in such a plan. A challenging discovery has emerged from various studies of long-term marital happiness. Satisfaction levels tend to decline as the years pass unless couples learn to work and play together to keep their relationship alive and well. Married people who continue to be friends and lovers after even a few years together usually have done this. Using a relational growth plan does not, of course, guarantee a blissful relationship. But it does increase the odds that mutual need-satisfaction and stimulation to growth will flourish rather than flounder in a relationship.

Relationship Caring Exercise: Reflect on the two suggested questions as they relate to developing a relationship-nurturing plan. / Then write notes about your insights and/or share them with your partner. Toward the end of this session, you'll be asked to firm up such a plan.

Love-Nurturing Strategy 12

If you don't have time to care for your intimate relationships in ways such as described above, you need to revise your priorities and how you spend your time. Are you investing only leftover time in your most important relationships? How often do you take or, more accurately, *make* time to communicate heart-to-heart? Perhaps you feel what couples in pain and alienation often say, wistfully or angrily: "We only communicate on the run, like ships passing in the night." The problem many couples have today is stated in these simple words: *Love takes time!*

In our hectic, harassed lives, it's easy to let the pressure of other important things squeeze love-nurturing out of our prime time. But let's be frank. The moment-by-moment decisions regarding how we will invest our time each day are guided by our working values and priorities. So if you want more time to enjoy communicating and loving, the way to start may be by revising the priorities that guide your life. The Time-Values Inventory in Session 2 may be helpful in doing this.

Relationship Caring Exercise: Reflect on the two questions suggested at the beginning of these strategies as they relate to making time for your relationship. / Then write notes about your insights and/or share them with your partner.

_____

_____

_____

_____

_____

_____

_____

Love-Nurturing Strategy 13

Add one or more of your own strategies, based on your unique insights, needs, and interests as individuals and as a couple. It is likely that those you yourselves develop, using your own hard-earned fragments of wisdom, will prove to be among the most useful in enriching your particular relationship. The responsibility for developing and implementing a workable self-other care plan rests with you and your partner. So please add your own strategies here:

_____

_____

_____

_____

_____

_____

Liberating Yourself and Your Relationship

The barriers to developing your full, God-given potentials and the special health hazards you face as a woman or man are well documented in our society. High levels of stress-induced illnesses reduce the life expectancy of men, and high levels of clinical depression and lower levels of self-esteem are found among women. Take concrete steps, individually and as a couple, to protect yourselves and to nurture greater wellness by seeking to liberate yourself from whatever sexist programming you received in your childhood and youth. You can move toward the healthy objective that is called "androgynous wholeness." This means the balanced development of both sides of women's and men's personality potentials—the emotional, nurturing, intuitive, receptive gifts of your mind and spirit, and the rational, assertive, leading, analytical-thinking abilities.

In many traditional families, girls have learned to overdevelop the first set of capacities, erroneously called "feminine," while neglecting the development of the other side. Conversely, boys have learned to overdevelop the second side, erroneously called "masculine," while neglecting to develop the first side. Empirical evidence shows that this lopsided development is bad for people's mental, physical, and spiritual health. Macho males have been shown to be more inflexible and less able to respond appropriately when nonaggressive behavior was called for by the situation. Women who fit the traditional stereotype of "feminine" have been shown to be more inflexible than even the macho men. They tend to be unable to respond assertively to the needs of a crisis situation.

When both women and men free themselves from the shackles of sexism, their relationships tend to improve. They often become closer as well as more honest and trusting after they have gone through the conflicts the changes have stimulated. Traditional one-up, one-down relationships spawn dishonest, manipulative power games between the sexes. In contrast, as the two genders' power, educational, and economic opportunities become more fair and equal, *genuine* partnerships between women and men can take place so that together they can enhance the wholeness of families, churches, communities, and governments.

A New Day for Marriage and Women-Men Relations

With all the gloomy statistics and reports about marriages and families, are you ready for some good news? All the chaos shows that our society is in the challenging early stages of a new era for women-men relationships. Many couples are struggling to develop healthier, more egalitarian

partnerships between themselves. Such relationships based on equality and justice will become the norm in the twenty-first century, producing healthier families in which healthier children can grow. More and more men and women will work together to create lifestyles aimed at fulfilling both persons' dreams and enhancing their lives and those of their children in all seven dimensions of living.

As in any time of traumatic social transition, conflicts and chaos increase as some people resist and others push for needed changes. Congregations and all of us as Christians are called by God to commit ourselves to do all we can to help birth this promising new day of liberating relationships in our own lives, families, and congregations, and eventually in the human family everywhere!

A Conflict-Healing, Love-Feeding Communication Tool

The Intentional Relationship Method (IRM) is a do-it-yourself communication exercise that you and another person (or persons) can use to strengthen and enrich your relationship in three ways:

1. by responding more intentionally to each other's needs and wants;

2. by preventing and reducing conflict that most frequently occurs around conflicted needs and wants;

3. by renegotiating the working agreement or covenant in your relationship to update it and make it more fair and satisfying for each person.

Of the numerous communication tools that I have devised in relationship-enrichment and counseling work over the years, the IRM is the clear winner. It has been evaluated "most helpful" by far more couples and families than any other. Some who have learned it report that they continue to use it regularly, particularly when tensions and conflicts arise in their relationship. To my happy surprise, clergy and congregational leaders have adapted and used this simple communication model effectively in various ways. Several use the inventory in preparation for marriage training, parenting seminars, creative events for singles, women's and men's renewal retreats, family camps, church membership classes, and planning retreats of church leaders.

Based on this feedback, it is clear that the IRM is the most useful love-nurturing and conflict-preventing tool in this book. Try it with your partner if you are studying this chapter together, or with a close friend. If you are alone, doing it solo can be good preparation for doing it with a partner later. Just picture the significant person you want to use it with and complete the sentences as you would with that person. Doing this can awaken insights about how you can build and enrich close relationships. Remember that this sign / means to stop reading while you do what has been described.

Step 1: *Affirming the Strengths in Your Relationship*

One person begins by completing this sentence to the other, "I appreciate in you . . ." as many times as wished. The one receiving should just listen and enjoy the warm glow of affirmation from the partner. / Now reverse roles. / Jot down below what each of you appreciates in the other. / Share with each other what you experienced as you were giving and receiving warm affirmations. / As mentioned, appreciation is the language of love. New lovers know this intuitively and practice it spontaneously, but some of us longer-coupled folks forget this love-nurturing truth. Step One provides a firm launching pad for the other steps.

Step 2: *Identifying the Growing Edges of Your Relationship*

Every relationship has room to grow, even those that are working well. This step lets you focus on places where you can grow together, if you choose. Building on Step One, begin with each person's thinking of the things you wish your partner would do to make your relationship better. / Then one of you completes this sentence aloud to the other, as many times as she or he wishes, "I need (or want) from you . . ." (Don't concern yourself at this point with whether your partner can or will respond to your statements.)

When receiving, listen as carefully as possible, remaining as nondefensive as you can. The purpose of this step is simply to get your "druthers" (or wishes or desires) out on the table and thus to have them available to work with, if you choose, in the third step. Remember that meeting all of each other's needs is neither desirable nor possible in any relationship. /

After each person has completed her or his list of needs and wants, jot down what you heard your partner express. / Then, as a communication check, compare your list with your partner's list. Discover how clearly each of you stated your needs and how carefully each has listened. / Now discuss how you feel about this step. / Remember that unmet needs in any close relationship are where conflicts occur most often but also the place where change has the greatest payoff.

_____

_____

_____

_____

_____

Step 3: *Planning Love-Nurturing Changes to Increase Mutual Need-Satisfaction*

Commend yourselves for completing the preparation toward intentionally making your relationship more mutually satisfying. There are three types of needs in close relationships—shared needs, conflicted needs, and parallel needs, which are not in conflict but are simply different. It's easiest to make changes in shared needs, since both of you will find the changes rewarding. So discuss the shared needs on your two lists and decide on one or two that seem important and achievable to both of you. /

Now, work out a *mutual change plan* that you agree will meet the shared need(s) you have selected, describing the changes each of you will make to implement your plan. / Write down the plan so that you can check on the progress you have made together in fulfilling it. / Some couples find it helpful to confirm their plan with a brief prayer by each person and then congratulate themselves for their commitment to creative change. If it feels meaningful to both of you, do something like this now in your own way. /

_____

_____

_____

_____

_____

_____

Step 4: *Implementing Your Mutual Change Plan*

This is the payoff step. As you put your plan into action, discuss and keep notes on your progress. Be sure to reward yourselves for each small step you take toward your change objectives. You deserve this because, through intentional affirmation and planning, you have strengthened or improved one or two small but significant clauses in your relationship covenant. Through your actions, you are intentionally making your relationship more fulfilling for both of you. If a particular plan does not work for whatever reason, modify or scrap it and work together to devise a more workable plan. /

_____

_____

_____

_____

_____

_____

_____

Step 5: *Choose Another Shared Need or Two Parallel Needs and Repeat the Steps*

By continuing this process from one unmet or partially met need to another, you walk forward on the path of intentional self-renewal in your relationship. Be sure to repeat the "I appreciate in you . . ." step regularly. /

When you move from shared to parallel needs, you'll be working out a mutual change plan to meet one partner's need and then the need of the other. Developing workable plans to satisfy conflicted needs is the most challenging because this requires effective negotiation that produces win-win compromise agreements. In these win-win agreements, each person gets some but not all of what he or she needs or wants.

If you want more time together, for example, and your partner wants less, a win-win compromise would be to meet in the middle. Win-lose "solutions" of conflicted needs are not solutions at all in intimate relationships. If a couple has a regular pattern of adopting win-lose solutions that favor one partner, both people lose because their creative closeness will be hurt by this unfairness. In contrast, win-win solutions tend to nurture love by satisfying some of each of your needs and wants in a fair way.

Beyond Mutual Need-Satisfaction

Negotiating a more reciprocally fair and fulfilling relationship is an excellent place to start but not to stop in enlivening your love. To do so is simply enlightened self-interest, meaning in the self-interest of each of you. If you are suffering from considerable mutual need-deprivation and therefore feel painful hostility and emotional alienation, intentionally increasing mutual need-satisfaction is the most effective way to gradually heal the hurt and distancing. But then, with God's help, you may discover that giving each other pleasure and need-satisfaction actually is self-rewarding in two ways.

By giving more love and satisfactions, one eventually receives more in the relationship. In addition, as a relationship deepens, people tend to own more of each other's needs. This means that each person begins to experience the desire to respond to more of the other person's needs, not just to get one's own needs met but because one feels satisfaction in meeting the needs of the other cared-for person. Each partner gets more pleasure from the act of giving the other pleasure.

At this point, people whose love is growing begin to move beyond reciprocity and enlightened self-interest to what can be called the "second-mile principle" in the Christian context. In such relationships people give loving care when the other is in a crisis or has special needs without expecting or receiving direct reciprocity at that time. Of course, self-serving needs continue in all of us to some degree. Being willing to ask for what one needs is healthy in relationships, provided it is a two-way exchange over time. The give and take of any functional adult relationship must be fairly balanced if wholeness is to be generated in both partners.

Going the second mile in relationships is healthy if this balance exists and each partner feels esteemed and cared about and also cared for by the other. Going the second mile is an embodying of grace on a human level. Experiencing the graceful love of God that undergirds and transcends all imperfect human love enables spiritually alive people to enjoy the partial grace they at times are able to give and receive.

Loving becomes most mutually transforming as people move beyond enlightened self-interest. The spiritual pioneer Thomas Merton illuminates this transition beautifully: "In reality, love is . . . a transcendent spiritual power. It is, in fact, the deepest creative power in human nature. . . . When people are truly in love, they experience far more than just a mutual need for each other's company and consolation. In their relation with each other, they become different people; they are more than their everyday selves, more alive, more understanding. . . . They are transformed by the power of their love."[3]

What to Do If Self-Help Is Not Enough

If people have a deeply toxic relationship, suffering from negative communication and cycles of mutual attack, they need the help of a trained relationship counselor or therapist. Such a caring, competent professional can help them learn how to reconnect the broken lines of communication, escape from self-perpetuating cycles of mutual attack and need-starvation, and stop relating today in terms of yesterday's obsolete programming. Many of us marry for unhealthy subconscious reasons that continue to sabotage our best efforts to make close relationships healthier.

If, in spite of all that you do, your painful conflicts continue, it is wise to give yourselves the gift of the skills of a marriage and family therapist. Your pastor may be trained to help couples with relatively functional relationships weather the storms of family crises. She or he probably can recommend a qualified family therapist in your community or a pastoral counseling specialist who is trained to do longer-term marriage therapy.

Questions for Reflection

1. How well am I (or are we) doing the things that will keep our love going and growing? What are the most important things that I (or we) must do to enhance our relationship-nurturing behavior? What makes this difficult for us?

2. Does the central theme of this session—that love grows as people learn to respond intentionally to more of each other's human needs—seem problematic?

3. What topics on Christian marriage and family life were overlooked or discussed inadequately in this chapter?

4. What can I (we) do to involve people in our congregation in relationship-enrichment experiences such as learning to use the Intentional Relationship Method?

Strengthening Your Self-Other Care Plan

Whether you are working on self-care solo or with a partner, review by yourself the insights and ideas for changes that you gained during this session and from your

reflections on the issues you scored OK or NS in the checkup. / Then write out a brief self-other care plan for your relationship(s) and add this to your overall self-care plan. / If you're working with a partner, discuss and integrate your two care plans. (Remember to include concrete, realizable objectives that you really want to achieve; practical strategies for moving toward these; rewards you will either give yourself as you take each step toward an objective or withhold if you don't move ahead. Keep your plan love-centered, playful as well as serious, and energized by your Christian faith.) /

Then choose one or two attractive and achievable objectives and begin implementing them together soon. I trust you'll experience the rewards of improving the care-giving love in your relationships.

Closing Prayer, Song, and Evaluation

Whether you are doing this session alone or with a partner or group, end this session with a brief and lively period of worshipful celebration. Sing a favorite folk song or hymn about God's love and human love. Share prayers of thanks for new insights that can help your love flower. Take time to evaluate this session and to discover how the next sessions may be improved.

Continuing Your Self-Care

To continue your wellness work between sessions and, equally important, to prepare yourself for the next session, take time to do the following:

• Individually and/or with your partner, begin implementing the high priority objectives in your self-other care plan, keeping track of what you learn and how your relationship is affected.

- Enjoy a daily talk and a minivacation or two with each other, and have a fun evening out together during the time between sessions.

- To prime the pump for the next session, take and tally the Work and Play Well Being Checkup. Highlight the things you find interesting or problematic. If you are especially interested in work wellness or play wellness, be sure to read Chapters 6 and 7 in *Well Being*.

- Each day, in a prayerful spirit, form a mental picture of the people you love most, surrounded by the warm, healing light of God's love and yours.

- Reflect on how the positive benefits you have experienced in your well being program could be enjoyed by other members of your church. Share these with your clergyperson, education director, or lay leader.

Session 6

Increasing Well Being
in Your Work and Play

Even if I were a hedonist, I wouldn't enjoy it.

—Bumper sticker

A person becomes a flowering orchard. The person that does good work is indeed this orchard bearing good fruit. . . . Whatever humanity does with its deeds in the right or left hand permeates the universe.

—Hildegard of Bingen[1]

I have said these things to you so that my joy may be in you, and that your joy may be complete.

—Jesus to his disciples
at the Last Supper (John 15:11)

The religious life is to be danced, not just believed.

—Zorba the Greek

A Work and Play Well Being Checkup

 To help you gain the greatest benefits to the well being of your work and play from this session, take and score this checkup first. Remember, it is not a test but a tool to increase your well being in two very important dimensions of your life. It will give you a quick evaluation of areas in which your work and play wellness is robust and those that

need to be strengthened. The first part of this checkup is a list of things you can do to enhance your work wellness. The second half is the same for your play wellness. In this session you will be asked to refer back to the findings of this checkup as you develop your self-care plan for work and play.

Instructions: Mark each statement in one of three ways:

E = "I'm doing *excellently* in this."

OK = "I'm doing *acceptably*, but there's room for improvement."

NS = "This is an area where I definitely *need strengthening*."

Work Wellness

____ I have a sense that my work is a calling, that I'm fulfilling God's purpose for my life by what I'm doing and that it has both constructive consequences for people and some value to society.

____ Whenever possible, I plan my evolving work life intentionally as a part of my life planning and goal setting.

____ My work life increases my general well being and zest for living because it uses many of my talents and I feel competent, set realistic objectives, and achieve many of these in it.

117

____ The stresses and frustration in my work don't diminish my mental or physical health seriously.

____ I'm paid adequately for my work so that I have reasonable economic security.

____ I often use the principle of prioritizing and focusing on one thing at a time during a busy work schedule. I usually avoid cramming my workday with appointments and deadlines or frustrating myself by trying to do several things at once.

____ I don't paralyze my effectiveness by chronic procrastination.

____ I give myself several brief "breathers" or minivacations of a few minutes during my work day. Occasionally I enjoy a brief, release-valve fantasy when work pressures become heavy—for example, of being on a flowering tropical island with a delightful companion with no telephones, fax machines, copying machines, or E-mail

____ I'm not compulsive about my work and keep a healthful balance between work and play. My work time and my free time often complement and balance each other.

____ I like many of the people with whom I work and have relatively constructive relationships with most of the others. I give and receive appropriate warmth and appreciation to and from work associates.

____ I have a constructive relationship with my boss or supervisor, and I feel appreciated by her or him. When I supervise others, I do so with fairness and empathy.

____ I eat a healthy breakfast before work and a nutritious lunch without high-pressure lunchtime business. I don't drink alcohol or use recreational drugs during the workday to prop up my self-confidence or anesthetize my anxieties.

____ When conflicts or frustrations arise at work, I do everything I can to resolve the underlying causes quickly. When something unfair happens, I raise objections and work with others for changes that increase fair play.

____ I savor small or large work successes, learn from my mistakes, and don't waste valuable energy brooding over them.

____ I usually don't take my work home with me literally or in my thoughts, preoccupations, and feelings, and I don't lose sleep over job problems.

____ Fear of failure doesn't keep me from taking creative risks in my work.

____ I function well in the system within which I work without feeling I am selling my soul to it.

____ I don't participate in or tolerate sexual, religious, or ethnic harassment in the workplace, and I protect myself from this and other misuses of power by others.

____ I laugh frequently with others at work, and I often chuckle at myself and with them over some of the work world's absurdities.

____ If my work situation became chronically frustrating or in conflict with my values, I'd be open to changing jobs. If I lose my job, I know how to cope and search effectively until I find a new one.

____ If I weren't paid to do my work, non-monetary satisfactions would motivate me to continue some of what I do now for pay.

____ When I look back over my job history, I'm generally glad that I chose the line of work I did. If I could live my life over several times, I would choose the same work in at least one of them.

Play Wellness

____ Playfulness, laughter, and celebration are essential ingredients in my understanding of a healthy Christian lifestyle.

____ I enliven my spiritual life by a playful as well as a serious relationship with God, who laughs as well as cries with us humans. I also tend to respond to especially pious people with playfulness.

____ I enjoy laughing at myself and the crazy things I do on occasion. When I get bogged down in taking myself too seriously, a chuckle at my self-inflation helps rescue me.

____ I enjoy the playful kid within me who enables me to enjoy laughing and playing with other people in ways that enrich those relationships.

____ I practice the healing power of play regularly by giving myself several laugh breaks and minivacations during work each day.

____ In serious situations, I often see or think of something at least mildly funny. When things get boring or tense, lightening the tension with humor often helps.

____ My smile comes from my center. It is seldom "put on" for appearances or to manipulate others.

____ I frequently enjoy funny movies, comic plays, TV humorists, and humorous books.

____ I usually take at least one real "day off" each week, protecting it from spillover from work and saving it for relaxation, self-care, and just plain fun.

____ I regularly enjoy a variety of playful activities that are stress-reducing, energizing, and rejuvenating for me.

____ I take a substantial vacation each year, planning it carefully to make it genuinely fun and renewing. I'm able to loaf, play, and take fun vacations without feeling guilty and punishing myself before or afterwards.

____ I occasionally use light TV programs, films, and reading or joking or playing games with friends as temporary escape hatches when things get too heavy.

____ I can laugh at the absurd expectations I put on myself or allow others to put on me, thus lightening my load of self-expectations.

____ I don't tell sexist, racist, and ethnic jokes; and I let those who tell them know that I find them offensive and not funny.

____ Laughing inwardly, if not aloud, at stuffy bureaucrats and mini-dictators, protects me from their power trips by letting me keep my inner strength when I'm in their presence.

____ There is an intermingling of work and play in my life, meaning I'm sometimes playful when I'm working and productive at times when I'm playing. This makes both my work and my play more creative and less stressful.

____ My laughter and tears often complement and enrich each other. Each deepens the other.

____ I find a checkup on laughing and playing something of a joke.

Using Your Findings to Enhance Your Work-Play Wellness

Take the following steps to help you use the results of this checkup in developing your self-care plan for work and play:

1. Tally your responses and write down the totals below. This will provide you with an overview of your well being in work and play. / Give yourself a pat on the back for those you honestly scored "E."

E: _____

OK: _____

NS: _____

2. Go through the list and put a star beside those OK and NS items that seem either urgent or especially important to you. /

3. What is your overall "feel" concerning the general wellness of your work and play? In the space below, jot down your evaluation of the strengths and weaknesses of your work and play wellness.

_____

_____

_____

_____

_____

4. Beside the starred items, make notes about how you could strengthen your well being by implementing some of them, thus enhancing your work and play. / In this session, you will be asked to come back to these items and elaborate on your ideas as you develop an achievable self-care plan for your work and play.

_____

_____

_____

_____

Biblical Perspectives

 Work allows us an opportunity to express our stewardship, responsibility, and gratitude for the countless good gifts of God, including the greatest gift—life itself. The Hebrew wisdom lore includes guidance about the spiritual significance of work and the ethics of living a good life. Here is an invitation to Christians as well as Jews: "Commit your work to the LORD, and your plans will be established. The LORD has made everything for its purpose, . . . Better is a little with righteousness than large income with injustice. . . . Honest balances and scales are the Lord's" (Prov. 16:3-4, 8, 11). This scripture expresses the ancient understanding of work as a vocation, a task that serves God's purpose for the world, and to which one feels called because of possessing certain gifts. Having such an understanding is a major key to well being in our work.

Let's shift gears now and consider a biblical story that points to the place of laughter, joy, and playfulness in a wellness lifestyle. The gala wedding feast at Cana, attended by Jesus with his mother and disciples, must have been an occasion of joy. Consider the spiritual significance for living a Christian lifestyle of one simple fact: Jesus chose to use his miraculous powers for the first time to replenish the refreshments at such a party. According to the story, he supplied good wine—asking that six water jars be filled, each holding twenty to thirty gallons—so that the joyful celebration of a loving, committed relationship would have adequate refreshments to continue (John 2:1-11).

Would you agree that it's no wonder that some of Jesus' very "religious" critics could not understand such a joyous, people-loving, life-celebrating young man? Today in a comparable way, some very "religious" Christians have trouble with the view that laughter and playfulness are two of God's very good gifts to humankind. They are enlivening, health-nurturing gifts to be used like God's other gifts—responsibly and constructively with gratitude. If used in this way, they can balance, lighten, and energize the parallel gifts of hard work, commitment, responsibility, and discipline.

God intends for all humans, including Christians, to use and enjoy the gifts of play and work in constructive and health-enhancing ways. In this session, we will explore the problems we encounter in or bring to our work and play and strategies for using both work and play to bring strength and vitality to our Christian lifestyles.

 **Learning Exercise: Take a few minutes to reflect on how this view of the important role of work and play in a Christian's living relates to your own experience. What are the issues with which you struggle in trying to balance work with play, particularly if your life is pressured by nonstop responsibilities and challenges? / Now make notes of your insights or discuss them with others. /

_____

_____

_____

_____

_____

Major Objectives and Themes

 To clarify your personal learning goals for this session, put a check mark in front of those objectives and themes listed below that are important to you as you seek to live as a

Christian in today's world. In this session, you will have opportunities to learn the following:

❑ Resources for increasing self-care for wellness in your work and play.

❑ Insights from the Bible to illuminate these two key areas of living.

❑ How to use your checkup to evaluate the strengths and weaknesses of your work and play self-care.

❑ Strategies both for avoiding burnout in your work and for implementing your Christian mission in your vocation and avocation.

❑ Playful self-care strategies to enliven and energize your lifestyle.

❑ Suggestions for encouraging family members to increase their wellness by balancing their work and play.

❑ Suggestions for encouraging leaders and teachers of your congregation to integrate more healthy work and play in their programs and teaching.

The objectives you have identified constitute your learning goals for this session. Keep them in mind and develop ways to move toward them. If you are working with a wellness partner or group, share your goals so you'll be able to encourage each other to find ways to accomplish them. /

Biblical Roots

Take a few minutes to jot down in the space below a few Bible passages that shed light on how work and play can best be incorporated in your life as a Christian. These will help provide a strong biblical foundation for this session's themes.

_____

_____

_____

_____

_____

_____

_____

_____

_____

_____

_____

Other Biblical Resources for Work Well Being

Work was often a heavy burden in biblical times, as it still is for many people around the world today. In the second creation story, part of God's punishment of the disobedient Adam and Eve in their expulsion from the garden of Eden was the necessity to work all their lives in order to eat: "By the sweat of your face you shall eat bread until you return to the ground" (Gen. 3:19).

Given the drudgery of work in ancient times, Jesus' words have a poignant ring: "Come to me, all you that are weary and are carrying heavy burdens, and I will give you rest" (Matt. 11:28). The vision of heaven in the last book of the Bible predicted that those who die in the Lord will "rest from their labors" (Rev. 14:13).

 Learning Exercise: To get in touch with another dimension of the Bible's view of work, pause and picture Jesus in your imagination, seeing him engaged in the work roles of most of his adult life—as a carpenter, builder, and businessman. Carpentry was a skilled trade Jesus undoubtedly learned from his father. Watch him work in the shop as he carefully constructs a table and a chair, a bed or a baby's cradle, or other objects that will help transform his customers' houses into attractive, functional, welcoming homes. /

These were Jesus' so-called "hidden years" between his experience in the temple in Jerusalem when he was twelve and the beginning of his active ministry. Do you picture him as a skilled, creative craftsman whose competence, integrity, spirituality, and caring about people made him warmly respected by those whom he served in his trade? In your imagination, see him relating to his friends and neighbors who come to his shop to ask him to design and make something they need, or to pick up a beautiful and highly functional object. /

In my mind, it seems safe to assume that Jesus regarded his work as the practice of his first vocation. I have no doubt that his work reflected the ethical and spiritual understanding of work from the Jewish religious heritage that shaped his personality and character. / Integrate what you have learned from this experience by sharing with another person or by making notes in your journal. /

The writer of the book of James, who according to one ancient tradition was the brother of Jesus, lifts up work in his letter to first-century Jewish Christians. He reminds them that to be faithful followers of Christ, their beliefs must be translated into the down-to-earth work of service, reaching out with caring to those in need.

James declared, "What good is it, my brothers and sisters, if you say you have faith but do not have works? Can faith save you? If a brother or sister is naked and lacks daily food, and one of you says to them, 'Go in peace, keep warm and eat your fill,' and yet you do not supply their bodily needs, what is the good of that? *So faith by itself, if it has no works, is dead. . . .* Show me your faith apart from your works, and I by my works will show you my faith" (Jas. 2:14-18, emphasis added).

Biblical Resources on Play's Importance for Well Being

The Bible has little *explicit* guidance about how to include health-giving playfulness in our lives. But certain themes recur in the biblical record that affirm the positive value and spiritual significance of joy and play in the lives of people. The Hebrew Scriptures contain numerous such guiding images. For example, the wisdom sayings in Proverbs include this oft-quoted gem: "A cheerful heart is a good medicine, but a downcast spirit dries up the bones" (Prov. 17:22). A hearty laugh a day probably does more than an apple to keep the doctor away, although some of each would be even more effective in preventing the need for medical attention.

Substantial evidence exists in the Bible that Jesus was a man of laughter and joy, as well as a man of sorrow who had compassion on those who suffered, as he is often pictured. As was described above, his first miracle at the wedding at Cana certainly suggests this. Years ago, Elton Trueblood wrote a little book called *The Humor of Christ*[2] that gives a picture of laughing, playful spirituality. Trueblood cited thirty passages from the Synoptic Gospels (Matthew, Mark, and Luke) as evidence that Jesus was a person of wit and humor who laughed and expected others to laugh. His examples show Jesus using the wit and wisdom of Jewish humor and irony in his teaching and ministry. Jesus was accused by his critics of being "a glutton and a drunkard," as contrasted with the ascetic John the Baptist, because Jesus came "eating and drinking" (Luke 7:34). He obviously enjoyed lively fellowship and conversation with all kinds of people.

Think about the overtones of joy as well as sorrow in this vivid image used by Jesus to describe the response of many who heard the "good news" about God's love he was announcing: "To what will I compare this generation? It is like children sitting in the marketplace and calling to one another, 'We played the flute for you and you did not dance; we wailed, and you did not mourn'" (Matt. 11:16-17).

The Gospel of John describes at length the spiritual wisdom that Jesus shared with his closest friends at his last meal with them. Jesus gave them this new commandment: "Just as I have loved you, you also should love one another. By this everyone will know that you are my disciples, if you have love for one another" (John 13:34-35). He then clarified the nature of this love: "As the Father has loved me, so have I loved you; abide in my love. If you keep my commandments, you will abide in my love, just as I have kept my Father's commandments and abide in his love" (John 15:9-10).

After highlighting the primacy of love, Jesus explained his reason for sharing this wisdom: "I have said these things to you *so that my joy may be in you, and that your joy may be complete*" (John 15:11, emphasis added).

Jesus' joyful intentions were fulfilled repeatedly in the early church. The disciples did experience spiritually rooted joy in their passionate mission to communicate the good news, in spite of all the opposition and dangers they encountered. For example, immediately after Paul and Barnabas experienced persecution and rejection in Antioch, they traveled on to Iconium where the same thing happened. Yet, "the disciples were filled with joy and with the Holy Spirit" (Acts 13:52). Note that the Greek word for "joy" is used sixty-six times in the Christian testament, and the equivalent Hebrew word appears 103 times in the Hebrew Scriptures.

Other biblical illustrations show the prominence of joy in a healthy religious life. The Bible emphasizes celebration, singing, and joy as fitting responses to the goodness of life as a gift of God. "Make a joyful noise to the LORD, all the lands! Serve the LORD with gladness! Come into his presence with singing!" (Ps. 100:1-2, RSV). A harvest of joy occurred when God restored the fortunes of God's people: "Then our mouth was filled with laughter, and our tongue with shouts of joy. . . . The LORD has done great things for us, and we rejoiced" (Ps. 126:2-3).

Two different expressions of laughter appear in the Genesis story of Sarah and Abraham. When Sarah overheard the messengers of the Lord telling her husband that she would give birth to a son, she laughed and said to herself, "After I have grown old, and my husband is old, shall I have pleasure?" When the Lord confronted Abraham about her laughing at the message, Sarah, in fear, denied what she had done. The Lord responded, "Oh yes, you did laugh" (Gen. 18:9-15). (Apparently God didn't have a sense of humor, in their view.) When Isaac was born, Sarah rejoiced, as parents often do today. She exclaimed, "God has brought laughter for me; everyone who hears will laugh with me" (Gen. 21:6).

The psalmist's spiritual wisdom about the usefulness of laughter in dealing with small or large dictators is demonstrated by an unusual and fascinating image of God: "He who sits in the heavens laughs" (Ps. 2:4). The divine Spirit laughs derisively at the arrogant rulers of the earth. To some, this may seem to be an undignified way of picturing God. But directing laughter at puffed-up bosses, as well as at authoritarian political and religious power brokers, is mentally healthy therapy for us humans.

The cutting jokes made by Jews, African Americans, and other oppressed groups have demonstrated amply the protective and healing impact of such humor. This kind of levity helps to lighten the load and lift the spirits of oppressed people. In a society where the majority group still puts them down on occasion, self-deprecating humor actually increases their sense of inner power and worth as persons. By sticking pins in the inflated ego-balloons of pompous people in authority, their humor helps them feel less of what Martin Luther King Jr. called "nobody-ness." Oppressed people usually know that it is prudent to laugh *with* other oppressed people at the pretensions of those in power, but to do this behind the backs of the authority figures.

In most cases, the oppressed also know that laughter is no substitute for justice-making but that it can provide strength to carry on during the struggle to achieve justice and that it also can bring energy and perspective for engaging more effectively in the struggle.

In light of these biblical images and insights, it seems clear that enhancing con-structive work, play, and laughter are very important for Christians' wellness. Let's look now at the meaning of healthy work and play and at how we can translate this awareness into our day-by-day living.

The Meaning of Work Well Being

In finding our way through the present workplace wilderness, a radically new under-standing of the spiritual significance of work is needed. Such a new paradigm may help us find paths through the thicket to healthier lives in a healthier world of work. Theologian Matthew Fox describes well the escalating work crisis:

The work-machine [created by the industrial revolution] is running out of steam, even in the so-called First World. The basics of human living, including work, health care, politics, education, and religion, are increasingly beyond our grasp. And so a new era is upon us. We are being challenged today—in light of a wounded Earth, the one billion unem-ployed adults, the billions of despairing young people who see no guarantees of either work or jobs, and the needs of other species around us—to redefine work. . . . Changing our ways includes changing the way we define work, the way we compensate work, the ways we create work, and the way we let go of work and learn to infuse it with play and ritual.

Here is Fox's succinct description of spiritually centered work: "Work is the expression of our soul, our inner being. It is unique to the individual; it is creative. Work is an expression of the Spirit at work in the world through us. Work is that which puts us in touch with others, . . . at the level of service in the community."[3] This paradigm has some deep roots in our religious heritage, but it also has new and innovative dimensions because of the unprecedented aspects of the global work situation.

Creative work is a key dimension of whole-person health for Christians for a variety of reasons. Work that you love and find challenging gives feelings of meaning, esteem, competence, and accomplishment plus the spiritual reward of knowing that you are contributing something of value to others in a very needy society. Furthermore, for most people, work involves the largest single investment of our limited and precious resource—time.

Consider the impact on your overall well being of finding satisfaction, joy, and increased self-esteem in your work, on the one hand, versus anger, frustration, and diminished esteem, on the other. Then imagine that this positive or negative impact continues for forty-plus hours a week, for fifty weeks (totaling over two thousand hours) a year, for forty or more years.

Unfortunately, countless millions of people around the world miss the health-giving benefits of creative work. They are victims of the global pandemic of work problems that have skyrocketed since the thawing of the Cold War. Reducing the economic props the Cold War produced, although constructive in terms of our society's overall health, has triggered necessary and widespread downsizing. Greater multinational economic competition and computerizing of production increase the work woes of countless people.

Millions are suffering diminished wellness from unemployment or from work that is menial, boring, unappreciated, and underpaid. These people experience nothing approaching joy in their jobs. For many the only sources of work-related satisfactions are the money and merciful escapes from work on weekends, on vacations, and in retirement. Many others struggle with chronic or creeping burnout or burnup that robs them of zest, purpose, and satisfaction in their jobs. At the same time, economic injustice proliferates, causing the underclass to live in health-robbing poverty. While rich families and rich countries get richer, the poor get poorer.

In such a chaotic work world, many people find their jobs (or lack of them) the greatest single source of chronic stress, frustration, anger, and anxiety. Work-related pain is matched, in many cases, by problems in home life and other intimate relationships. Such domestic problems are often triggered or intensified by burnup from job stress, burnout from job conflicts and frustration, painful tension between job demands and family needs, and the necessity in two-parent households for both parents to be employed in order for a family to survive financially.

 Learning Exercise: If you are with a wellness partner or group, talk together about how you really feel about your work. Is it a source of self-esteem and satisfaction that nurtures your well being, or the opposite? Do you find anything like the work-generated spiritual meaning and joy described above? / If you were not paid for your work (or if you are not paid because you are retired), are parts of your job satisfying enough that you would do them "for free" as a volunteer? /

If well being in your workplace is crucial to living life in all its fullness, what is a Christian response to individual and societal work crises? / If you are studying solo, discover what insights come to you as you reflect on these questions, then note things to remember in the margins of this workbook or in your journal. /

What are the characteristics of work well being? Work well being flourishes to the degree that people derive the following rewards from their work life:[4]

• adequate and secure income so they can meet their basic needs as well as some of their wants;

• secure health care and other perks, including a retirement plan, adequate vacations, sick leave, child care benefits, etc.;

• adequate time off—free from work worries—for regular relaxation, fun, renewal, self-care, and enjoyment of family and avocational interests;

• satisfactions from knowing they are appreciated for their work and that it creates something others value;

• the challenge and stimulation of using their intelligence and creativity;

• a sense that their work somehow expresses their vocation or purpose in life. For Christians, this means they have an awareness that they are using their God-given talents in some significant ways that meet the needs of persons, of society, and of God's creation. They have a sense that in these ways they are making their family, community, or world a better place for their own children and the children of the human family, as well as the earth's other species.

An encouraging indication in recent years of the importance of a sense of vocation is that many men and women in successful careers have taken a daring, expensive leap of faith. They have decided, often during their midyears, to leave lucrative careers and invest the considerable time and money necessary to prepare for work such as the ministry, which they believe is their true vocation.[5]

Burnout and the Christian Lifestyle

Burnout is the common cold of vocational health. It's important that we understand the nature, causes, and cures of burnout so that we will respond more appropriately when this widespread and growing but often unrecognized problem occurs in ourselves or those around us. The space-age term *burnout* refers to rockets that have consumed all their fuel but race on at great velocity pushed only by sheer momentum. Do you ever feel this way? Can you identify, as I can, with an apt image that George Donigian, editor at Upper Room Books, shared with me: "Today's schedule is a hungry bear!" If this feeling becomes chronic, it is burnout. If you adopt this pattern of behavior while you are pushing to complete an important project (as I'm doing on this workbook now), it does not lead to burnout unless it becomes chronic.

Even if you are not a go-it-alone workaholic, you are vulnerable to burnout if you tend to be idealistic, perfectionistic, hard-driving, and people-pleasing and if you suffer, at times, from shaky self-esteem. Christians who are overcommitted to meeting the needs of dependent people, even to the point of chronic neglect of their families and their own self-care, are especially vulnerable. Burnout is very prevalent among teachers, health professionals, and clergy as well as those in high-pressure business and government jobs, single parents, and mothers of young children. A conservative "guesstimation" suggests that at least one out of five clergypersons suffers from some degree of burnout, often unrecognized by them.

Because burnout is a gradual process, it easily sneaks up on its victims. As in cancer or alcoholism, knowing the early warning signs can help you avoid the advanced stages. If you have any inkling that you may be vulnerable, put a check mark in front of the symptoms that apply to you:

❏ A creeping loss of zest, energy, purpose, passion, and excitement in your life and work.

❏ Chronic fatigue, in spite of getting what previously was enough rest.

❏ An inability to handle the appropriate demands or to say "no" to the inappropriate demands by others in your work and relationships.

❏ Decreasing efficiency, accompanied by feelings of needing to run in order just to stand still.

❏ Increasing feelings of depression, cynicism, inability to cope, defeat, and negativism which eventually lead to deadening apathy.

❏ Frequent or multiple psychosomatic illnesses such as colds and back pains.

❏ Chronic feelings of falling behind which produces frantic, inefficient efforts to catch up.

❏ Spiritual illnesses such as hopelessness and despair and a loss of any sense of vocation in one's work.

 Learning Exercise: As you read the causes of burnout listed below, identify the internal causes that are present in yourself or a family member and the external causes that exist in your work setting. Remember, self-diagnosis is the first step in self-healing. / Note your

findings for use later in developing your self-other care plan. /

_____

_____

_____

_____

_____

Burnout results from the interaction and convergence of a variety of internal and external causes.

• Internal causes may include low self-esteem; lack of a strong sense of identity and purpose; inner conflicts between human needs and impulses and one's idealized self-image (often increased by religion); and inner struggles to meet the time conflicts and demands of work, family, and self-care (with the second and third being sorely neglected).

• External causes of burnout appear in people's work environments. These may include unhealthy, "craziness-making" jobs with inadequate pay; low levels of appreciation, creativity, and morale; high levels of criticism; authoritarian or flabby leadership; poor communication; chronic overload of employees; little mutual support; and racist, ethnic, sexist, classist, ageist, or religious discrimination. Keep in mind this good news—*external causes are much more likely to produce burnout in people made vulnerable by inner causes, and you have more ability to change causes within yourself.*

Work burnout is widespread among Christians as well as in society in general. For many, it is a huge barrier to living life in all its fullness. It affects all seven dimensions of life, particularly the physical, mental, spiritual, and relationship dimensions. As a caring Christian you should equip yourself to respond in three ways: preventing burnout, helping heal mild burnout, and finding professional help for persons suffering advanced, immobilizing burnout.

The overall strategy of burnout prevention is to increase your self-care. If you have begun to implement the self-care plans you developed in previous sessions, congratulate yourself! You already are on the road to preventing future burnout as well as healing early-stage burnout that otherwise might increase or become chronic. Furthermore, the numerous action-options in the checkup for this session are tailored to enhance your work wellness and reduce the internal causes of burnout listed above.

The Spiritual Key to Preventing Burnout

The most crucial thing you can do to prevent burnout and enhance your work wellness is to enliven the sense of meaning and purpose you gain from your Christian faith and relate this to your work life. In my own efforts to avoid burnout through the years, as well as in counseling with those suffering from this malady, one thing has become ever clearer. The energy and passionate vitality derived from the meanings and purposes in our lives nurture work wellness and thus surpass all other factors in preventing burnout. One of my favorite one-liners is a bumper sticker you may have seen, "There are lots of people complaining of burnout who never seemed to have been on fire!"

This is the spiritual key to burnout prevention and work well being. From a Christian perspective, people who have the fire in their hearts of passionate commitment to life in all its fullness—for themselves, others, and their world—often have unusual resources that defend them against burnout. You may wonder why so many "good Christians" who have a sense of God's purposes suffer burnout. It is usually because they have not learned that renewing self-care is an essential prerequisite for offering ongoing loving care to others.[6]

A holistic Christian view is that *all* constructive work is of value in God's sight; therefore, all persons who are so engaged are fulfilling their unique vocation or calling. As Christians, God invites us to use our personalities, intelligence, creativity, imagination, love, and skills to actualize God's intention that all people (including ourselves) have opportunities to develop their gifts as fully as possible. Individuals who accept this invitation and use their gifts in this way are aligning their lives with the purposes of the spiritual universe. They thus become imperfect but real channels through which a little of the creativity of that universe becomes available in everyday life to ordinary people.

Such individuals demonstrate the health-wisdom of Christian commitment to the abundant life by the way they live. They work very hard for the things in which they believe—for their "causes"—and naturally suffer the frustrations and disappointments of such actions. They often become tired, of course, but they are not exhausted at their center, which would be a sign of burnout and depression. They frequently are highly productive in their work without becoming work addicts.

If you are searching for clues to identify your sense of vocation, a key question has helped many of us zero in on our calling. Simply ask, *At what points in my life do my unique gifts, needs, and interests intersect with the needs of the world?* By searching, listening, and praying with open hearts, answers gradually come that can help locate those points of intersection, letting people discover their vocational options. Then, if a choice is difficult, it is wise to have a few sessions with a trained vocational counselor.

Preventing Burnout by Enhancing Work Wellness

Here are some guidelines for burnout prevention and work wellness, viewed from a Christian perspective. As you peruse these, identify those that you may need to use in your work situation and incorporate into your lifestyle. Then make notes for developing your work self-care plan.[7]

1. *Schedule regular time for renewing self-care,* and then commit yourself to honoring your schedule when trivial or important things threaten to sidetrack self-care. Bear in mind that self-care is an application of self-love, both of which enable you to care for others. Periodically each day give yourself brief breaks to replenish your inner springs of vitality. Use methods such as meditation, humor and playfulness, music, intentional breathing and relaxation, prayer, art, inspirational reading, or opening yourself to being nurtured by nature's rhythms and beauty.

It is possible, as some Christians have discovered, to find emotional and spiritual renewal by unobtrusively using focused prayer and meditation during brief breaks from working. Be sure to do whatever is necessary to take at least one real "day off" each week and a renewing vacation at least once each year. People who consistently ignore their need for days off and vacations are cases of burnout waiting to happen.

2. *Schedule regular time to enjoy the circle of mutual caring among your family and close friends,* and then commit yourself to protecting this time from intrusion by other demands, trivial or important. This is an expression of your Christian commitment to nurturing love in these life-giving and health-sustaining relationships. (See Session 5 for "how to" methods.)

3. *Get into the driver's seat of your time*

and thus your life, so that you will run your schedule instead of allowing your schedule to run you—into the ground, perhaps. A Christian lifestyle takes self-responsibility and self-directed intentionality seriously. The best tools for taking charge of your schedule and your day-by-day life are Life-Work Planning (LWP), developed by pioneer work-guru Richard Bowles, and the methods developed by Alan Lakein and described in his classic book *How to Get Control of Your Time and Your Life.*[8] Here is Lakein's convincing philosophy in a nutshell: "Time is life. . . . To waste your time is to waste your life, but to master your time is to master your life and make the most of it."[9]

 **Learning Exercise: Give yourself the gift of a brief introduction to two valuable self-help methods. Turn to pages 141–42 in *Well Being* and take a few minutes to try the "Life-Work Planning Tool." / Then try the "Goal-Setting Exercise" on pages 143–44, which is my adaptation of Alan Lakein's basic time-management approach. / Each of these tools is useful in sorting out both short- and long-term objectives and then prioritizing them according to their relative importance in a schedule that expresses a Christian's lifestyle.

4. *Take better care of your body with healthful nutrition, vigorous exercise, adequate rest, and satisfaction of your skin hunger.* You become especially vulnerable to burnout when you are physically depleted and run down. Body self-care makes it possible to glorify God in your work as well as in your body.

5. *Balance work with humor and playfulness, whenever this is possible and appropriate.* Laughing with others and at yourself, as well as at the absurdities and craziness that are present in most workplaces, is good for your health and also your work

relationships. Such laughter may also help reduce the craziness that otherwise resists change. Adding a humorous touch whenever you can will lighten your workload and bring a gift to other workers.

Playfulness may be quiet as well as vigorous. Among the prized memories from my early boyhood is of my mother, standing at the kitchen sink, softly humming loved hymn tunes. She did this while doing what must have been dull, monotonous chores in those low-tech times before modern labor-saving devices. In retrospect, my heart is warmed by the awareness that Mom was drawing on the riches of her spiritual life in those moments of spirit-centered renewal and playfulness.

6. *Don't store up anger or resentment, guilt or grief on or about your job.* Burnout thrives on accumulated pressure from these negative feelings. Be on the alert to avoid the distortions of Christian attitudes that result in the repression of such feelings. Repression often eventually leads to an explosion.

7. *Practice the healthy principle of alternation,* moving back and forth periodically between different types of activities during your workday. Albert Schweitzer, the pioneer medical missionary in French Equatorial Africa (now Gabon), is reported to have alternated activities several times during his long workdays. He interspersed his primary work of treating patients with brief interludes of doing carpentry on a needed building and with playing Bach compositions on his piano. If your work utilizes mainly left-brain analytical, verbal, and mathematical skills, your well being will be nurtured by taking a right-brain renewal break occasionally, doing activities such as those listed above in Guideline 1.

8. *Develop ways to treat yourself and others in your work setting with more grace as precious persons, loved daughters or sons of God.* This may seem a little strange to you if you work in a secular setting, but it can be done in subtle attitudinal ways as a quiet, nonaggressive application of your Christian faith. Such behavior may bring unexpected healing in relationships with yourself and others. An important part of grace-full workplace behavior may be self-forgiveness for your own work foibles and mistakes.

9. *Give occasional gifts of deserved appreciation to others at work, and welcome appreciation from friends and colleagues.* Many problems and conflicts in the work-place result from depleted self-esteem. Mutual self-other esteem enhancement in work settings may help increase working effective-ness and reduce unproductive conflicts among colleagues. Although it is wise to satisfy most of your self-esteem and all of your affectional needs outside job relationships, sincere appre-ciation from a boss or colleague may enhance the wellness of working relationships.

Reaching out to build friendships with work associates with whom you feel rapport is time well invested and can contribute to work wellness for them and for you. One of my losses in retirement, with all of its gains, is that I no longer have frequent opportunities to have lunch and mutually supportive conversations with a dear colleague. He became a trusted and esteemed friend as well as a much-needed sanity-saving confidant during my years of seminary teaching.

10. *If you suspect that your present life-investment plan—your priorities, values, and goals that guide your use of time—may be contributing to burnout-causing conflicts in you, take action.* Your Christian ethical life and spirituality both may benefit from your evaluating and improving your life-investment plan. The values-revision tools in Session 2, the Time-Values Inventory, and the Life-Work Planning Tool recommended above can be useful in this process.

11. *Practice the fine art of saying "No" when you are overloaded or when others*

make excessive demands that will preclude adequate time for yourself and your family. To do this, you must curb any tendencies to be a people-pleaser, remembering that the inability to say no is a major cause of stress overload. Saying no can be a way to say yes to your own needs by giving you adequate time for self-care and mutual care with family and friends. This, in the long run, will be good for the well being of your work.

12. *Keep creating and growing and stay excited about things that are important to you, to others about whom you care, and to your community and world.* If being a Christian is having a love affair with life and the Author of life, there is no shortage of things that Christians should find challenging and exciting. People who continue to learn and grow and use their creativity in fresh ways usually do not burn out.

13. *Use intentional life- and work-planning regularly, particularly at difficult transitions and decision points in your life.* Career planning is effective only if you do it in the context of intentionally planning your lifestyle. Periodic life-career replanning can help you avoid going off in all directions instead of moving in a more focused way toward those objectives that you most prize as a Christian. (Use the resources by Richard Bowles mentioned in Guideline 3.)

14. *Devise ways of expressing the larger purposes of your life—your Christian vocation—in your avocation as well as in your work.* If you are unable to fulfill your Christian calling in your job, and changing jobs is unfeasible, find a way of fulfilling your Christian calling in your free time. Many people in spiritually unsatisfying work find rich nonmonetary and spiritual compensations in the volunteer work they do through their churches and/or community organizations.

15. *Deal with the pressures, conflicts, and frustrations inevitable in any workplace peopled by human beings by confronting these problems and dealing with them quickly and directly.* Use win-win solutions whenever possible to eliminate sources of conflict, and also do those things that will prevent conflicts by strengthening work relationships. Some studies show that the leading cause of burnout in businesses is chronic conflict and unresolved hostility.

16. *If do-it-yourself methods like these don't suffice, make a worthwhile investment in your life and work well being by having some sessions with a competent, caring pastoral counselor or psychotherapist.* To admit you need such professional help and then to seek it are signs of personal strength, not weakness.

Increasing the Wellness of Your Play

I link play wellness with work wellness for two reasons. Work and play complement and balance each other, and both have to do with how we use our time, for better or for worse. Laughter, playfulness, and recreation can nurture your well being not only in the area of your work but in all the other dimensions of your life—during times of health and of sickness.[10]

From a Christian perspective, the most important health benefit of increasing your playfulness and laughter is that they can enliven your spirit. Trying to walk on the path of a Christian lifestyle is a challenge, to say the least—a challenge in which most of us stumble or fall at times. Taking a playful attitude toward your faith helps liberate your spirituality from shallow legalisms and moralisms, thus releasing your ethical energy to use for justice and other important values that guide a Christian lifestyle.

Playfulness is a channel through which joy can flow into your life. As the Christian good news increasingly becomes someone's personal good news, that person tends to experience more *joie de vivre*, a fine French term that means "joy of life." It brings a warm, vibrant aliveness that can express itself in many ways. These include quiet, gentle joy; joy through intimacy with people and nature; hilarious celebration and rambunctious clowning; and, most precious of all, what some spiritual pioneers across the centuries have described as "holy joy."

This is the joy that flows from intimacy or, some would say, oneness with the divine Spirit. It flows from loving God and celebrating a love affair with God and the life God gives us. Such healthy love and spirituality are the very heart of human well being. When the streams of this kind of love and spirituality flow together in our inner lives, we can drink deeply from the cup of joy.

The spiritual pioneer and scientist Pierre Teilhard de Chardin observed that joy is the most infallible sign of the presence of God. Deepening our sense of the basic wonder and goodness of life, in spite of its troubles and tragedies, can help us open ourselves to experiencing God's smile. It can rescue our Christian faith from heavy religiosity as well as fruitless moralizing, refreshing it with the blessing of what I like to describe as the music of God's cosmic chuckle.

Living a healthier lifestyle has many obvious physical rewards, such as increasing the likelihood of living longer with a higher quality of life. The ultimate reward, which has special significance for Christians, is living with more spiritual aliveness and joy at the center of your life, however long or short, happy or painful, it turns out to be. Joy, as used here, is not the same as happiness or pleasure, although both of these may be present at times of experiencing joy. This joy does not depend on external circumstances. It comes from a deeper source—your life-loving spirituality and the celebration of life's everyday miracles that are so easy to ignore or take for granted.

Playfulness can be a delightful expression of this spiritual joy. And here is some more good news—there is a circular or reciprocal relationship between your level of well being and your joy and playfulness. Each tends to increase the other. To be joyful and playful is good for your body-mind-spirit health, and healthy people tend to experience and express joy-full playfulness more often.

Laughing can activate our immune systems to increase our body's healing capacities and give our overall health a boost. A striking illustration of this fact is the increasing therapeutic use of laughter in hospitals, including its use with people suffering life-threatening illnesses. In this time of soaring costs and anxieties about health care, laughter is certainly among the most cost-effective forms of healing.

 **Learning Exercise: Stop reading and give yourself the quick, free gift of a health-enhancing break. Just recall and enjoy again something hilariously stupid that you did or that happened to you recently. / If you are with a partner or group, share your "funny" with them and invite them to tell you one of theirs. /

I often think of the late great holistic health-peacemaker Norman Cousins and his description of laughter as "inner jogging." Laughing, however vigorous, should not be considered a substitute for aerobic exercise, but it certainly can enhance your body's wellness. For example, laughter is a medically proven stress and depression reducer, and it stimulates the flow of life-giving oxygen in our cardiovascular system.

In addition to their physical benefits, laughter and playfulness have numerous psychological benefits. They help to reframe problems, reduce depression, and awaken hope. If you can shift from a gloomy perspective and adopt an energetic and humorous attitude toward the unchangeable frustrations in your daily life, you may reduce their ability to provoke stress and to trigger depression and burnout.

 Learning Exercise: The next time you are stuck in a boring or frustrating church meeting, where voting with your feet by leaving is not feasible (I assume that these may occur occasionally), use the "inward smile" technique of self-nurture and self-therapy. Keep looking until you find something ludicrous or absurd in the people or the situation. Then instead of doing a slow burn, which will not help your mental health, let yourself smile or chuckle inwardly as you playfully enjoy the absurdity of that scene.

Incidentally, you can do this in your mind while you stay aware of what is happening on another mental level, if that seems desirable. It is prudent to resist the temptation to laugh out loud, or your church colleagues may decide that you have really gone off your rocker. (Having used this technique for years in boring academic meetings, I can vouch for the fact that it works, at least sometimes.)

Taking Ourselves Lightly

Laughing at ourselves can also be self-liberating. It can help free us from being stuck in our little ego boxes. When you're uptight over concerns about yourself or your life, try shifting gears. Try laughing or at least chuckling at the heavy seriousness with which you and I often take ourselves and our small concerns—concerns that in the larger scheme of things don't deserve such weighty treatment. Laughing at our own super-seriousness is a neat way to deflate it so that we don't float off on an extended ego trip like a hot-air balloon that will eventually deflate.

My students and I once met a Buddhist monk at a Zen center halfway up Mount Baldy, my favorite mountain. Garbed impressively in his monk's flowing brown robe, he shared with us this delightfully wise spiritual saying, attributing it to "an ancient Zen Buddhist seer": "Angels can fly because they take themselves so lightly!"

I have enjoyed several hearty chuckles since that experience, when I have come across the same saying two or three times, attributed to other writers who lived some time during the last two centuries. (As an unrecovered former academic, I can't help wondering who was quoting whom while forgetting to footnote the source.) But all joking aside, the saying is healthy advice for us Christians to follow, no matter who expressed it first. When we are tempted to take ourselves, our problems, our beliefs, churches, politics, and opinions too seriously, letting go of some of our ego baggage via what might have been ancient Buddhist wisdom, may even free us to soar spiritually.

A playful attitude toward your life and work also can stimulate the flow of creative juices. The familiar phrase "playing with an idea" sheds light on the creative process. Playing with an idea is a way of using our ingenuity and our fertile imaginations to come up with something useful or fun or something that gives a little touch of the novelty, excitement, and beauty needed to transform some of the boredom and ugliness in life.

Laughter and playfulness give welcome gifts to the playful inner child who, if she or he is anything like mine, feels ignored or neglected at times. Playfulness gives that little girl or boy within each of us a chance to enjoy life in ways that are natural for children. To let your inner child play, and better still, to play with your inner child, can enliven your adult self and improve your ways of relating to flesh-and-blood children around you. Give it a try!

Learning Exercise: If you are aware of any workaholic leanings in yourself, try this experiment. Take out your all-important date book or pocket schedule and scan what you have planned and expect to accomplish during the next week or two. If you are a budding workaholic, your schedule probably will reflect some excessive, even grandiose, self-expectations. If so, let yourself have a thigh-thumping time of laughing loudly at yourself and your self-punishing expectations. /

I hope you found that this lightened the inner load you were putting on yourself. You might even consider canceling, postponing, or delegating to someone else some of the many things you had planned to push yourself to do. If so, your inner child will give you a hug and a hearty "thank-you!" (If you like theological ways of thinking about matters, just remind yourself that you'll be exercising some needed grace toward yourself in this way.)[11]

Laughing as a Way to Deal with Conflict

Playing and laughing with (not at) those you love most is a delightful way of enlivening those all-important relationships. It can remove the cutting edge from conflictual conversations. It may even awaken slumbering romantic feelings in your marriage or other loving relationships. Sharing in jokes has long been a way both of expressing and strengthening bonding among groups of people.

As was pointed out in the earlier discussion of God's laughter in Psalm 2, when oppressed people laugh derisively at the oppressor, they often experience energy, perspective, and strength to continue their struggle for justice. Laughter can strengthen your self-esteem and give you the perspective and courage you need to handle challenging,

absurd, or unjust situations more constructively. When you're the target, laughter can help you sidestep the temptation to sink into feelings of being a helpless victim.

The English writer George Eliot (1819–80) provides a poignant illustration of the use of such survival humor. She wrote in *Adam Bede*: "I'm not denying, the women are foolish. God Almighty made them to match the men." As a target of sexist oppression from the male-dominated literary fraternity (I use the term advisedly), she must have experienced the value of such knife-edge humor. She had felt it necessary to use the gender-hiding pen name "George Eliot" for a sad reason. She knew that trying to publish using her real name Mary Ann Evans would have caused her fine writing to be ignored generally.

Another value of exercising your laughter muscle is that it can open up a partially blocked emotional valve, releasing pent-up pain, tears, and anger as well as love. This may seem strange, but it is true because the same emotional channel within yourself carries the flow of laughter and tears, love and grief, affection and anger. If that channel is partially closed, for whatever reasons, it will restrict the flow of all those vital feelings. Psychotherapists who specialize in "laugh therapy" have documented this. They point out that one reason some people don't let themselves laugh spontaneously and freely is that they fear the release and expression of their repressed tears, anger, or grief. But if people willingly "go with the flow" of these painful feelings, the healing effects can be dramatic.

A playful attitude toward life's downside certainly is better for our mental health than gloom-and-doom responses. Take, for example, the persistent problems in most intimate human relationships, from everyday arguments to family chaos and chronic conflict. These problems obviously are serious and growing in number. Often they elicit only what Transactional Analysis therapy calls "ain't it awful" responses. Refusing to take such problems solemnly and gloomily does not prevent us from taking them seriously.

At the other extreme, the pop psychology circuit has an oversupply of superficial answers that are variations on "just love each other more." Given the complexity of many marriage and family problems, these good answers are really nonanswers. Actress-comedienne Lily Tomlin gives this tongue-in-cheek response to such superficial advice: "If love is the answer, could someone rephrase the question?" [12]

In my practice of marriage counseling and family therapy, I encourage couples to awaken playfulness in their relationships by doing things they both enjoy. For such encouragement to be effective, timing is crucial. It must be after much of the built-up anger from their mutual hurting is diminished, if not resolved. It is not necessarily true that couples who play together stay together, any more than it's always true for those who pray together. But some couples in crises who begin to recover the ability to be even a little playful at times—as they probably were as lovers—discover that playfulness releases tensions, helps heal their mutually wounded feelings, and supplies the energy of hope, which they can use to find deeper solutions.

The careful use of humor often has even more immediate and dramatic effects in marriage enrichment events designed to "make good relationships better." In leading such events, I have discovered that a nonthreatening way of introducing humor is to share something stupid and funny that I do or have done in my marriage or my relationship with our children. (These are not hard to find.)

Sharing one incident in a way that does not put down my family members, encourages couples to see the absurd humor

in their own mutual-hurting patterns or their problems with their children. When this happens, it's a hopeful sign. They are becoming less defensive and a little more understanding of what each brings to the problems in their relationship.

Joking together in nonattacking ways can be a healthy way for couples to give themselves a minivacation from the chores of being a wife, husband, or parent. When the whole family begins to laugh together, it can be both a sign of increased relational wellness and also a path to greater health.

 Learning Exercise: If your life is overloaded with wall-to-wall "oughts" and "shoulds," leaving little space for fun, self-care, or self-renewal, I recommend that you take the following four steps:

1. Reserve regular blocks of time at least a month ahead in your date book—a minimum of two or three times each week—that are yours to use for fun and self-care in whatever ways you will enjoy. / Also, with members of your family or with friends, set aside regular time for playing together, perhaps taking turns in planning what you will do during these times. /

2. Jot down a tentative list of things you (and they) would enjoy doing during these times that will give all of you renewal, pleasure, and health.

3. Number the activities on your list in order of their priority, and tentatively put them in the times you have saved for this on your schedule.

4. Move ahead with your plans to enjoy priority number one. I trust that this exercise will lighten up your lifestyle and let you laugh and play more often.

Let's look at humor and laughter in a larger context. As the human family enters a new century and millennium, it is a time of astonishing global changes that are baffling and often scary, bringing an uncertain future of unknown dangers and opportunities. In this time, a vital spiritual faith enlivened by a robust sense of humor can be very important to our individual and collective well being. Because we can only imagine the emerging shape of what promises to be a whole new era in human history, lighthearted openness to the future will be needed, along with faith, hope, courage, and love.

Thank God for the spiritual guidance we have as followers of Christ. Jesus embodies all these strengths and can help us continue to laugh as we celebrate the new possibilities that await the whole human family, including ourselves. And thank God that God laughs—because if the divine Spirit lacks a sense of humor, humankind is probably in big trouble, don't you agree? Such a God calls us into this new future with the joyous knowledge that spiritually we are never alone.

Guided Meditation to Enhance Work-Play Well Being

 This guided meditation, one of my favorites, provides an opportunity to explore ways to make your work life healthier and your play life more enjoyable. Like other guided meditations in this workbook, it uses one of your many creative abilities—the ability to form moving pictures in your imagination and to use them for enhancing your health. Simply read the following instructions until you come to this mark /, then stop while you close your eyes and do what has been recommended.

Using methods you have experienced in previous guided meditations, take a little while to relax your whole body-mind-spirit until you are very relaxed but also very alert. This is the optimal condition for experiencing guided wellness meditations so that they

provide the most benefits. You will recall that an alert but relaxed condition may be facilitated by alternately tensing and releasing all your muscles, deepening and quieting your breathing, and focusing your consciousness on a single point such as a candle, a flower, a word or phrase, or on your breathing. /

Using your imagination, picture a large box big enough for a person to be inside. / Now, see yourself getting into the box and having the door closed. / Be inside the closed box for a little while, letting yourself experience how that is. Push on the sides of the box to feel how it limits you. / As you are there inside the box, let it represent those things in your life and work that cause you to feel "boxed in." Become aware of what things constrict your playfulness, freedom, and well being. /

Now decide how you will get out of the box. If it's latched or locked from the outside and you must ask for help, be aware of how this feels. / Now get out of the box and be in a beautiful spring meadow or some other free, open place. / Take a little while to enjoy playing in the fresh air and freedom of the meadow. Just let your playful inner child frolic and have fun doing whatever she or he chooses. Be aware of what you're doing and how you are feeling, compared with your feelings inside the box. / Now have a friend with whom you enjoy having fun join you in playing in the meadow. See how this changes the experience. /

Now if you'd like to explore how your spirituality relates to your play, send your friend away and invite Jesus to come and play with you in the meadow. / Go back to where you left your box and see how you feel as you have another look. If there is something you'd like to do to or with the box, it's yours, so feel free. / Finish the meditation in whatever way you choose to give it a sense of closure. /

Keeping your eyes closed, think about

what you just experienced and learned. Does your work or family life ever feel like a box? If so, do you stay in it psychologically more than is good for your well being? / Did you enjoy the freedom and play in the meadow? / Do you need to relax and play in the meadow more? Can you take some of your meadow experience into your workplace or family? (It's your box and meadow so you can go there whenever you choose.) Did you have trouble playing with Jesus? If so or if not, what's your message to yourself in this? / When you returned to your box after the fun and freedom of the meadow, what did you feel and do? / Open your eyes and make a few notes of things to remember or to do. / Then share your experience and insights with someone else. /

I hope that this guided meditation was valuable. Perhaps it shed light on any parts of your life that feel boxed in, helped you learn what you can do to liberate yourself, and gave you the enlivening experience of letting yourself enjoy playing. If you had trouble asking for help in getting out of the box, this could be a useful awareness concerning your feelings about being dependent, independent, and interdependent. If you had trouble playing with Jesus, you may have a clue about how your spirituality needs to be integrated with your play to enrich both. / If you are bordering on burnout, I suggest that you use this meditation whenever the pressure builds up in you. /

Enhancing Your Church's Programs for Work and Play Well Being

If you believe that your congregation is missing some important opportunities to help people grow through their work and play, consider recommending programs such as these:

• A support group for persons experiencing work crises and difficult workplace transitions. Congregations who have tried such groups usually have found that they meet the needs of a variety of people not only from among their members but also from their surrounding communities. The majority of those who come are struggling to cope with unemployment, which has wounded their self-esteem and shaken their confidence in themselves, as well as causing severe financial problems. The programs may include instruction in writing resumes, role playing to practice for job interviews, coaching in job hunting skills, discussion of changing jobs, and moving back into the world of paid work in the midyears. Finding a sense of Christian vocation in one's work should be a key topic discussed.

• Educational units for youth on career choices and the Christian faith that lift up the central value issues that they should consider in such decisions. Adult church members in a variety of professions and fields could describe to interested young people how they understand their work to be an expression of their Christian vocation.

• More occasions when people laugh heartily and play together with childlike abandon (as I hope you did in your meadow). In our highly competitive society "winning isn't just important, it's everything," but is this an appropriate response to God? A few people feel buoyed up by winning and many others feel hurt by losing (often repeatedly). Churches can provide a countercultural environment by sponsoring games in which everyone wins, at least some of the time. A book by Matt Weinstein and Joel Goodman entitled *Playfair: Everybody's Guide to Noncompetitive Play* is a compendium of games in which the fun of playing rather than winning is the main objective.[13]

• Playful involvement in vigorous sports by church teams and more involvement in nearby Special Olympics events. Team competition has important learning potentials concerning values such as cooperation and sportsmanship. Such learning is increased if coaches encourage participants to discuss ways that Christian values can relate to their sports behaviors. One of the strong points of the Special Olympics is that all those who participate get some kind of recognition and award in the form of ribbons.

Many overworked clergy, church volunteers, and secretaries will probably identify upon retirement with the Apostle Paul's sports image of having "finished the race" (2 Tim. 4:7). Before they retire, they may identify with the gallows humor behind the sign I once saw in a business office: "An employee who doesn't have a hernia isn't carrying his share of the load!" Congregations can practice as well as preach work well being by avoiding overloading church employees and willing volunteers who "can't say no." Such people are usually a small group, and overloading tends to make them feel resentment that contributes to burnout.

Questions for Reflection

1. Does the idea that constructive work and play should be major contributors to Christian well being fit with your understanding of the faith?

2. What are the main conflicts and tensions you experience in your efforts to balance time for your work, time for your family and friends, and time for yourself? Which ones of these important areas in your life get shortchanged? If this is happening, how do you plan to improve the balance?

3. What are the two most important things you need to do so that your work contributes more to your health? your play? How do you plan to overcome the obstacles to these actions?

4. Does your congregation need to offer a greater number of educational and caregiving programs that focus on workplace problems and possibilities, given the present society-wide work crises? If so, how can it begin to offer such programs?

5. Do you need to expand the opportunities in your family for recreation that really re-creates? in your church? in your community? What can you do to help this happen?

6. Does the picture of Jesus' laughing fit your understanding of his life and teaching?

Strengthening Your Self-Care Plan

If you took and tallied the Work and Play Well Being Checkup before this session, you came to the session with some awareness of things you need to do to improve your work and play self-care. You undoubtedly have acquired other ideas during this session. Now you are ready to strengthen and enrich your self-care plan by doing the following:

1. Look over your tally of the checkup and any notes you made, giving special attention to NS and OK items, remembering the ones you checked as being important or urgent for taking action. /

2. Review the ideas and action-options to which you were attracted during this session because they felt useful for enhancing your work or play. /

3. Now, using these ideas from the checkup and the session, beef up your self-care plan by adding a brief section listing the most important work or play action-options. / Spell out specific objectives you want to achieve, feasible plans for moving toward these, a time schedule, and rewards you will give yourself or withhold as you step forward or backward. /

4. Select one high-priority action-option in the area of work and one in play. Choose ones that are achievable, and begin implementing them within the next day or two. Be

sure to pick options that are relatively simple to implement. This will let you begin to enjoy the rewards of improved work and play well being in the short-term as well as long-range. Trying to change long-standing, unhealthy lifestyle patterns is difficult. This is a good place to begin because in self-change, nothing succeeds like success. /

5. Pray each day from your heart for God's guidance and help in implementing your plan so that you can celebrate life and a God who laughs as well as works in all creation.

Closing Song, Prayer, and Evaluation

Close this session by doing the following things:

• Sing a hymn, spiritual, or folk song that celebrates the good gifts of God, including satisfying work and joyful play.

• Highlight and celebrate useful insights and new plans you have made during this session by listing these, and then committing yourself in heartfelt prayer to implementing them.

• Do a brief evaluation of the strengths and weaknesses of the session, aiming at increasing the benefits of the last two sessions.

Continuing Your Self-Care

Whether you're doing these sessions alone or with a well being partner or group, these activities will help you continue wellness care between study sessions. They also will prepare you to use the next session to gain maximum benefit for your well being.

• Read chapter 7 in this workbook and chapters 9 and 12 in the companion text *Well Being*.

• Each day, spend at least a brief time in imaging prayer for the wellness of yourself and others about whom you care, including work colleagues, your well being study partner, and family and friends with whom you play. Visualize yourself and them enveloped in the warm healing light of God's love. Ask for inspiration and guidance as you seek to become a better channel of that healing love to anyone you know who is in a work crisis or a playless vacuum.

• Take and tally the Crises and Losses Well Being Checkup before the next session.

• Each day, implement several of the plans now included in your overall self-care plan, including the work and play items you chose just now. It probably will help to keep a record of how this is going. The rewards will come as you put your plans into action.

• Consider how you will encourage your congregation to increase programs for work and play wellness.

Growing through the Crises and Losses on Your Life Journey

Life is what happens to you while you're busy making other plans.

—John Lennon

Lord, don't move that mountain, but give me strength to climb it.

—Lyrics of a Mahalia Jackson song

The way I see it, if you want the rainbow, you gotta put up with the rain.

—Dolly Parton, actress and singer

Gentle horse for gentle people. Spirited horse for spirited people. For people who don't like to ride, we have a horse who doesn't like to be ridden.

—Sign in a riding academy (a crisis about to happen)

A Crises and Losses Well Being Checkup

 To help you gain the greatest benefits to your well being from this session, take and score this checkup first. It will give you a quick evaluation of ways in which your ability to handle losses and crises constructively is strong and how this ability could be strengthened. You will find that the items in the checkup are attitudes and actions you can implement to enhance your ability to cope whenever dark, difficult days come your way.

Later in this session, you will be asked to use the findings of this checkup as you develop your self-care plan for coping with crises and losses.

Instructions: Mark each statement in one of three ways:

E = "I'm doing ***excellently*** in this."

OK = "I'm doing ***acceptably***, but there's room for improvement."

NS = "This is an area where I definitely ***need strengthening***."

____ For me God is a very present help in trouble. My Christian faith is a valuable resource in times of darkness and distress, as well as in times of sunshine and joy.

____ When trouble strikes, I give myself the gift of more self-care. I continue to eat and rest adequately, even if I don't feel like doing so, and I avoid the tempting trap of trying to deaden the suffering with alcohol, drugs, or frenetic activity.

____ When life seems horribly heavy, it helps me cope to take the future in small pieces, one at a time—an hour and then perhaps one day.

____ I'm able to find healing by expressing and talking through my full range of agonizing feelings for as long as I need to until I eventually can release them.

_____ I'm able to sort out the pieces of a complicated crisis and take action on one part at a time rather than being paralyzed by the whole intertwined mess of problems.

_____ I usually avoid the temptation to retreat for long into a cul-de-sac of denial or despair even when I cannot feel any hope. I know that my hope eventually will be reborn, if I do everything I can to improve things little by little. I know in my heart that the sun is still shining even when it's completely obscured by dark clouds.

_____ If I feel wiped out by a crisis or loss, I have enough courage and good sense to seek the guidance of a competent, caring clergyperson or other counselor.

_____ I often reach out to others going through crises and losses like mine for mutual support and understanding of each other's pain.

_____ When confronted by the expectation of a loss or by a prolonged stressful situation, such as a terminally ill loved one or a highly stressful life transition, I let myself begin to grieve in anticipation of the loss rather than allowing it to hit me all at once.

_____ I don't waste spiritual energy for long by feeling that God is punishing or discriminating against me when crises and losses hit, because I know they are a normal part of everyone's life sooner or later.

_____ I've learned how to eventually find some spiritual meaning and comfort even in tragic situations that seem unfair.

_____ When my old faith feels shattered by tragedy, I'm able "to hang in there" while spiritual renewal gradually occurs, probably with a little more spiritual maturity.

_____ After making corrective amends, I forgive myself and accept God's forgiveness for my contributions to crises and losses.

_____ Whenever possible, I avoid making irreversible decisions while I'm still in shock after a shattering crisis or loss.

_____ I try to listen to what physical, mental, or interpersonal pain is telling me about the need to change something in my life.

_____ If I experience a socially stigmatized loss, such as a death by suicide or AIDS, I have spiritual resources and people I can turn to for coping with the judgmental attitudes of others and the lack of social support.

_____ Among the uninvited lessons that sometimes come from crises is the discovery that with God's help I _can_ survive more than I could have imagined.

_____ I see my life as a gift from God, a journey of growth with new assets, insights, and possibilities as well as new problems and losses at each life stage. I'm learning to handle the problems of the present stage by developing some of its new possibilities.

_____ My experience of today is enriched by prized memories from many yesterdays and hopeful expectations about the tomorrows.

_____ I have personally and socially worthwhile life goals, and I'm doing all I can to accomplish these.

_____ I prize the things I've learned the hard way in the past and have made some peace with my past so that I seldom waste time and creative energy on unproductive remorse and regrets.

____ I have made some peace with my tomorrows by careful planning and by not wasting creative energy on unproductive worry. My feelings about the future are energized by a reality-based hope.

____ I enjoy living in the present moment, aware of both its joys and its pain, thankful for the precious gift of just being alive.

____ I'm open to learning from and sharing my understandings with those who are younger as well as those who are older.

____ My Christian faith helps me accept my own mortality, so that knowing my time on earth is limited motivates me to live today more fully, joyfully, and lovingly for others.

____ I'm committed to doing everything I can to help make my world a little healthier and whole when I leave it than when I was born.

Using Your Findings to Sustain Your Well Being in Crises

Take the following steps to help you use the results of this checkup to learn how to find sustenance in the midst of crises and losses:

1. Tally your responses and write down the totals below. This will give you an overview of your self-care in crises and losses. / Give yourself a deserved pat on the back for the things you honestly scored "E."

E: _____

OK: _____

NS: _____

2. Go through the list and put a star beside those OK and NS items that seem either especially important or urgent to you. /

3. What is your overall "feel" concerning your general ability to cope with and grow through crises and losses? In the space below, jot down your evaluation of the strengths and weaknesses of this area of your life.

_____

_____

_____

_____

_____

4. Beside the starred items, make notes about how you could begin to implement changes to help you grow through crises and losses. / Later in this session, you will be encouraged to come back and elaborate on your ideas as you develop a workable crisis-loss self-care plan.

Two Biblical Perspectives

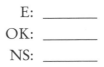 To set the tone for this session, here are two stories from the New Testament that shed light on losses and grief. In his sermon to a throng of spiritually hungry listeners gathered on a mountainside, Jesus declared, "Blessed are those who mourn, for they will be comforted" (Matt. 5:4). (Luke phrases this verse as "blessed are you who weep now" (Luke 6:21.) Those among Jesus' hearers who were feeling overwhelmed by devastating losses must have wondered how either comfort or blessing could come from their empty agony.

The power and insight of Jesus' statement is illuminated by the meanings of the key words. The word used for *blessed* in Greek (the language in which the New Testament was written) means spiritual fulfillment and joy that arise out of suffering and pain. Among the several Greek words for *mourn*, the word used is the one for the most open and demonstrative form of grieving. The Greek word for *comforted* implies strengthening as well as consolation. This demonstrative kind of mourning, as contemporary studies of grief confirm, may help produce the growth of new personal and spiritual strengths.

The second story relates to Paul's pastoral letter to the conflict-ridden church in Galatia in Asia Minor. He reproves his readers for their conflicts and reminds them what freedom in Christ means for human relationships: "For the whole law is summed up in a single commandment, 'You shall love your neighbor as yourself'" (Gal. 5:14). He then states that Christians should "bear one another's burdens, and in this way you will fulfill the law of Christ" (Gal. 6:2). The law of Christ is the primacy of love experienced in a caring community of faith where all are valued, supported, and needed for mutual care.

Then just three verses later, Paul lifts up what seems to be a contradictory guideline for Christians about carrying the heavy burden of crises and losses: "For all must carry their own loads" (Gal. 6:5). In Paul's day and still today, caring empathy and love *do* help people carry their personal loads. At the same time, only as people develop the will and strength to carry their own loads will they grow stronger in crises and losses.

 Learning Exercise: Pause and ponder these two biblical stories, thinking about your own pattern of giving and receiving care in crises and losses. Do you find it easier to be a giver or a taker of care? Do you tend to lean heavily on others, on the one hand, or be superindependent in crises, on the other, or are you able to maintain the healthy balance between dependence and autonomy that is interdependence? / How does your understanding of living a Christian life influence your response to crises and losses—your own or those of people you care about in your family, friends, or congregation? Do you need to rethink your faith in light of your health needs, knowing that it is blessed both to give *and* receive? / Note in your journal ideas to remember, or share them, if you are working with a wellness partner or group. /

Because our painful problems affect all seven dimensions of our lives, how we handle crises is a major determinant of our overall well being. In this session we will explore practical strategies and Christian resources for carrying our own loads while also sharing mutual support with others who are struggling to carry their loads, perhaps in lonely isolation. The strategies presented here are not only for catastrophic megacrises and losses but also for everyday minicrises and losses, which often occur with painful frequency. As you know, in life "when it rains it may pour." The cumulative impact of clusters of smaller problems sometimes hits us like a "ton of bricks."

Major Objectives and Themes

 To clarify your learning goals for this session, put a check mark in front of those items listed below that are important to you as you seek to enhance your Christian lifestyle. In this session, you will have opportunities to learn the following:

❏ Resources for handling crises and losses more constructively.

❏ Wisdom from the Bible on dealing with crises and grief.

❏ Awareness and appreciation of all that you already have learned about coping with crises.

❏ Strategies for helping yourself and others when you or they are going through deep water.

❑ Ways to strengthen your self-other care plan by adding care before, during, and after times of crises and losses.

❑ Ways for your congregation to develop innovative educational and caring group programs so that it can better help people find healing and growth in crises and losses.

The objectives you have identified as significant concerns constitute your self-selected learning goals for this session. Keeping these in mind as the session unfolds will increase the focus of your learning.

Experiencing Healing in a Crisis or Loss

**Learning Exercise: You probably know lots more than you think you do about how to use Christian resources and other skills for coping constructively with crises and losses. This exercise will increase your awareness and appreciation of things that life has taught you, including those you did not expect or want to learn.

Go back in memory and pick a painful crisis, loss, rejection, failure, accident, disability, or acutely frustrating situation on which to focus. Choose one that happened prior to the last six months or year but about which you still have some unresolved feelings. (Remember, this sign / means to close your eyes and do what has been described.) /

Now let yourself *relive* that painful experience as vividly as you are able. Re-experience the whole sequence of events and of your feelings. / Become aware of healing that has occurred but also of pain that is still in your heart. If you feel unhealed fear, guilt, shame, or anger, remember that letting yourself reexperience these painful feelings can be an essential initial step on the road to healing. /

Stay with any remaining painful feelings, and in a prayerful attitude, visualize yourself and these feelings in particular enveloped by the gentle healing light of God's grace and peace, compassion and caring love. / Experience this healing light touching your whole body, mind, and spirit with God's healing energy, like those who were healed in the Gospels after being touched by the strong, gentle hands of Christ. / Continue this, opening yourself to experience the here-and-now healing that we are promised in the New Testament. / If it feels appropriate, express in your own way of praying what you are feeling now. /

Before you open your eyes, reflect on what you just relived and experienced. / How did your Christian faith help you when the crisis first occurred? Was it a source of healing as you relived it? / Did your faith change or grow because of the crisis, initially or just now? / Think about which things and people were helpful or were not helpful. / Become aware of what you have learned, then or now, from this painful experience—any small strengths, bits of wisdom, spiritual insights, empathy, or growth that you gained from coping with the crisis and using your Christian faith. You can, of course, intentionally use in future crises and losses any tested-in-the-fire wisdom you gained. /

Even if you feel you only "muddled through," remember that you *did* mobilize enough strength and inner resources to do this. So commend yourself for hanging in there and perhaps learning something useful about how to cope more effectively. /

Please note: If reliving and seeking further healing of the trauma has left you with considerable unhealed pain, it is important for your well being that you talk through the whole experience. Find someone you trust to listen without judging you or giving uninvited "let me fix it" advice. By doing this, you help keep the painful memories from again going underground in your mind and thus causing you to miss what may be an opportunity for fuller healing. A caring, trusted pastor who is trained in crisis and grief counseling would probably be an ideal person.

If you found this exercise at all helpful, I strongly recommend that you try another guided meditation that I have found to be of great value to many people who are searching for healing of emotional wounds and residual griefs from childhood or any other stage of life. You will find detailed instructions for "Re-parenting Your Inner Child" on pages 289–93 of *Well Being*.

Biblical Roots

Begin to construct a biblical foundation for this session's exploration by jotting down in the space below one or two Bible passages that shed light on how a Christian can handle, transcend, and learn from crises and losses. I recommend that you discover which passages are meaningful to you before you look at the passages I have listed below. /

_____

_____

_____

_____

_____

_____

_____

_____

Of all the books in the Bible, Job confronts most fully the major spiritual problem with which many good people struggle when they are hit by huge misfortunes. Job lifts up the reality that life is often not fair or just. Painful experiences are among the strands that frequently are woven into the fabric of everyone's life. Experiencing crises and grief is not an anomaly or punishment. Instead, such experiences are "par for the course" for a finite, vulnerable human being who loves other finite, vulnerable human beings. As Job declares out of his pain, we "humans beings are born to trouble just as sparks fly upward" from a fire (Job 5:7). He weeps and says, "My eye pours out tears to God" (Job 16:20). Job also shows an appropriate response to the "windy words" with which his so-called "comforters" try to help him, words that actually increase his distress and bring no comfort (Job 16:3).

Wisdom about coping with crises and griefs from both personal and societal causes is sprinkled throughout the Psalms. Just after depicting in moving words the way our souls thirst for God's spirit, the psalmist expresses what must have been grief from a crisis of spiritual drought: "My tears have been my food day and night" (Ps. 42:3). The liturgical songs of the psalmist also describe the fruitful inner joy that follows effective healing of grief: "O LORD my God, I cried to you for help, and you have healed me. . . . Weeping may linger for the night, but joy comes with the morning" (Ps. 30:2, 5). "May those who sow in tears reap with shouts of joy. Those who go out weeping, bearing the seed for sowing, shall come home with shouts of joy, carrying their sheaves" (Ps. 126:5-6).

Jeremiah's reputation as the "weeping prophet" is well deserved. Out of deep pain for his nation's well being, he cried out, "O that my head were a spring of water, and my eyes a fountain of tears, so that I might weep day and night for the slain of my poor people!" (Jer. 9:1). Now picture Jesus weeping as he looked out over Jerusalem on Palm Sunday. What was the source of his deep grief? Like the prophet Jeremiah, it came from knowing his country had strayed from the road to spiritually empowered well being—the road to shalom (Luke 19:41).

Recall Jesus' powerful, poignant story of the man beaten and robbed on the road winding from Jerusalem to Jericho (Luke 10:29-37). Recall the contrasting responses of the religious leaders who passed by on the other side and the despised, socially rejected Samaritan, the story's real hero. Through this confrontational parable, Jesus made it crystal clear to his followers how they were called to be caring neighbors when people are in painful crises and losses.

The Bible also contains gems of wisdom about handling developmental crises constructively as we grow older. The psalmist prayed, "So teach us to number our days that we may get a heart of wisdom" (Ps. 90:12, RSV) and prophesied, "They still bring forth fruit in old age, they are ever full of sap and green" (Ps. 92:14, RSV). The book of Ecclesiastes in the Hebrew Scriptures includes wise guidance about making peace with time and change in the various seasons of life. A familiar passage begins, "For everything there is a season, and a time for every matter under heaven: a time to be born, and a time to die; a time to plant, and a time to pluck up what is planted; . . . a time to weep, and a time to laugh; a time to mourn, and a time to dance" (Eccles. 3:1-2, 4).

When the early church was spiritually empowered at Pentecost, Peter quoted Joel's prophecy (Joel 2:28) that God's spirit will be poured out on everyone so that "your sons and your daughters shall prophesy, and your young men shall see visions, and your old men shall dream dreams" (Acts 2:17).

Why Constructive Coping with Crises Is Crucial

Learning to cope constructively with crises and losses is crucial to sustaining health and well being. Sooner or later, most of us experience heavy frustrations, losses, failures, or disappointments. As we grow older, sad good-byes become as frequent as joyous hellos, if not more so. In churches, Christians often play the phony hiding game called "Let's pretend." But in small church groups, such as a grief recovery group where real trust grows, people often feel safe enough to risk letting others see behind their protective masks. When they do, they generally make the surprising discovery that most people have at least one, if not several, painful things about their health, family, or job that they wish passionately they could change but cannot.

As I grow older and am clobbered by more losses, these wise words of the admired and loved minister of my boyhood congregation come back to me: "Walk softly, for everyone you meet is carrying some cross."[1] These words make sense to me today—more so than when I heard them and thought they must be exaggerated. I now see that most of us have lots of practice in hiding our personal crosses from each other, even if they weigh a ton.

 **Awareness Exercise: Pause and think of how surprised you feel when you greet someone with the nonquestion "How are you?" and they actually tell you the truth. / Then reflect on how Christians can open up so we can receive and give the loving Christian care for which we hunger when we or others are passing through the shadowed valleys of our lives. / Record your thoughts or share your insights with your wellness partner or group./

Have you discovered, perhaps in the earlier exercise of reliving a trauma, that your faith has been shaken and changed as a result of personal pain? Learning effective and growth-enhancing strategies for handling crises and losses is important for the vitality of our Christian faith and lifestyle for the very reason that traumas can threaten our faith. I recall a brilliant philosophy professor who said to our class at DePauw University many years ago: "The rock on which more philosophies of life break up than on anything else is why good people suffer unjustly." Making some peace with the reality that confronted Job—that many bad things happen to good people—is a tough challenge for most of us. But it is also essential so that our Christian faith can help us when tragedies hit us again.

Christians are called to be gardeners of the Spirit. You may not be familiar with plows, but the plow serves as an important spiritual image for me because of my boyhood and early teen experiences on my maternal grandparents' farm in southern Illinois. Sharp plow blades slicing deep furrows through the soil became for me a fitting image of what often happens to our spirituality when crises and tragedies cut through our lives. They sever any shallow spiritual roots. But disturbing the soil also prepares it for receptivity to new seeds of meaning, helping them take root and grow. In due season, some will flower. The deeper the plow goes, the deeper the new roots of faith can penetrate.

Right after plowing, the furrows become tiny rivers when the spring rains send needed water. From a spiritual perspective, the furrows cut by crises and losses can become channels for either the toxins of bitterness toward God (as often is true, at least initially) or the living water that nourishes life in all its fullness. Gradually we can let the living water of healing love—ours and God's— flow through this channel in our souls. When this happens, new flowering of faith can be nurtured in grief-parched, crisis-stricken lives—beginning with our own.[2] In recent years one fact about this story has become clear: The quiet, simple but profound Christian faith of my Grandpa Whittenberg is what gives this image its spiritual significance for me.

Understanding Crises and Griefs

We now know many valuable things about the spiritual impact of painful life experiences and the dynamics of recovery from them. A summary of these may be of practical help in coping with and even growing through crises and losses.

 **Reflection Experiences: After reading each of these sections, pause and consider whether your own experiences of crises and losses confirms them. / Then learn from your reflections by making a few notes to yourself, or if you are working with a wellness partner or group, share your reflections and discoveries with one another.

• Crises and grief are really twins, not identical but deeply related and often alike in terms of the help that is needed. To have a crisis there must be either a loss or the expectation and fear of losing something that is important to the persons involved. This means that most crises involve some grief, and major losses trigger feelings of crisis.

• What may feel like small crises to others often loom large over those experiencing them firsthand. When I was a hospital chaplain, the hospital humor pool included this quip: "A minor operation is one that happens to someone else." I also recall a lapel button that eloquently and ironically stated, "It's easy to be philosophical about a toothache—providing it's someone else's!"

• Crises happen *in* people rather than *to* them. The same event or loss may produce in different people intense, moderate, or no feelings of crisis. When people encounter external or internal changes or stressors, how they perceive, feel, and choose to respond determines the degree to which they experience crisis-related feelings such as fear, loss, anger, guilt, despair, powerlessness, disorientation, and paralysis of coping skills. Because crises occur within us, we have more power to change our attitudes and responses to the external stressors triggering them than most people assume. Of course, some stressors, such as the death of a loved one, are so huge that it is impossible as well as inappropriate for people to respond without feeling grief and experiencing the event as a crisis.

• Both crises and griefs trigger spiritual turbulence, large or small, and therefore offer spiritual growth opportunities. Old beliefs and values by which we have created security, order, and meaning in our lives often seem irrelevant. We discover that old values are unreliable compasses for guiding healthy decisionmaking in stormy spiritual seas.

When old gods die, the deep human hunger for believable and worthy objects of devotion is left unfed. Thus, when people are in spiritual chaos from anxiety-causing crises, they may clutch at old authority-centered beliefs. Or they may take a risky leap of faith, hoping that they will discover new objects of devotion and reliable values to guide them in the future. Jumping across a chasm of meaning of unknown width or depth requires faith and courage. The resulting spiritual growth and health enhancement usually is visible only in retrospect, which makes such a leap of faith even more threatening and risky.

• Crises and grief come from many losses, actual or threatened, and have many different faces. We often associate grief exclusively with losses by death. But the number of griefs from losses unrelated to physical death is undoubtedly much larger than the millions that result from death. Consider these prevalent sources of grief not associated with the death of humans: lost childhood and youth by those deprived of experiencing and working through these essential life stages; lost lovers or the lost hope of finding a lover; the multiple, often-infected wounds from divorce and the shattering of families; the deep grief of

couples who desperately want a baby and cannot have one; the awful betrayals of domestic violence and incest; the death of pets who are loved family members.

Also consider the following: the countless losses that immigrants and refugees experience in losing their home and place, even their homeland; the spiritual anguish of lost purposes, hopes, and dreams that brings emptiness of meaning and value vacuums; the loss of cherished beliefs that often result from severe losses.

• Remember that there are four distinct types of crises, each with its own special spiritual impact and patterns of loss:

1. The so-called *accidental crises* that come "out of the blue" often destroy the comforting belief that such things happen only to other people.

2. *Developmental crises* occur at every significant life-stage transition, including moving from the teens to adulthood, marrying, having a child, retiring, and dying. Fortunately, many of the same spiritual strategies are helpful in coping constructively with both accidental and developmental crises.

3. *Chronic trauma and grief* occur when the cause is ongoing. Chronic traumas usually require demanding, oftenwrenching lifestyle and spiritual changes. Families in your congregation with a severely disabled child, someone with Alzheimer's disease, or a chronic alcoholic who does not accept treatment all know the agony of chronic grief and the acute spiritual needs caused by ongoing trauma.

4. *Collective crises and grief* affect whole groups. These are caused by social factors such as injustice, discrimination, and oppression, often linked with racism or sexism; national, cultural, and international catastrophes such as wars, political violence, genocidal pogroms, and ethnic "cleansing"; or natural disasters such as earthquakes, floods, fires, and hurricanes that traumatize whole

regions in many parts of the world. Such collective traumas have their own dynamics, needs for help, and spiritual consequences.

• Love is linked inseparably with grief; and love, along with faith and hope, is required for the healing of grief. The deeper our love for a person or thing, the more profound our grief when loss occurs. Love from some person or persons and a measure of hope and faith are essential if healing and growth eventually are to follow severe losses. Again we discover the wisdom of 1 Corinthians 13:13, in which the Apostle Paul tells us, "Faith, hope, and love abide, these three; and the greatest of these is love."

Studies of death camp survivors revealed that those who managed to survive the extreme deprivation, humiliation, violence, and massive losses were, in most cases, those who had three things. They had found ways to see at least a little meaning in the experience (faith); they held a belief that they would somehow survive to fulfill some intense dream, such as being reunited with someone they loved deeply or writing about their ghastly experiences so the world would know the truth (hope); and they received at least occasional caring from another human being (love). Those who suffered from vacuums in faith, hope, and love tended to drown in despair and die sooner because their will to live had been stolen.

When far less severe losses strike people, the same three keys are crucial. Their spirituality is a source of faith, hope, and love, and it helps them transcend the trouble they encounter. This is why the quality of our spiritual lives is so vital in coping with and even growing through grief. Persons whose Christian faith is alive and well often discover an adequate supply of these lifesaving resources in their faith when crises and losses strike.

• Grief and crises are whole-person experiences, affecting the well being of our total lives in all seven dimensions. Severe trauma profoundly disturbs our bodies, minds, and spirits, making us highly vulnerable to a plethora of illnesses. These may range from the common cold to immobilizing depression or other mental and spiritual disorders. Major crises and losses frequently disrupt our work life and rob us of the rejuvenation of play. They cut us off for a time from both the social and the natural environments, leaving us feeling disoriented, isolated, and dismally alone—like persons in a strange land where everyone else communicates in an unknown language that we have no hope of learning.

 Learning Exercise: What does all this mean to us as caring Christians? Pause and remember a recent crisis or loss, reflecting on queries such as these:

• Did I develop a significant health problem soon afterward in one or more of the important dimensions of my life?

• Did I give myself the extra self-care I desperately needed?

• Did I ask for increased care from others who love me?

• Did the care I received from my church community address some of my needs?

• How can I use what I have learned from my own experiences of loss and grief to make the Christian care I give to others suffering from comparable experiences more holistic? /

Make notes about your answers, or if you are studying with a partner or group, share your responses so as to learn from each other. /

Sudden, unexpected losses usually take much more time and "TLC" (tender loving care) to heal than expected losses. This is because there is

• no time to do "anticipatory grief work" before the loss;

- no opportunity to say "good-bye," "I love you!" "Please forgive me!" or simply "Thank-you!"
- greater shock, denial, depression, anger, and guilt;
- more likelihood of the grief wound being deeply infected and never healing;
- no opportunities gradually to refill the place left by the persons or thing lost.

The process of the healing of grief from stigmatized losses generally is much more difficult and longer than from socially accepted losses. Grief from such losses as AIDS, suicide, a crime, or a messy bankruptcy or divorce usually are complicated and protracted. Many such wounds become so deeply infected that they heal very slowly, if at all. Factors that complicate or block healing include attempting to hide the loss because of shame, rejection and judgmental attitudes encountered in others, and a lack of the social supports that are usually available to one mourning a socially acceptable loss such as death.

To help fill this aching void, a Christian response must communicate grace and acceptance of the sufferers, sensitivity to their devastating feelings, and a willingness to move slowly in gaining their trust. It also involves a willingness to continue providing frequent, nondemanding caregiving for as long as needed, which is often several years.

 **Learning Exercise: If persons you know have lost their health or loved ones unexpectedly or from a stigmatized illness, ask them if they would be willing to share with you what they have learned from the devastating blow of a sudden trauma or from a loss in which they received little healing care from their family, friends, or church. / If they share their painful but precious insights, decide how you will express your heartfelt thanks in some appropriate way.

Learning to Recognize and Respond to Blocked Grief

A variety of studies, as well as my own counseling and clinical teaching experiences, have revealed that a high percentage of people who consult counselors, psychotherapists, and health professionals have severe unhealed grief wounds among the hidden causes of their problems. At the pastoral counseling and growth center where I seved as clinical co-director, an informal survey showed that more than 60 percent of those who sought help had suffered a catastrophic crisis or a series of painful crises and losses during the months just before the onset or dramatic worsening of their problems.

In most cases they did not recognize that grief was among the major causes of problems that pushed them toward help. Because these wounds of their minds and hearts were hidden and infected, they probably would never have healed fully if they had not sought and received help from a trained pastoral psychotherapist.[3]

In most, if not all, congregations, numerous Christians suffer from grief that a casual observer might think has healed based on surface behaviors, but at a deeper level the grief wounds fester. The marvelous, God-given healing processes are blocked because the grief wounds are infected by powerful and unacceptable feelings that go unresolved. Often the sufferer has pushed these feelings out of awareness into the closed rooms of the unconscious. There these repressed feelings continue to grow, robbing the person of energy for living because creative energy is being wasted in maintaining denial and repression.

Caring people need to learn to recognize infected grief wounds, as well as how to encourage victims to find appropriate counseling help. The problem of the "walking wounded" whose grief is hidden even from themselves is widespread. The cost to people's overall well being, aliveness, and joy in living is enormous. Studies over the last half-century have identified certain physical illnesses as often being grief-related: heart disorders, hypertension (high blood pressure), hyperthyroidism, arthritis, diabetes, neurodermatitis (a severe skin disorder), psychosomatic problems, and certain cancers. Blocked healing of infected grief wounds is a frequent cause of alcoholism and other drug addictions, chronic depression, sleep disturbances, phobias, obesity and other eating disorders, sexual dysfunction, and marriage and family disturbances.

What are the identifying symptoms of infected grief wounds? The single most significant warning sign of unhealed grief is that the feelings normally associated with any major crisis or loss—depression, guilt, anger, fear, disorientation—continue in undiminished intensity over weeks and months or longer after a major loss. Certain spiritual symptoms also may be caused by repressed grief. These include an ongoing loss of faith, persistent intense anger or fear toward God, an upsurge of fears about death, and continuing spiritual depression marked by feeling hopeless and utterly alone, abandoned in the universe.

How can persons with this problem best be helped? If the grief blockage began recently and is relatively mild, as it is in many mourners, caring listening over time may be enough to unlock the energies of healing. A trusted friend or family member who is a good listener needs to keep inviting the person to express and talk through all his or her unresolved feelings about the loss. As the intensity of these feelings begins to diminish, healing is occurring. Persons whose losses occurred longer ago—and whose resulting wound is therefore more deeply blocked—may need the skills of a pastor, priest, or rabbi who is trained in methods of grief counseling.

A trained pastoral psychotherapist may be needed if grief is long-repressed. The general rule to follow is that the longer ago the loss occurred or the more unaware a person is of continuing pain, the more likely that person will need the skills of such a specialist or psychotherapist. A referral to such a professional can be an invaluable gift of Christian caring to that person.

Six Strategies for Healing and Growth in Crises and Losses

Are you ready for some good news? You already are acquainted with a wide variety of strategies for helping yourself or others experience healing and perhaps even growth during crises and losses. The items in the checkup early in this session introduced a number of strategies. Strategies listed below are organized into six tasks that include some of the insights you have encountered. Completing these basic tasks often helps people cope constructively and helps prevent infected grief wounds by facilitating the healing process. A summary of these grief-healing tasks follows with comments about their spiritual dimensions and suggestions for helping yourself and others accomplish them.

Grief-Healing Task 1

Gradually let go of denial and accept the painful reality that your problem or loss has really occurred. In agonizing tragedies, people's minds go back and forth from refusing to believe that the tragedy has happened to experiencing the grim reality for a short time. Denial is a gift from God to protect our minds from being overwhelmed until we can slowly absorb awful truths. But if this protective defense becomes frozen, continued denial blocks acceptance of reality, an essential step that lets us move ahead to the other tasks necessary for recovery.

What kinds of care and support do people

need as they struggle after a tragedy to move beyond shock and denial to accept the realities with which they must now begin to cope? Most important of all is simply what has been called the "ministry of presence"— the comforting presence of loving family and close friends during the first agonizing hours and days. Caring people also can help with practical things like food, transportation, and assistance in making wise decisions about matters that must be handled almost immediately. They can help by phoning those who need to be informed of what has happened and finding housing for persons who may come from a distance.

A trusted minister can help in a variety of ways. Very important is the minister's presence as a spiritual leader and representative of a congregation's faith tradition. He or she also can provide comforting prayers, scripture, and familiar rituals to the family and circle of friends as well as guiding them in planning ritual events such as a funeral or memorial service.

Congregational leaders and care team members can give ongoing emotional, spiritual, and practical support and help with logistics as requested. The common practice of providing food for several days after a family trauma obviously is an example of such practical help. If the food provided is both delicious and nutritious, it will encourage family members to eat in healthy ways and to avoid the health hazards of neglecting to eat or living on junk food in the time immediately following a loss. Furthermore, gifts of food are a deeply symbolic way to communicate caring, and they may bring oral comfort to the inner child of adults. Reaching out to bereaved persons in ways like these is practicing the scriptural call to "bear one another's burdens, and so fulfil the law of Christ" (Gal. 6:2, RSV).

 **Learning Exercise: Recall a recent significant loss and, in light of your spiritual needs at the time, formulate a brief prayer that you can use to address those needs. / If you are working with a partner or group, share your prayers with one another. /

_____

_____

_____

_____

_____

_____

Grief-Healing Task 2

Experience and express the full range of your agonizing feelings repeatedly, as the cutting pain slowly diminishes. This task is difficult because it must begin almost immediately, and it continues as people reluctantly tackle the other tasks. People need a certain kind of listener who will encourage them to express their feelings, especially those about which they feel some shame and guilt as they talk about their loss again and again. If people continue "talking through" (to use counselor's jargon) their swirling feelings and are heard by a caring person, the overwhelming pressures on their minds and spirits are diminished. They then will have more strength to cope with their new reality.

As they accomplish this task over what may be days or weeks or longer the life energy that had been tied up in denying and repressing a mass of painful feelings becomes available for dealing with the new reality. The importance of this second task is shown by the fact that the healing of grief is most often blocked by the repression of painful emotions.

The most effective method of helping people accomplish this task is to practice *responsive, focused, caring listening*. Such warm, empathetic listening involves paying careful attention to whatever is being communicated by words, feelings, and body language and responding so that the suffering person will know that the listener is trying to understand. It also involves asking questions that will encourage the continued expression of feelings, while avoiding giving advice unless it is requested or unless it pertains to practical and pressing issues with which the bereaved is wrestling.

Learning Exercise: Pause and think of questions that you believe will encourage grieving people to continue expressing their memories and feelings. Write them down in your journal or in the margins of this workbook. / If you are meeting with a partner, take turns practicing responsive, focused listening, using the questions you formulated. (If you had difficulty thinking of such questions, try these: "What happened?" "How are you doing, really?" "What are your real feelings about what has happened?") One person should describe a personal experience of a loss, while the other listens intently and tries to draw out any other painful feelings.

As you take your turn as listener, resist trying to make the other person feel better or offering quick solutions to the problem. Neither of these is possible in the early stages of loss. / After ten minutes or so, each person, especially the one who was describing a loss, should evaluate candidly what was and was not helpful. / Then reverse roles and repeat the practice. / Caring listening is a valuable skill to know and can help you respond more sensitively to a grieving person.

Grief-Healing Task 3

Cope as constructively as possible with all the decisions and actions that occur in the first hours and days after a tragedy. These new demands hit people while they are most vulnerable. Without help, they are in danger of making unwise decisions or taking irreversible actions that they would avoid if their minds were clear and not paralyzed by grief.

Therefore, people often need a trusted, caring person or two who can be with the acutely bereaved to encourage them to make sound decisions and to take actions that are likely to seem prudent and wise a month or more later, after the worst of the crisis has passed. This helping process includes encouraging the acutely bereaved to consider various options and the probable consequence of each before making decisions. If grief has immobilized the deeply bereaved persons, it is important that they consult with other family members or, if these are unavailable, with the pastor in making significant decisions that cannot be postponed.

Grief-Healing Task 4

Rebuild the structure of your life, minus whatever has been lost. In major losses, this task usually takes months or even several years. It involves *unlearning* the ways that important needs had been met by whomever or whatever is now gone and learning alternative ways of meeting these needs or accepting the hard fact that this may be impossible.

**Learning Exercise: If you have lost a significant person from your life, stop and enumerate in your mind and then on paper all the things you received from and gave to that person. (This may be difficult but valuable to do, depending on where you are on your journey from grief to recovery.) / Beside each item, note how you now meet or do not meet the needs listed. Which needs have you met in new relationships and which have you had to relinquish, at least for now? / If thoughts come to you about what you need to do to satisfy some of the empty places in your life, jot these down beside those items. / I hope that this exercise enabled you to gain new understandings of where you are in your recovery process and how you may be able to continue moving out of your shadowed valley.

_____

_____

_____

_____

Grief-Healing Task 5

Evaluate and enlarge your Christian faith in light of the crisis or grief, so that it will bring you needed meaning and purpose in your new situation. If your faith has been strained, weakened, or shattered, think back to the plow image discussed earlier. The fertile soil of faith can be made more receptive to the seeds of spiritual growth by being turned upside down in a crisis or loss. Growing spiritually in such experiences does not happen by chance or easily, but it can happen. As discussed in Session 2, every crisis and grief exposes beliefs and values that are obsolete and perhaps even harmful. Unfortunately, sufferers miss many of these opportunities for spiritual growth because they stop growing after licking their wounds.

A church, as a garden in which to grow whole-person well being centered in healthy spirituality, is the ideal setting for people to help each other use opportunities for spiritual and ethical growing. As a sign on a church bulletin board put it with a chuckle, you can "come in and have your faith lifted." Sharing and caring groups, personal Bible study groups, prayer and healing groups, and certainly Christian grief recovery groups all are productive settings where people help one another walk the walk, as well as talk the talk that heals crises and grief.

Grief-Healing Task 6

Join hands with others who are struggling with similar problems for the purpose of giving each other understanding, affirmation, and guidance. Jesus' expression of this spiritual wisdom (mentioned earlier) appears in all four Gospels: "For those who want to save their life will lose it, and those who lose their life for my sake, and for the sake of the gospel, will save it" (Mark 8:35). The meaning of this enigmatic statement often is taken by Christians to be an affirmation of self-sacrifice. It may be this, but what if we understand it in the context of Jesus' central life purpose—that people have life in all its fullness? In this interpretation, the statement can be paraphrased in this way: "To find life in all its fullness, in the midst of our own brokenness and that of others around us, we must reach out with caring to others in pain. To keep the new life we discover as Christians to ourselves will cause us to lose what we have found. To keep it and let it grow involves giving it away in mutual covenants of caring in which we share the new life we have found with each other."

Let me tell a little about Clem Lucille, my mother. I am very thankful for the way she kept her faith and her sanity when Ruth, her baby daughter, died on her first birthday. (See the Window of Wholeness on page 223 in *Well Being*.) Writing short notes to other parents whose children had just died was a loving expression of Mom's deep Christian faith. But it also was an expression of a truth that she must have known intuitively in her heart—*that one's own healing is nurtured by reaching out in healing ways to others who also are going through profound losses.*

I am sorry that I did not ask her before she died if she received any responses to the many notes she wrote over several years. She probably did receive some grateful responses. But there is absolutely no doubt in my mind that her own mental health was sustained and her faith enriched through the loving outreach involved in writing these notes.

A cynic is alleged to have said that if you cast your bread on the water, all you get back is some soggy bread. My mother taught me by her living that sharing love, the bread of life, operates on a radically different principle. The only way to keep it is to give it away. And when you give loving care to another with a need like yours, what you receive back is a double bonus of mutual healing and wholeness. This principle of Christian outreach is explored in more depth in the next session.

 Learning Exercise: If you have been moving through dark days of crisis and loss, reaching out to another person or family experiencing similar problems is enlightened self-interest. Your pain and theirs might become a bridge of mutual understanding and help. Offering to walk beside them on their lonely way can help transform their loneliness and yours, as you both experience the warmth of walking together. Joining hands can release the energy of mutual caring within each person—energy that can be used to light a single lamp for both journeys. So if you feel ready to do this, devise and implement a plan to create such a caring alliance with someone else in grief. /

In spite of her severe disabilities, Helen Keller once declared: "We bereaved are not alone. We belong to the largest company in the world—the company of those who have known suffering. . . . Believe, when you are most unhappy, that there is something for you to do in the world. . . . no one is so bereaved, so miserable, that he [or she] cannot find someone else to succor, someone who needs friendship, understanding, and courage more than he [or she]. The unselfish effort to bring cheer to others will be the beginning of a happier life for ourselves."[4]

Helping in Crises

You can use a simple but effective tool called the ABCD method, which employs the principles of crisis counseling, to help yourself or others cope constructively with many types of crises. The ABCD steps overlap and complement the six tasks of healing grief described above.

(A) *Achieving a trusting helper-helpee relationship* is the foundation of most counseling methods, including those that focus on crisis and grief. Listening to the helpee's feelings and description of the problem is the same as task two of grief healing—experiencing and expressing fully all the feelings involved.

(B) *Boiling down the problem to its smaller parts* is one of the helpful things to do in tasks three and four of grief healing work. These are the tasks in which the bereaved person deals with the immediate and longer-term problems posed by the new situation.

(C) *Choosing one or two parts of a crisis on which to take action first* is also an effective way to begin coping constructively with the new reality produced by a loss.

(D) The same is true of *developing and implementing an ongoing action plan.*

In summary, the ABCD steps are useful for helping people in crises of all types, as well as those whose primary problem is a loss. It works by helping people mobilize their inner resources to sort out and take carefully planned action that will help them improve their situation, one part of the problem at a time. (For more on this approach to crises, see pages 222–24 in *Well Being*.)

Strategies for Coping with Developmental Crises

A man named Henry Swan once said, "The older I get, the better I used to be!" He was a retired plasterer with a sense of humor who coped with the crisis of retirement in an incredibly ingenious way. Henry Swan wrote a book called *Being Henry*, in which he described his experiences in his small Arizona hometown. He then opened a "one book bookstore" in the little town and sold over 25,000 copies of his self-published volume. (Perhaps authors like myself who keep hoping more people will read their books might emulate Henry by developing their own creative solutions.)

As I have worked with older people through the years, and, for the last decade, struggled myself to age a little more gracefully if not creatively, an annoying truth keeps rearing its head: the frequency of painful losses and grief experiences keeps accelerating as one gets older. People in the older years seem to lose more and more things they cannot replace. Also as I look back now over a series of life stages, it is clear that each transition from one life stage to the next, from the cradle to the grave, brings significant losses as one passes through "developmental crises." So wherever you are on your life journey, a key to growing older constructively is to strengthen your skills for coping with crises and healing your griefs.

Each age and life stage has new losses and liabilities, new problems and challenges. But like many other people, have you overlooked the good news that balances and brings hope to this bad news? Each emerging life stage also brings new strengths and insights, new possibilities and fragments of wisdom not available to you earlier.

What's the key to enhancing well being in your present life stage? *It is to cope with the problems and pains that this stage brings by developing some of the new assets and gains it offers you.* Using this strategy as a guiding compass becomes more of a challenge, but it also becomes more essential to your overall well being with the passing years. In short, staying alive and well in all the downs and ups of your future requires developing some new strengths in your mind, body, spirit, and relationships in the present.

 Learning Exercise: On numerous occasions, while leading workshops on topics such as "Staying Alive All Your Life," I have been surprised by the power of a simple do-it-yourself tool. It involves focusing more sharply on both the gains and pains of your present life stage. Such a candid evaluation can provide insights on how you can use more of your partially hidden assets and gains to cope with the crisis of aging, including your losses and pains. Turn to pages 286–87 in *Well Being* and do the "Inventory of Your Present Life Stage.

Another strategy for aging more creatively comes from T. S. Eliot's "Four Quartets": "Old men [and women] ought to be explorers."[5] Actually in our Jewish and Christian religious heritages, younger as well as older women and men are called to dream new dreams and glimpse new visions (Joel 2:28; Acts 2:17). Would you agree that as Christians, whatever our age, we all should continue to explore the marvelous mysteries of life—of ourselves and other people, of God and the earth—as Jesus did so brilliantly and so fearlessly?

Learning Exercise: Stop and form a picture in your mind of an elderly woman or man you know who loves life and therefore continues to enjoy exploring new intellectual landscapes and discovering new spiritual vistas. Such people seem determined to keep on enjoying the good gifts of their minds, hearts, and spirits, and by so doing to "die young (in mind and heart) as late as possible." / If you do not know such a person well, do yourself a favor and find one in your church or community. If that person is interested, visit and ask him or her to share some gems learned during their long life. /

Discover what you can learn from such persons about growing through crises, coping with losses, continuing the adventure of openness to learning, and thus staying very alive all one's life. / Then reflect on your own strategies for growing older with well being. How would your present or future wellness be enhanced by what you learned from the wisdom of this older person?[6] Remember that the strategies for creative aging described here are designed to help you enhance your well being at *any* adult stage, including your present one. The best way to prepare for well being in the future is by developing more of your present possibilities. In light of all this, what do you need to do today or perhaps tomorrow? / Go for it!

Another strategy for coping with developmental crises and grief is expressed in a line by Madeleine L'Engle: "The great thing about getting older is that you don't have to lose all the other ages you've been."[7] Think of all the things you have learned about living and loving and crises and losses in earlier life stages. These experience-derived insights are little pieces of wisdom you now have stored in your memory bank. You can draw on them as you go about aging more constructively.

 Learning Exercise: From a psychological perspective, who you were at each previous life stage is still a valuable part of who you are today. The inner child, teenager, young adult, and so forth are still a permanent part of your identity. They also are valuable sources of insights for how to live a Christian wellness lifestyle in your present stage. To increase your conscious awareness of what you can learn from your inner child, for example, begin by forming a vivid moving picture in your imagination of yourself as a small child. / Then have a spirited inner dialogue with the little girl or boy within you, paying special attention to what that little person says in response to your queries. /

Most adults, including myself, could benefit from befriending, listening to, and playing with our inner child more often. He or she may help us rediscover the healing power of play or the adventure of learning something new and exciting. As you experience this learning exercise, you may also discover fresh meanings in the words the prophet Isaiah used to describe the peaceful kingdom—"A little child shall lead them" (Isa. 11:6)—and in Jesus' words about becoming open to God's kingdom—"Whoever does not receive the kingdom of God as a little child will never enter it" (Mark 10:15).

Christian Guidelines for Well Being on Your Journey

Here are some suggestions for adding life to your years and perhaps years to your life.

1. Be aware that life itself and your life in particular, from a Christian perspective, is a precious gift from God to be used well in each new stage.

2. With God's help, celebrate the present moment by moving from regrets about your

past and fears about your future to gentle self-forgiveness for your past stumbling, action-supported hope for the future, and thankfulness for God's loving gift of being alive and aware in the present moment.

3. In the midst of the routine of life, directed by your wristwatch and calendar, become aware of the spiritual meaning and opportunities of this time in your life. Your everyday life is structured by *chronos* (clock and calendar time), but don't lose touch with *kairos* (a Greek word from the Bible), which conveys the spiritual meaning and opportunities of time. By prayer, you can experience God's here-and-now presence in your life, a presence that can keep you in touch with the sacred in the secular, the transcendent in the mundane routine of your life.

4. Awaken in your heart the hopes and intentions of God as we know these in Christ—a vision of a transformed future of greater well being for yourself, for those you love, for God's whole human family, and for all of God's creation. Then open yourself to God's empowering presence that can invite, guide, and energize you to make small but significant contributions in your own unique ways to translating this dream into a transformed reality.

Enhancing Your Congregation's Crises and Grief Programs

Our society desperately needs an innovative strategy for helping the countless people in every community and congregation who suffer from unhealed grief. Churches (along with schools) should take initiative in helping to develop and implement such a strategy for the following reasons:

• Churches have regular, face-to-face relationships with more adults of all ages than any other institution in our society.

• Clergy and church leaders have contact with more people in accidental, developmental, social, and natural crises and disasters than any other group, professional or nonprofessional. Most clergy have some training in the skills needed to help people with crises, including dying and death.

• Congregations already have numerous small groups, as well as some lay leaders who can be trained readily to lead innovative crisis-grief programs.

• Religious organizations have many spiritual and ethical resources that people long for when they are in days of darkness.

What are the major dimensions of innovative crisis-grief programs in congregations? Congregations that have effective programs frequently include four parts:

1. *Regular educational units on the Christian resources that can help in coping with crises and grief.* Such units should be offered in the religious education program on all age levels, from elementary school through the older years and in multigenerational educational events. All wellness programs should include educating people on how to prepare for future problems and how to cope constructively with present crises.

2. *A crisis and grief-recovery class, group, retreat, or workshop offered regularly.* Those in special need should be encouraged to attend.[8]

3. *A lay caring team* composed of carefully selected people who themselves have grown through crises and who have received special training and ongoing coaching by a pastor and/or mental health professional. Such teams often double the caregiving effectiveness of their congregations by working with the pastor in visiting the homebound, the disabled, and those in crises and griefs.

4. *Pastoral crisis and grief counseling available from a minister who is trained in this skill.* I would estimate that at least 75 percent of all crisis and grief counseling is done by parish clergy. They are on the frontlines where people live and pray, curse and

die, hurt and hope. Supporting and providing backup to these pastors is a growing group of qualified pastoral psychotherapists who are clergy with advanced clinical and academic training in pastoral psychology, counseling, and psychotherapy.[9]

Questions for Reflection

 1. Do your personal experiences support or contradict the idea that crises and losses can be used as opportunities for psychological and spiritual growth?

2. As you think about the six tasks of grief recovery (and growing through grief), which are the most difficult? What kinds of help have you needed to accomplish these tasks?

3. If your faith was shaken or shattered by major trauma, have you been able to rebuild it? If so, how has it been changed by this process?

4. How adequate are the crisis and grief counseling and the education program in your congregation or community? What are the next steps that may help to strengthen these?

Strengthening Your Self-Care Plan

If you took and tallied the Crises and Losses Well Being Checkup before this session, I trust that it primed the pump and brought you some cold, clean water for use in the desert of crises and losses. You came to the session with an overview of the issues and some awareness of things you need to do in this area of your life. I hope you have acquired a variety of crisis-care ideas during this session.

Now is the time to strengthen and enrich your self-care plan by taking the follow steps:

1. Look over your tally of the checkup and any notes you made after taking it, paying particular attention to NS and OK items that you checked. These are options that you picked as particularly important or urgent for taking action. Also review any initial notes you made about what you can and should do to implement these action-options. /

2. Review other ideas or tools to which you were attracted during this session—things that now seem important to help you find healing and growth not only in present crises and losses but also in those that will come in the future. /

3. Now, using these ideas from the check-up and session, enhance your self-care plan by adding the important items for crisis and grief self-care. Spell out the concrete objectives you want to achieve, practical plans for moving toward these, a time line, resources and people you will need to help you, and rewards you will give yourself as you take each step or withhold if you backslide. /

4. Select one or two high-priority items that are both attractive and achievable, and plan how to begin implementing these in a current crisis or loss. Be sure to pick options that are relatively easy to implement so that you can enjoy the rewards of improved self-care in the short term.

5. From your heart, pray for God's guidance and help in implementing and also reshaping your crisis-grief plans as new ideas develop.

Closing Song, Prayer, and Evaluation

 Whether you are studying alone, with a wellness partner, or group, close this session by doing the following:

• Sing a hymn, spiritual, or folk song that celebrates the fresh insights that dawned in this session about self-other caregiving in crises and losses.

• Highlight and celebrate the new plans that you made during this session by listing these. Commit yourself in passionate prayer to implementing them.

- Do a brief evaluation of the strengths and weaknesses of the session, aiming at increasing the wellness benefits of the next and final session.

- Make plans for the final session, including a closing celebration and a commitment to ongoing wellness self-other care.

Continuing Your Self-Care

These activities will help you continue enhancing your wellness between study sessions. They also will prepare you to use the next session to gain maximum benefits:

- Read chapter 8 in both textbooks, highlighting or underlining the things that seem problematic or important for enhancing your care of your well being by caring for the well being of your community and earth.

- Each day spend at least a brief time in imaging prayer for the wellness of yourself and that of others about whom you care, especially those in crises and losses. Visualize yourself and them enveloped in the warm healing light of God's love. Ask for guidance as you try to become a better channel of that healing love to people suffering in difficult days.

- Take and score the Ecology-Justice-Peace Well Being Checkup before the next session.

- Each day implement several of the action-options you have in your self-care plan, including those you have added in this session. Remember that the wellness payoff comes gradually as you put these plans into action.

- Consider how you will encourage those who plan your congregation's education and holistic wellness programs to increase innovative crisis-grief self-care offerings.

Session 8

Helping Heal God's Wounded World

Every creature is a word of God and a book about God.

> —Meister Eckhart (thirteenth-century German mystic)

The Earth laughs in flowers.

> —Ralph Waldo Emerson

Never doubt that a small group of thoughtful, committed citizens can change the world. Indeed, it is the only thing that ever has.

> —Margaret Mead, anthropologist

An Ecology-Justice-Peace Well Being Checkup

 To help you gain the greatest benefits from this session, take and score this checkup first. This checkup can be useful to you in two ways as a self-discovery instrument. First, it will give you an evaluation of the health of your Christian lifestyle and the values that shape it as these relate to the health of your society and the natural world around you. Second, the items in the checkup are a list of concrete options from which you can choose as you increase your own wellness by helping to increase the wellness of your world.

Instructions: Mark each statement in one of three ways:

E = "I'm doing *excellently* in this."

OK = "I'm doing *acceptably*, but there's room for improvement."

NS = "This is an area where I definitely *need strengthening*."

____ My love of people, nature, and life energizes my concern, study, and work for a healthier world.

____ I love the earth and feel an intimate connection with the amazing network of living creatures, of which I am a small but significant part.

____ I know that my personal wellness is woven inextricably with the wellness of my society and the natural world around me. Therefore, doing everything I can to make my community and natural surroundings healthier really is enlightened self-interest.

____ I often experience the spiritual lift of God's living presence in the mystery, power, wonder, and beauty of nature.

____ Knowing that there are no individual solutions to society's problems, I work with others for institutional and social change.

____ I enjoy relating to people of diverse backgrounds, languages, cultures, and faiths, seeing them all as God's children and therefore my sisters and brothers in the human family.

____ I often feel energized and renewed when I am in lovely places in nature or near a favorite indoor tree, plant, or pet.

____ I enjoy sharing experiences in the natural world with people I love, and I feel our love is enriched by this sharing.

____ I have mutually supportive people who share my active passion for peace based on justice and for loving the earth.

____ I pray regularly for guidance on working for peace with justice; for environmental caring; and for the victims of violence, injustice, and environmental pollution.

____ In my Christian faith I find spiritual power to avoid "compassion burnout" and to "keep on keeping on" when working for community change is an uphill struggle.

____ I work with others in my congregation for a better world in which all children, youth, and adults have fuller opportunities to develop their talents as good gifts from God.

____ I experience spiritual aliveness and empowerment for wholeness when I open myself to be nurtured by the natural world.

____ I know how to be nurtured by nature, even in a city, by relating to outdoor plants, to trees and birds in a park, or to beautiful houseplants.

____ I'm working to help change two basic causes of damage to God's creation, the earth—the population explosion in poor countries and the lifestyle of greedy consumption in more affluent countries.

____ In the spirit of the Prince of Peace, I vigorously oppose the arms race, which causes huge waste of natural resources and environmental damage.

____ I recognize that both violence against nature and violence against persons falsely labeled by society as weaker or less valuable (e.g., women, children, minorities) have similar causes: sexism, racism, classism, ageism, destructive religion, and economic inequality.

____ I regularly examine my Christian lifestyle and the values that guide it to find ways of making them more earth-friendly and just.

____ When feelings such as anger, grief, and guilt hit me, triggered by my learning of gross injustices or environmental degradation, they often motivate me to take constructive action.

____ I know how to "ground" my body, mind, and spirit in a supportive awareness of the earth and the Creator who brought it into being.

____ I try to stay current and knowledgeable about the complex causes and cures of social and environmental problems.

____ I support and work with others in groups that are committed to justice, peacemaking, and protecting the environment for children everywhere.

____ I know that my personal peace is intertwined with the peace of my family, community, and world and that justice is the only firm foundation for peace at any of these levels.

____ I am open to learning new ways to nurture the inner peace that is valuable in itself as well as indispensable for effective peace and justice work.

_____ For my own health and the healing of God's earth, I often get involved politically, supporting and voting for candidates who favor strong programs for economic justice, ecology, and peacemaking.

_____ I know and use methods for renewing my hope and energy for action when feelings such as despair, denial, or powerlessness hit me.

_____ When I work for society's healing and wholeness, a sense of partnership with God's spirit gives me needed hope and strength.

_____ My Christian faith and values build bridges, not barriers, with people of goodwill who have differing faiths and views of social problems.

_____ Laughter—at myself and with others— reduces stress and gives me a lift for living a socially responsible Christian life.

_____ I try to practice justice, earth-caring, and peacemaking in my family, work, social life, and congregation.

_____ I have a vision of a healthier future for the human family and for God's creation, toward which I am drawn to work, walk, and worship.

_____ When the same community and social problems keep recurring, Yogi Berra's remark could give me a chuckle: "It's *déjà vu* all over again!"

Using Your Findings to Enhance Your Ecology-Justice-Peace Wellness

Take the following steps to help you use the results of this checkup in preparing to develop your self- and earth-care plan:

1. Tally your responses and write down the totals below. This will give you an overview of the health of your lifestyle with respect to the wider society and the world. / Give yourself a pat on the back for the things you honestly scored "E."

E: _____
OK: _____
NS: _____

2. Go through the list and put a star beside those OK and NS items that seem either urgent or especially important to you. /

3. What is your overall "feel" concerning the general wellness of your lifestyle with respect to issues of ecology, justice, and peace? In the space below, jot down your evaluation of the strengths and weaknesses of your well being in this area.

_____
_____
_____
_____
_____

4. Beside the starred items, make notes about how you could begin to implement changes to care for your community and environment. / In this session, you will find many other suggestions for strengthening your plan for self-other-earth care.

A Biblical Perspective

 Let's reexamine a powerful story in the good news according to Luke. Jesus was visiting Nazareth where his parents lived. On the Sabbath, he went to the hometown congregation where he must have received his childhood religious education. He was handed the scroll of the prophet Isaiah to read aloud during the service. Jesus chose to read this prophetic declaration: "The spirit of the Lord is upon me, because he has anointed me to bring good news to the poor. He has sent me to proclaim release to the captives and recovery of sight to the blind, to let the oppressed go free, to proclaim the year of the Lord's favor" (Luke 4:18-19; from Isa. 61:1; 58:6). He then rolled up the scroll and, with all eyes on him, declared, "Today this scripture has been fulfilled in your hearing" (Luke 4:21).

When Jesus thus interpreted the prophet's scripture in a way that confronted the people and announced his prophetic mission, they rejected him in self-righteous rage. They forced him to leave his hometown, even trying unsuccessfully to cause him serious bodily harm.

By choosing this passage from the courageous Hebrew prophet of the sixth century B.C.E., Jesus lifted up social evils, including oppression, poverty, and the health problem of widespread blindness. His choice made clear that he identified his ministry with the central motif of the prophetic heritage: to challenge and correct the institutional evils that produce widespread human brokenness in his society and in ours.

 Learning Exercise: Try to put yourself inside Jesus' experience, perhaps by imagining that you have returned to your childhood congregation and have been asked to take part in the worship service. Imagine the courage it would take to speak honestly to the congregation about their community's evils. See if you can feel something of the agony of being rejected violently by many former friends and neighbors. Bear in mind that whenever Christians speak the honest truth about society's people-hurting problems, they face the risk of being ignored or vigorously opposed by Christians and others who like the status quo because they benefit from the inequalities and injustices. Take a few minutes to jot down your responses for future reflection or share them with your wellness partner or group. /

This session explores how God calls Christians and congregations to emulate Jesus by enlarging our horizons of caring beyond self-care and the care of those we love to include two interrelated dimensions—care of a wounded earth and care of society's institutions so that they will support rather than diminish people's well being. This session will focus most of its attention on the environmental crisis, but issues of social justice and peace are so intertwined with this crisis as to be inseparable.[1]

Major Objectives and Themes

 To clarify your personal learning goals for this session, put a check mark in front of those objectives and themes listed below that are important to you as you seek to live as a Christian in today's fractured world. In this session, you will have opportunities to learn the following:

❑ Why seeking individual and family well being, while ignoring the well being of society and the earth, is an ineffective way to enhance your own wellness or that of your loved ones.

❑ Why working to heal society and the earth is essential to an enlightened and relevant Christian lifestyle in today's turbulent, deeply troubled society.

❑ Spiritual and ethical causes at the roots of the ecology-justice crisis.

❑ Special roles of women and men in saving a healthy earth for future generations.

❑ Resources in the Bible that you can use as the foundation of earth-caring and justice-making expressions of your Christian faith.

❏ The unique and essential contribution that all religious people, including Christians, can make to transforming society and saving a viable planet.

❏ How to understand and use the three dimensions of the "ecological circle" model of earth-caring.

❏ Insights and methods for healing ourselves by healing the earth and society.

❏ Methods to motivate Christians in a faith community to become involved in earth-caring, peacemaking, and justice-creating work.

❏ Practical strategies by which Christians and congregations can make a positive difference in their world.

❏ Two earth-awareness guided imaging tools.

❏ Suggestions for strengthening your self-other care plan by adding earth-caring, and suggestions for continuing to use your overall self-care plan after this session and series.

A Tragic Story with a Hope-Filled Sequel

Maintaining hope is essential for effective and ongoing involvement in the struggle to heal society and the earth, as well as people's alienation from themselves, other people, God, and the earth. While absorbed in writing my book *Well Being* in the early 1990s, I was saddened to read a tragic story in the *Los Angeles Times*. A wave of profound grief and anger swept over me when I read that the last Palos Verdes blue butterfly in the world was dead. This beautiful, diminutive creature had been on the endangered species list since it was discovered in 1977. In spite of its vulnerable status, the city of Rancho Palos Verdes (California) had destroyed a field of locoweeds, its only food and habitat, to build another sports field. The article said that the city was being taken to court for destroying the species, a charge that is only a misdemeanor.

My feelings came, I discovered, from realizing that my children and grandchildren (and all children and grandchildren) would never again be able to see a Palos Verdes blue butterfly. In the larger scheme of human tragedy, this loss may seem almost trivial compared to the agonizing suffering and deaths of thousands of children each day from hunger and war. But it cut into my psyche like a razor-sharp knife as a painful symbol of the countless species that are destroyed every day somewhere on the earth, each one a small thread ripped from the fabric of God's awesome and incredible creation. I remembered that *extinction is forever*!

I'm delighted that I can now share this hopeful sequel, because it brings good news both about this beautiful butterfly and a young former prisoner in Los Angeles. I was surprised with joy to hear, four years after the news about the death of the species, that the Palos Verdes blue butterfly had been discovered to be not quite fully extinct. A patch of locoweed with a few survivors was discovered unexpectedly in a U.S. Navy fuel depot near the Los Angeles harbor. A young man named Arthur Bonner was working to save their habitat and also to incubate and care for larvae in a program aimed at increasing the numbers of this still-vulnerable butterfly species.

In the mid-1980s, Bonner was a tough "gangbanger" in the Los Angeles ghetto, describing himself as a "natural gangster." Shortly after his eighteenth birthday, he began a prison sentence of about three years for shooting a man in the face. In prison, he decided to try to turn his life around when released. He joined the California Conservation Corps program and was assigned to the program that hopes to reestablish the Palos Verdes blue butterfly. This has become his passionate commitment. Of his precious butterflies he declares, "They are saving me as I am saving them!"

Although Bonner's former gang friends think that he has gone soft, his new friends know better. They know a man who loves to read and who hopes to go to college. His moving story superbly illustrates the healing power of relating intimately with nature. It also shows how a passionate investment in working with others to help save even one tiny part of the threatened network of living creatures can release healing, transforming energy in a person's life.

Learning Exercise: I hope that you have experienced the remarkable healing, growth-enabling energy that can flow from having an intimate relationship with God's natural world. Have you known a person who has experienced healing and transformation like Arthur Bonner? / Pause now and take a few minutes to jot down responses to this story in your journal or, if you're working with a partner or group, share your responses with one another.

Biblical Roots

Before reading further, take a few minutes to jot down some passages from the Bible that teach us to care for the earth and for all of God's people.

_____

_____

_____

_____

_____

_____

Here are some biblical passages that illuminate the Christian understanding of our responsibility for earth caring and justice-based peacemaking:

• "The earth is the LORD's and all that is in it, the world, and those who live in it" (Ps. 24:1). We humans do not own the natural world; rather, it belongs to God who loaned it to us to care for respectfully and with love.

• The refrain repeated after each stage or era of the first creation story in Genesis 1: "And God saw that it was good." Our ways of living often treat the earth as something that exists only for our use or abuse as we choose in meeting our often-greedy desires.

• The creation story in Genesis 2 pictures the basic earthiness of us humans by portraying us as being created by God out of the soil—the soil into which our bodies will someday be recycled. Modern science has shown this image, unlike many biblical images, to be literally true chemically. Our blood has chemical affinity with the water of the oceans. Our genetic roots are in the earth and the sea.

• This same creation story pictures God as a gardener: "And the LORD God planted a garden in Eden" (Gen. 2:8). In the fourteenth century, Julian of Norwich, a passionate pioneer of creation spirituality, wrote, "Be a gardener. Dig a ditch, toil and sweat, and turn the earth upside down, and seek the deepness and water the plants in time. Continue the labor and make sweet floods to run and noble and abundant fruits to spring. Take this food and drink and carry it to God as your true worship."[2]

• All the Hebrew stories of the covenant (or sacred contract) between humans and God emphasize our obligation to be good stewards of God's creation. The flood story climaxes with these words of God to Noah and his sons, "This is the sign of the covenant that I make between me and you and every living creature that is with you, for all future generations: I have set my bow in the clouds, and it shall be a sign of the covenant between me and the earth" (Gen. 9:12-13).

The ark story and rainbow covenant paint the most dramatic portrait of our responsibility to care for the other animals. Prophetic descriptions of the new covenant for the future (see Hosea 2:18 and Isaiah 11:6-9) include responsibility for the animals and the establishment of *shalom*, meaning wholeness for God's entire creation.

• The Hebrew prophets cared passionately about healing both the violence against nature and the human brokenness produced by oppressive institutions. They saw that ecology, peace, and justice issues cannot be separated. The truths they spoke twenty-eight centuries ago are painfully relevant to our present global ecojustice crisis.

Isaiah declared, "The earth dries up and withers. . . . The earth lies polluted under inhabitants; for they have transgressed laws, . . . broken the everlasting covenant" (24:4-5).

Speaking in the name of God, Jeremiah mourns, "I brought you into a beautiful land to eat its fruits and its good things. But when you entered you defiled my land, and made my heritage an abomination" (2:7).

Hosea saw that creation suffers because of human sins against one another: "Therefore the land mourns, and all who live in it languish; together with the wild animals and the birds of the air, even the fish of the sea are perishing" (4:3).

• The book of Job reveals awareness of nature's celebration: "the morning stars sang together" (38:7). Job also includes a statement about learning from nature, including the other animals, "Ask the animals, and they will teach you; the birds of the air, and they will tell you; ask the plants of the earth, and they will teach you. . . . Who among all these does not know that the hand of the LORD has done this? In his hand is the life of every living thing and the breath of every human being" (Job 12:7-10).

• Jesus grew up immersed in the Hebrew worldview these scriptures describe. His frequent use of teaching images from nature— birds of the air, wild flowers of the field, weeds in a field of grain, a farmer planting seeds, and a woman using yeast to bake bread reflect his intimate bond with the natural world. He did most of his teaching outdoors, and he retreated to places of wilderness in nature to find renewal and to struggle with difficult issues. In his marvelous healing work, he used water and earth symbolically on occasions.

• Throughout the Bible, both human shalom (meaning peace and wholeness) and salvation are understood as being possible only in a shalom community. This is a spiritually empowered, transformed, and transforming faith community where people find well being together. Privatized health-seeking and salvation-seeking that ignores the social and ecological contexts in which we all live are not only ethically wrong; they are unbiblical and ineffective in the long run.

Our health is inescapably dependent on the health of our society and the natural world. We should work in our church and community to improve these because this is our Christian responsibility. It also is *enlightened* self-interest, as contrasted with stupid, shortsighted selfishness. Enlightened self-interest knows that my real well being can prosper best in covenants of mutual well being with other people, institutions, and nature.

• Sad to say, two creation story themes have contributed to the environmental crisis. The first, "Be fruitful and multiply" (Gen. 1:28), has been used to justify the runaway population explosion, a major cause of many social problems, including environmental degradation. The second theme, "have dominion over [all] . . . the earth" (Gen. 1:26), has been misunderstood and used to justify the exploitation and waste of the earth's limited natural resources.

 Learning Exercise: Take a few minutes to reflect on these biblical gems as they relate to your Christian lifestyle. / Then jot down or share with your partner or group your insights about a Christian's responsibility to care for the earth and to have a commitment to justice, peace, and environmental work as an essential expression of your ministry as a follower of Christ. /

_____

_____

_____

_____

_____

_____

Discovering What Nature Gave You in Your Childhood

 Learning Exercise: The purpose of this exercise is to discover how your early relationship with nature continues to influence who you are today. Close your eyes and remember your early childhood home. Picture it as vividly as you can. / For a short time, see yourself as a child walking around outside that home. Relive the natural environment in which you grew up. If there were trees, bushes, birds, and animals in the area surrounding it, be aware of those living things. Whether you grew up on a farm, in a small village, in a suburb, or in a large city apartment, see whatever things of nature were present, and be aware of how they influenced your life then. /

Go inside that home now; walk through the rooms and become aware of how any houseplants or pets influenced your feelings about that place. / Reexperience the social environment, the people who lived there with you. Experience again how your parents and other adults felt about nature and the plants and animals around you. / Now let yourself relive one or two very vivid experiences of nature in your childhood—for example, an enjoyable family camping trip or a violent, even traumatic, storm. / Think about how all these early experiences with nature may have influenced the person you are today and your present relationship with nature. Did they help to shape your feelings and attitudes toward nature? /

Now integrate what you have learned from this memory trip to your childhood home by sharing with another person or recording your insights in your journal. /

Why Are the Social and Ecological Twin Crises So Crucial?

Your health and that of your family cannot be separated from the health of either your natural environment and that of the key institutions in your life. As the Bible makes clear, God made us humans deeply interconnected with one another and with the biosphere around us. From a biblical perspective, no one can have the fullest possible shalom or well being until all have well being. Therefore, investing some of our time, money, and passion to help heal social institutions and the earth is actually an important investment in our own well being.

Many eminent earth scientists agree that the current global environmental crisis is unprecedented in the eon-spanning story of life on our green, living planet. For the first time, one species—our species—has acquired the industrial power and chemical capability to damage the earth's remarkable self-healing systems beyond repair. In religious terms, our generation is the first to literally hold in our hands the future health of God's living creation.

The environmental crisis will not be healed until you and I, and countless other people of goodwill, learn to translate into action our love of our incredibly beautiful but terribly vulnerable planet. As Christians, we must develop the environmental know-how, consciences, and caring that will motivate us to live more earth-loving, ecologically healthy lifestyles. Helping to heal our little planet spaceship must include joining hands with others to enhance the health of those people-serving institutions that affect our lives every day in countless ways. Our goal must be to help shape them so that they will stimulate rather than stifle the body-mind-spirit well being of everyone whose lives they touch and the well being of the environment upon which both personal and institutional health ultimately depend.

Unless we humans save a healthy planet, opportunities to solve other serious health and social problems will disappear or have no meaning. Thus, the global ecojustice crisis is the most important ethical issue of our times. Unless we develop ways to become more earth-literate and earth-caring, our lifestyles will continue to make God's world an unhealthy place for all life. Because we have no options of escaping to other life-supporting planets so far as anyone knows, the stakes in this venture are incredibly high—our healthy survival on a healthy planet.

The things that each of us does to help save a healthy environment are precious gifts to the future. Our care for the earth now extends further into the future than ever before. Former President Jimmy Carter declared, "Each of us is part of an extended family that extends in time to include all who will ever be born. We have a responsibility to those family members separated from us by centuries."[3] A wise East African proverb communicates a similar imperative: "Care for the earth. It was loaned to you by your children."[4] Another observer noted, "If you can't picture your connection with the future, turn around and look at your children. They are the future!" Scores of decisions we make today are answering a most crucial question: Will our children, grandchildren, and great-grandchildren inherit a healthy and healthful planet?

On my birthday a few years ago, I enjoyed climbing a beautiful sacred mountain in South Korea with three young friends. It was a beautiful June day and the experience of being nurtured by nature in all its aliveness was wonderfully real. The wild flowers and birds, the sparkling mountain stream, and the welcome shade of the trees were nature's gifts as we climbed. As we descended the mountain via a different trail, we saw a large sign in Korean suspended over it. My climbing companions translated it for me: *"Love nature as you love your children."*

As I pondered that simple but urgent message in the days that followed, it dawned on me that none of us can love our children fully unless today we also love nature enough to protect and respect it as their precious home tomorrow. Only thus can we enable our children to inherit a green, clean, healthy planet home.[5] This is the ancient, very wise "great law" of the Iroquois Confederation of Native American Nations: "In every deliberation, we must consider the effect of our decision on the next seven generations." Today we must extend our ecological caring for the future beyond seven to seventy generations!

Learning Exercise: Close your eyes and picture your children or grandchildren. If you are single, picture your nieces or nephews or godchildren. / Be aware of what happens to your energy level as you get in touch with your deep love for these dear ones. / Now, feel this life energy flow into your doing all that you can to make sure that they have a clean, green, healthy natural environment in which to live and have their children after you have graduated (we hope) to heaven. / Make notes in your self-care journal about your learnings from this exercise, and share them with your wellness partner or group. /

Well Being in a Broken but (Let's Hope) Birthing World

One of my favorite cartoons shows a dog watching television with his master. The dog's thoughts, in response to the television news are in a bubble: "I find it increasingly difficult to remain man's best friend!" Would you agree that the world in which we struggle for wholeness is a mixed bag? Most people suffer from painful brokenness in some area of their lives—their health, families, jobs, spiritual lives, community, or country. For this reason, no approach to well being can be credible or helpful if it ignores the fact that our individual and social sins influence our lives day by day in profound ways.

Our society's epidemic of violence, sexism, racism, ageism, militarism, classism, economic oppression, chauvinistic nationalism, and sick religious movements affect us all. These institutionalized cancers hurt people's wellness in wholesale ways while parents, along with teachers, clergy, and therapists, try to prevent and repair woundedness on a retail basis. It is a losing struggle unless we also heal the institutional causes.

Martin Luther King Jr. wisely observed that we cannot understand or practice God's love unless we also understand and practice God's justice. I would add that we cannot fully practice God's love for the earth unless we also work to change the injustices that constantly damage the earth's health. We must express our love of God and all God's children—especially those whose lives we touch—by developing greater earth consciousness, conscience, and caring that will guide us in developing more ecologically healthy lifestyles.

Spiritual-Ethical Causes of the Ecojustice Crisis

Many complex causes contribute to the ecojustice crisis, including overpopulation, extreme poverty and wealth, and the military-industrial system. But, the deeper root causes of our damaging the earth are ecologically destructive spiritual attitudes and ethical priorities. Because the bottomline causes are religious and ethical, Christians, in cooperation with other faith communities, have special responsibilities and unique opportunities to take leading roles in saving the earth for future generations.

The global ecojustice crisis has little chance of being resolved until you and I and millions of our sisters and brothers in all countries and faiths change our lifestyles radically. This will not occur until we commit ourselves with *religious passion* to earth-caring aimed at healing our awesomely beautiful but wounded earth. The good news is that this is already beginning to take place in many denominations and faith groups that have mobilized "Caring for God's Creation" study-and-action programs.

**Self-Confrontation Awareness Exercise: Here is a list of some major, interrelated spiritual and ethical problems at the roots of the ecojustice crisis in your own community and around the world.[6] In the blank before each item on the list, enter a number between one and ten that indicates the degree to which it reflects your lifestyle. Use this scale:

0 = This behavior or attitude does not describe me at all.

5 = I sometimes feel or behave this way, but I am trying to change this part of my lifestyle.

10 = This behavior or attitude describes me perfectly.

____ 1. Shopping is one of my main joys in life. I like to shop till I drop (or would if I had the money). Shopping helps me forget my worries and feel a little more comfortable, at least for a brief time. I sometimes follow the urge to buy things I can't really afford, and I often don't use things I purchase very long, but soon pitch them in the trash.

____ 2. Feeling comfortable and nurtured when I'm in a natural setting is not something I experience. Pets and houseplants are not my thing. I usually prefer to be inside because I feel better there (for example, watching TV), rather than being surrounded by nature.

____ 3. I rarely if ever experience God's presence when I'm outdoors in a natural setting.

____ 4. I don't enjoy being in a wilderness, but want to get to a more comfortable, "civilized" setting as quickly as possible. When I feel "wild" energy, I experience uneasiness and a need to control it quickly.

____ 5. My religious and ethical concerns focus mainly on personal issues. Concern about political, social, economic, or ecological issues should not intrude into people's religious life. Such things are mainly the responsibility of political leaders.

____ 6. I'm not worried about the so-called environmental crisis because God won't let anything that bad happen to the world.

Are you wondering how these behaviors are symptoms of earth-damaging ethical-spiritual problems, particularly because many folks believe that they are normal, harmless ways of thinking and acting? Here is how they contribute significantly to the ecojustice crisis:

The behavior in item 1 is a symptom of consumerism or compulsive shopping, probably the most widespread addiction in affluent societies like the United States. This is not occasional shopping as necessity demands but rather shopping driven by psycho-spiritual needs in a futile effort to diminish or deaden anxiety, boredom, or stress. The ethical consequences are enormous for both the addicted and for the environment. In exchange for brief psycho-spiritual relief, consumerism wastes money because people purchase things that they do not really need and often do not use. Such consumerism squanders limited natural resources, making things unavailable to people who really need these articles.

From a religious perspective, consumerism is one form of psychological idolatry, making material things an object of worship to which victims sacrifice both money and precious time. Many of us suffer from this idolatry to some degree.

Item 2 describes symptoms of eco-alienation, a lack of close, positive bonding with nature and an inability to feel at home in God's creation and renewed by relating intimately with it. This is a personal loss, but it also reduces people's motivation to care for the earth. Why bother caring for something with which you do not have a valued relationship? Item 3 describes the spiritual loss that results from not feeling at home in the natural world, where many people have some of their most energizing spiritual experiences.

Item 4 describes a problem closely related to items 2 and 3: repression of that inner wildness that is a source of creativity, zestful living, and a spirit of joyful adventure. When a person denies or represses this God-given energy, often because he or she misunderstands what is important in living as a Christian, it tends to build up to an explosive level. Such a dynamic is illustrated in media stories of young people, known by others as "fine, churchgoing youth," who explode in violent behavior. Befriending one's inner wildness lets the energy be integrated in one's life so that it is channeled into creative living that enables people to blaze new trails for society.

Item 5 describes the privatized religion and ethics that focus mainly on helping individuals find salvation and righteousness. It ignores the prophetic heritage and detaches the religious life from any obligation to help heal the many societal and environmental sins that produce widespread hurt and brokenness. This contradicts the best in the biblical heritage.

Item 6 is what could be called magical, rescue-fantasy religion. This thinking is dangerous because it eliminates any Christian responsibility to become partners with God in helping the world that God loves to find healing, peace, and justice.

Christians Living the Ecological Circle

Here is a diagram that depicts the three dimensions of respecting and caring for the earth. It shows how we can make our lives

and lifestyles better serve the divine intentions that the good earth be sustained as a healthful home for all God's living creatures.[7]

The words around the circle describe two of the three interdependent dynamics of living an earth-caring lifestyle. "Nurtured by nature" refers to opening yourself more intentionally and frequently to the energy of healing and growth that are available as one bonds intimately with God's amazing network of interdependent living beings. This bonding is a major source of the energy and motivation for "nurturing nature," meaning protecting and caring for the earth with informed commitment as a part of your Christian living.

"Ecological spirituality" is the empowering center of the circle. It is that earth-grounded spiritual power that spiritual seekers through the centuries have discovered when they became quiet enough to experience the divine Spirit in nature. Energy for earth-caring comes both from being nurtured by nature and from the flowing stream of God's presence in the beauty, diversity, creativity, and awesome power of the natural world.[8]

I find that my awareness of the three dimensions of the ecological circle needs reviving whenever I become absorbed too long indoors with my computer, books, television, and professional and personal activities. My awareness often soars when I slow down and take a little time to reconnect with nature in our yard or to walk briskly outdoors along the hilly streets or to visit the nearby botanical garden. It also can happen if I take a minivacation and connect with our giant live oak tree or with a lone bird on the bird feeder. I hope that you have comparable experiences.

**Learning/Self-Teaching Exercise: Take a minivacation now, or perhaps later, by going for a brief walk alone outdoors. Be silent and become as fully aware as you can of whatever you are experiencing—the sounds, sights, smells, and touch of the natural world, including the outside air and the aliveness of nature, even if you are in a large city. Let yourself be nurtured by nature by opening yourself to the experience with all your senses. / As you experience the natural world around you more vividly, see if you also can become aware of the living presence of the Creator of this amazing, life-sustaining environment. / If you do experience even a little of the nurture and spiritual energy available in nature, become aware of how this affects your feelings about becoming more involved in nurturing nature as a Christian person. /

When you return from your eco-awareness walk, take a few more minutes to note anything you discovered that you would like to remember or on which you might reflect further. If you are working with a wellness partner or group, briefly share your experiences with one another once each of you has taken a walk alone in nature. / I hope that you discovered that you could awaken fresh awareness of one or more dimensions of the ecological circle in this exercise. /

Building On Your Discoveries from the Checkup

If you took and tallied the Ecology-Justice-Peace Well Being Checkup before this session, as recommended, you probably know some things you need to do to help heal God's creation and mend the torn fabric of our society. By doing these things, you may increase the possibility that all children will inherit both a healthier earth and a healthier society from your generation. You can now build on what you learned with the checkup.

Learning Exercise: Look over your tally and notes from the checkup with these things in mind: the NS and OK items that you checked as particularly important or urgent and your initial thoughts about what you might do about these options. / Take a few minutes now to reflect and make further notes about insights you gained. If you're working with a wellness partner or group, share what you discovered and the action you may take./

_____

_____

_____

_____

_____

_____

_____

_____

It is likely that the options you have selected from the checkup will form a basis for your self- and earth-care plan. The strategies that follow highlight some key ways to get more involved in this earth-saving cause.

Christian Strategies to Help Save God's Earth

• *As a Christian, begin by "greening" your own lifestyle and invite your family and close friends to do the same.* Making your home and your family life together more ecologically healthy and earth-caring has multiple rewards. It is a practical way to put Christian ecological ethics into practice right where you live. Your family's example may encourage other families to emulate your healthy earth-caring practices. Living in an ecologically friendly way also provides the most effective hands-on teaching and learning opportunities for children. It lets them learn how to care for God's creation at their fingertips. Chapter 6 in *Ecotherapy* (pages 155–69) has guidelines on "Making Your Living and Working Places Greener and Cleaner," as well as sections on "Understanding Ecological Illnesses," "Making Our Schools Environmentally Healthy," and "Plants as Living Air Cleaners."

• Include environmental issues in your spiritual reading and study.

• Encourage your congregation's education leaders to include eco-educational units that focus on "Caring for God's Creation" so as to equip children, youth, and adults to become Christian lovers of the earth. One goal of a congregation's education program should be to enable people of all ages to understand and implement the ecological circle in their lifestyles. This includes going "back to nature" but in a very different way than was practiced by people in the 1960s who tried to escape from the perils of technology and cities by moving into wilderness areas. Brief Walden-like vacations in national parks and wild places can give renewal and healing to those who are fortunate enough to have such experiences. But encouraging masses of people to move into wilderness areas is neither feasible nor desirable for the health of those areas.

Not long after the year 2000, more than half the world's population will be living in large cities. Fortunately, healthy bonding with the earth is possible in almost any setting if people open themselves to being nurtured by nature, however it is experienced there. From the standpoint of Christians' ethical witness, what is needed is not anti-technology or anti-cities campaigns but rather lessons in using technology in creative, innovative ways to make all settings in which we live—especially our cities—healthier, greener places for all people.

• Express your Christian commitment to the well being of God's children in all countries and cultures by nurturing an inclusive patriotism. The spiritual pioneer John Wesley once said that the world was his parish. As Christians, we are citizens of God's whole world. The health of yourself and your family is intimately intertwined, not only with the health of your neighborhood and nation, but with the health of all nations and peoples.

In a prophetic address at Stanford University, statesman Warren Christopher declared, "Our ability to advance our global interests is inextricably linked to how we manage the earth's natural resources. . . . We are determined to put environmental issues where they belong: in the mainstream of American foreign policy." In commenting on this lecture, an editorial writer observed, "The very idea of national security must be reconceived in relation to ecological disruption and international cooperation. Never was the ostrich approach to foreign policy less opportune."[9]

• Encourage your congregation to support research by earth scientists and ecologists that will generate the deeper understanding necessary to make earth-literacy more widespread. The medical researcher who discovered the first polio vaccine, Jonas Salk, declared, "The answers are in nature. It's up to us to find them."[10]

He probably was thinking of medical problems, but what is now clear is that the causes and cures of psychological, relationship, and spiritual problems also are deeply rooted in the natural order.

• Help clean and green your church's facilities, program, and outreach to the community and world. Begin by cleaning up your church's own act. How? Be more intentional at the church about such practices as recycling and energy and water conservation. Do not use toxic chemicals for building maintenance. Serve healthier food that is lower on the food chain than red meat and does not demand as much from the environment in its production. Adding living plants to all the rooms (and trashing any phony plastic plants) enlivens the ambience and enhances the healthfulness of the air people breathe by removing impurities and increasing the oxygen level.

• Encourage more outdoor church activities (in addition to church picnics and camps), including outdoor worship, education, recreation, and pastoral care, whenever this is feasible. The emotional and spiritual atmosphere of many church activities can be awakened and enlivened simply by holding them outside. It is also ecologically healthy to design church facilities that use environmentally friendly, sustainable architectural principles and building materials. These aim at reducing energy use for heating and cooling; placing windows so that green plants, sky, and natural views are visible; making surrounding green areas plentiful and easily accessible from church rooms; and landscaping with native plants that require less water and fertilizer.

Remember that to be nurtured by nature and to reexperience God in nature, there are no substitutes for intimate contact with nature. High-tech and electronic means for experiencing nature often are beautiful and inspiring. But this virtual reality is never an adequate substitute for touching and being touched by nature and by God in nature!

• **Work with other people of good will to protect the healing powers of nature hidden in the countless plants and animals whose medicinal properties are not yet discovered. A few years ago, a little girl named Jackie was diagnosed with childhood leukemia. She is in remission today with an 80 percent chance of continuing survival because of the discovery of the cancer-controlling properties of the flower of the rosy periwinkle.

Of all medical prescriptions written in the United States, nearly 40 percent are derived from medicinal plants or microorganisms or synthesized to copy natural substances. These include a powerful painkiller used to help terminal cancer patients (morphine derived from opium poppies); a medication widely used to treat heart problems (digitalis from the foxglove plant); aspirin (related to a chemical from the bark of the white willow tree); a variety of antibiotics derived from fungi, including penicillin and cyclosporin; and an immune suppressant to prevent rejection of transplanted organs (also derived from a fungus).

Persons with breast, ovarian, and other cancers are now being treated effectively with an antitumor substance from the bark of the Pacific Yew. Before this discovery, these trees were slashed and burned as worthless during the ruthless logging of old-growth forests in the Pacific Northwest.

Professor Thomas Ensnare, father of "chemical ecology," points out that only about 2 percent of the earth's estimated 250,000 plant species have been studied chemically to see if they might cure human diseases. He declares, "There can be no question that in the millions of species of nature many miracle drugs remain to be discovered." Ensnare holds that our obliterating countless plant species before their healing treasures are even discovered is as if we are burning the precious books of nature, God's creation, before their life-saving contents are known.[11]

• As part of your church's well being outreach ministry, educate its members to support constructive health-care, justice, and environmental legislation on all levels—local, state, regional, national, and global—in both church and governmental circles. Church people, as individual Christians and as the body of Christ, should collaborate with other groups to lead and support environmental, justice, and peace action in their community, their denomination, and the political arena.

This vital outreach ministry should include encouraging individuals to use their political voices and votes to support constructive public stands when the wellness issues involved seem clear from a Christian ethical perspective. On all issues, particularly those on which people of good will are sharply divided, it is crucial to offer accurate educational information on both sides fairly before presenting one's own position or that of one's denomination. In this prophetic, social-health, and environmental-health arena a familiar motto needs to be enlarged to say, "Think globally and act locally but also think locally and act globally."

• Network with regional, national, and international branches of your denomination as well as with ecumenical and interfaith groups, collaborating on programs aimed at healing society's social malignancies that foster ecological damage. These include extreme poverty in poor countries and the pockets of poverty in rich countries, excessive wealth in rich countries and among the privileged few in poor countries, environmental damaging practices by governments and industry, the global arms trade, and the oppression of persons with constricted economic and educational opportunities.

Undergird all approaches to justice and ecological and social responsibility with the prophetic voices in Hebrew Scriptures as well as with the policy statements of the mainstream Christian denominations.

Women's and Men's Special Roles in Earth-Caring

> The soul is kissed by God in its
>   innermost regions . . .
> And so, humankind full of all creative
>   possibilities,
>   is God's Work.
> Humankind alone is called to assist God.
> Humankind is called to co-create.[12]

The author of these poetic lines is Hildegard of Bingen, a remarkable twelfth-century author of a medical encyclopedia and several other volumes, preacher of reform among clergy, musician, spiritual leader, physician, physicist, dramatist, and Renaissance woman who lived in what is now Germany. She is a shining representative of the long history of women ecopioneers who loved God's creation with passion and earthy wisdom.

Women have a unique and vital role in helping to save a healthy earth for children. In my experience, many women have a stronger connection with the earth than many men. They are less alienated from the earth, perhaps because their bodies are equipped to be the instrument for one of the most earthy of miracles—birthing and nurturing a new human being! The fact that they can be co-creators of life with nature and God may well give them deeper, genetically based intimacy with and insights about the earth.

Many women have been key initiators of environmental action. Rachel Carson is an inspiring example whose courageous, farsighted book *Silent Spring* (1962) launched the modern environmental movement. She challenged her country with scientific evidence to support her claims and called for the protection of the "intricate fabric of life" by "sanity and restraint in the application of dangerous materials [like DDT] to the environment." She was attacked viciously by industrial leaders who feared that her call would threaten their corporate profits. Using their male sexism, they labeled her a "hysterical woman" and a "fanatic defender of the cult of nature."

Despite these attacks, Rachel Carson continued to work tirelessly for environmental sanity until her tragic death from cancer. Just before her death, her only fear was "that the cause for which she had struggled would be dropped after her death." Fortunately, others continue her struggle today.[13]

Consider another exciting story of a contemporary earth-empowered woman. When we were teaching in Kenya in the late 1970s, my partner and I were saddened by the emaciated-looking women carrying huge bundles of sticks and large earthen pots of water long distances along the country roads. Wangari Matthai, a courageous Christian eco-pioneer, was painfully aware of the desperate plight of women and their families caused by the environmental crisis in that part of East Africa. Widespread deforestation caused by the need for firewood and building materials had denuded large areas of the country, causing much of the precious topsoil to wash into the streams, polluting the water. Consequently, Kenya's food production had plummeted while hunger soared.

Wangari Matthai decided to take action. On a June day in 1977, she began by planting seven trees in her back yard. Then she visited schools in her community and eventually all around her country, inviting children to get involved in tree-planting. They responded enthusiastically when they understood the problem, quickly involving their mothers in helping to collect seeds of trees that produce edible fruit or are a fast-growing source of firewood.

In the years since that June day, what is now known as the "Greenbelt Movement" spread throughout Kenya. More than one million children from three thousand schools have been involved, often with their mothers, in this amazing grassroots reforestation program. More than ten million trees have been planted from seedlings grown in the fifteen hundred nurseries started and staffed mainly by women. The topsoil is being saved and renewed, while the water is improving in quality. Wangari Matthai now is able to declare, "The weight of the environmental crisis that rural women have been carrying on their backs is being lessened, one seed at a time."[14]

This moving story demonstrates dramatically how violence against God's creation is interrelated with other forms of violence—in this case against poor women and the health of their families, as well as the economic well being of their whole country. Think about what would not have happened there if Matthai had said to herself, *Someone ought to do something about the terrible problems of women and the environment!* Instead, she decided to *be* that someone, beginning by planting seven trees in her yard.

Stories like this can be a source of hope when people feel paralyzed by the magnitude of social problems or dodge their responsibility for taking action on the ecojustice crisis by "passing the buck" to governments or secular environmental agencies. These agencies have major and essential functions in the ecojustice struggle. It is important that individual Christians and congregations support them vigorously. But it is also important that all Christians who care about the healing and health of God's world become partners in innovative programs of eco-education and eco-action.

Christian men also have strategic opportunities in earth-protecting and earth-caring action. Because many of the handles of power in our society are still in men's hands (including the hands of many church men), they have an opportunity and responsibility to use their influence and power to encourage the institutions they are leading and in which they are working to adopt earth-friendly and socially just policies and practices.

**A Biblical Image for an Earth-Caring Christian Lifestyle

Read Matthew 13:1-9, a very down-to-earth story about a farmer. The parable tells about a farmer's planting, cultivating, and harvesting experiences. Jesus told this story as he stood on a boat and spoke to a crowd that was standing on the shore of the Sea of Galilee, eager to hear his message of hope and love, of justice and salvation. The crowd undoubtedly included numerous farmers. Perhaps in the distance they could see other farmers working. Spend a few minutes reflecting on how this story may help you as you sow seeds of Christian, earth-caring understanding and action in your family, community, church, and workplace.

What helps you to keep going when many of the seeds of love and justice you try to plant don't flourish or perhaps even survive because they are choked by weeds, eaten by birds, or fall where the soil is unreceptive to their putting down life-sustaining roots? Such things happen with discouraging frequency, sabotaging people's hard work for justice. When this occurs, do you find strength by remembering that if you "keep on keeping on" planting many seeds, some will take root in receptive soil where they will multiply and produce food for yourself and others, including the people you love? Does it help to remember that, like wheat seeds, the only ones that grow and multiply are those that create new life by their own self-giving

sacrifice? (See John 12:24.) And most importantly, do you remember that, as the Apostle Paul put it, the flourishing of the spiritual seeds you plant, including those cared for by others, ultimately is the gift of the creator God who gives the growth and the harvest? (See 1 Cor. 3:6.)

Take a few minutes now to write notes of things you have already discovered about living a Christian, earth-caring lifestyle, as you have planted the seeds of peace, justice, and environmental wellness in your relationships and institutions.

_____

_____

_____

_____

_____

_____

_____

_____

_____

_____

 An Exercise to Renew Your Sense of Wonder: One of the spiritual benefits of having knowledge about nature is that then your experiences in the natural world can renew your sense of wonder and give you a wider perspective on personal and social problems. Here is a simple experiment that may give you these gifts. On a moonless night, away from city lights, find Polaris, the North Star, around which the stars and constellations seem to rotate in the Northern Hemisphere. /

As you look at it, say to yourself, *This star actually is a huge sun many times brighter than our sun. Its light has guided sailors over trackless oceans for many millennia. The light*

that I see tonight has been coming through space, traveling at about 186,000 miles every second for the last 316 years. The light that I see now left that star only about sixty years after the pilgrim refugees from England landed at Plymouth. Yet, relatively speaking, Polaris is a nearby star in the immediate neighborhood of our own galaxy, the Milky Way.

Now if it is a crystal clear night, find the Milky Way and say to yourself, *What looks like a path of hazy stardust across the sky actually is a side view of the gigantic galaxy that is our little solar system's home. So vast is the Milky Way that it takes light, traveling so fast it could circle our tiny planet seven times in one second, 130,000 years to go from one side to the other of this galactic, circular star city composed of billions of suns.*

Then reflect on a recent discovery of the Hubble Space Telescope. Astronomers now estimate that there are probably fifty billion such gigantic galaxies in the whole universe. Light from the furthest of these galaxies photographed by Hubble has been coming through space at about 186,000 miles per second for some eleven billion years before it reached the photographic plate in this telescope. On a scale that the ancient stargazers could not begin to imagine, the heavens *truly do declare the glory of God* (Ps. 19:1, KJV).

Such a cosmic perspective from modern astronomy can give us a transcending perspective on our problems. It can make our own brief life and all life on our green, growing spaceship wondrously precious, even joyous. The book of Job declares poetically, "The morning stars sang together" (Job 38:7). Perhaps our hearts can sing with the stars.

 An Earth-Loving Wellness Exercise: The purpose of this guided meditation is to sharpen awareness of where our global abuse of the earth is leading and then how changes in our lifestyles can increase people's well being by helping heal the earth's wounds. Using this awareness exercise may help motivate you to make difficult but essential earth-loving changes.[15]

Use full-body relaxation and deep breathing methods to cause your body-mind-spirit to become very relaxed but also very alert. This is the optimal condition for receiving the insights that the exercise may awaken in you.

Form a moving picture in your imagination of your favorite place of beauty in nature, seeing it in your mind as vividly as possible. / Now, *be* there in that place and for a short time allow yourself to experience the healing, enlivening energies of nature that you know there. Enjoy experiencing that life energy flowing throughout your body-mind-spirit, bathing every cell with cleansing, new life, and healing. Continue this until your body-mind-spirit is more alive and well. /

Now shift mental gears and imagine that you are in your favorite place on a day like today but thirty years in the future. Imagine that the ecological patterns of consumerism, overpopulation, and other things that were destroying the good earth have continued unchecked for the last three decades. The population has nearly doubled, making congestion incredibly worse. A tidal wave of increasing violence, poverty, hunger, and disease continues, while the self-repair systems of the environment have sustained increasing and irreparable dysfunction. Religious people and their leaders have done little to heal earth-damaging ethical causes of the global crisis or to pressure industry and the government to move from earth-violating to earth-caring policies and practices. As you look around and become aware of the condition of your favorite place, be aware of your feelings about what has happened to it. /

Shift your mental picture again, imagining a radically different scenario. Imagine that in the twilight years of the old century and millennium, many Christians and people of goodwill in other faiths decided enough was enough. Knowing that the health of God's world is indispensable to human health, they formed a growing, planetwide, spiritual network of diverse religious individuals and groups, all committed to caring for the earth, protecting justice and making peace. They cooperated because they believed that joining together for the survival of a viable earth was the supreme ethical challenge, a challenge so important that they felt that it must transcend their profound differences that had bred continuing conflict and religious violence throughout history. They used the World Wide Web and the many existing ecumenical and interfaith structures to help save a healthy earth.

This spiritual network, working with an empowered United Nations, sparked the reversal of the population explosion. In addition, economic development became more sustainable, women and other oppressed groups gained fuller opportunities to contribute their talents to the well-being of the human famil;, the global arms race was halted; and the security of all nations was made truly secure by a genuine international peacekeeping force.

Look around your favorite place again and become aware that you are in a cleaner, greener, more beautiful place than ever before. For a few minutes, just let yourself be nurtured by that awesome aliveness and natural beauty. / As you are enjoying nature's healing energies, you notice a little girl of about eight or nine approaching you. She can tell that you have lived a long time and wants to ask you some questions about the old days at the end of the twentieth century. Have a brief conversation with her now, being aware of your feelings and your responses to her questions.

She asks: "What was it really like back then?" / "Was pollution poisoning the air and the water so that people and animals were getting sick?" / "Were there really bombs so big they could damage the whole world?" / "Were millions of children like me poor and hungry and sick because governments were spending so much on bombs?" / "Were people in many countries killing one another because they had different religions?" / "Did your religious beliefs cause you to work hard to help make things better?" / "What did you do to help give me and children like me a healthy, beautiful, peaceful place to live?" / "Did your faith give you strength to do this, even when it was very difficult?" /

When the little girl hears your answers, she spontaneously flings her arms around your neck and gives you a big hug of gratitude, saying with deep feeling, "Thank-you! Thank-you! Thank-you!" Then, a little embarrassed, she leaves quickly.

Sit quietly for a little longer and think about what you taught yourself by using this meditation. / Perhaps ask yourself, *How did I feel when she asked me what I had done, and did my faith cause me to work hard to give her and other children a healthy world?* As a caring Christian person, do I need to do more? If so, what? / Record your insights in your journal, and share them with your wellness partner or group.

To maintain reality-based hope about the future of the planet is not easy in light of the mounting evidence of global environmental degradation. It is important to be aware that there are many signs that today's ecological and social chaos may be the birth struggles of a more wholeness-making world. On what does the fulfillment of such hope for a more just and ecologically sane world depend? It depends on Christians and other earth-loving people in many faith traditions becoming midwives of active earth-loving in ourselves, our families, our churches, our communities, and our world.

We have two sources of hope as we do this work. We can remember that God, the ultimate source of hope in despairing situations, is working through us and countless others to help birth a new day of earth-caring, compassion, and community. We also can find hopeful energy in knowing that when we respond to the challenge with informed passion and disciplined commitment, we enhance our own earth-grounded well being.

Questions for Reflection

 1. Does the central theme of this session—that concern for the earth and society is an essential part of living a healthy Christian life—seem problematic?

2. What issues related to the environment and society's problems were overlooked or discussed inadequately in this chapter?

3. How well does my lifestyle reflect the biblical stewardship of the earth and the prophetic commitment to undergird love with justice?

4. What are the most important things that I need to do to become more involved in earth-caring and justice-making?

5. What can I do to involve more Christian people, including the leaders of our congregation?

Completing Your Self-Other-Earth Care Plan

 As you finish this session, complete and consolidate your self-care plan by taking these steps:

1. Go back and review the insights and plans for changes that came to you as you reflected on the issues you scored OK or NS in the Ecology-Justice-Peace Well Being Checkup and also the ideas for action that came to you in this session.

2. Then write out a short self- and earth-care plan and add this to the self-care plan you have already developed in increments in each of the earlier sessions. / Remember to include

• concrete, realizable objectives that you really want to achieve;

• practical strategies for moving toward these; and

• rewards you will give yourself as you take each step toward an objective or withhold if you do not move ahead.

Keep your plans love-centered and playful as well as serious and energized by your Christian faith. / Choose one or two attractive and achievable objectives from your earth-care plan and begin implementing them. / Experience the rewards of implementing the three dimensions of the ecological circle.

Continuing Your Well Being Self-Care

 To continue your wellness work on an ongoing basis, take time to do the following:

• Continue to implement the high-priority objectives in the self-care plan that you have developed over the eight sessions. Keep a record of what you learn and how these objectives affect your relationships with social institutions and the earth.

• If the plan that emerged as you added to it session by session turned out to be too time-demanding, go through it and put things that seem less important "on the back burner." Highlight those that seem crucial to your living a healthier lifestyle. Focus on implementing high-priority items in those dimensions of your life that you consider most in need of being strengthened.

• Enjoy a brisk daily walk in a natural setting if possible, to let yourself be nurtured by nature. While you walk, decide how you will implement your wellness plan that day and fit it into the day's schedule.

• If you have been working with a wellness partner or group, and it has been helpful, plan together how you will keep in touch with one another by phoning or meeting periodically for follow-up sessions. Continue to use the technique of forming a clear mental picture of this friend or group, as well as the family and friends you love most, surrounded by the warm, healing light of God's love and yours. Do the same with your home and natural surroundings.

• If you have enjoyed positive benefits from participating in such a well being program, consider ways to encourage friends and members of your church and community to become involved in such programs themselves.

Closing Song and Prayer

 Whether you are studying alone or with a wellness partner or group, close this session and the series by singing a favorite nature hymn such as "For the Beauty of the Earth"

or "Fairest Lord Jesus." Then, complete the following exercise. A well-loved verse from John's Gospel begins with the words, "God so loved the world" (John 3:16). Remembering that God loves the whole world, including all people and all of creation, complete the following three sentences with one, two, or three words that come to your mind. If you are working with others, take turns completing the sentences.

> God so loved the world that I feel . . .
> God so loved the world that I have hope
> and pray for . . .
> God so loved the world that I will seek
> to . . .
> Amen.[15]

Then if you feel moved to do so, end by offering prayers of thanksgiving for all that you have learned in this well being series.

Notes

Introduction

1. An insightful explanation of this significant medical revolution is *Manifesto for a New Medicine, Your Guide to Healing Partnerships and the Wise Use of Alternative Therapies* (Reading, Mass.: Addison-Wesley Publishing Co., 1996). Its author is a pioneer in this innovative movement, physician James S. Gordon, Director of The Center for Mind-Body Medicine (5225 Connecticut Ave., NW, Suite 414, Washington, D.C. 20015).

2. I am indebted to Gary Gunderson of the Carter Center's "Faith and Health" program for expanding my horizons on this challenge.

3. Trained leaders have used these books effectively to introduce the Adventure I healing program in some two hundred churches in forty-one states in the United States as well as Puerto Rico, Cuba, Sierra Leone, South Korea, and Australia.

4. If you are not familiar with traditional methods, it will enrich your understanding of Christian healing to study the Adventure I texts. The Adventure II materials differ from Adventure I in several other respects. Adventure I focuses on four key dimensions of everyone's life—mind, body, spirit, and relationships—and relates traditional spiritual healing approaches to these. Adventure II adds a variety of contemporary wellness methods to each of these and also focuses on three other dimensions of everyone's life—work, play, and the world, meaning both the world of God's creation and that of human institutions. Thus, the Well Being program is designed to help individuals and congregations implement more holistic approaches to Christian well being. Through this broadened channel, the power of God's healing love may flow to enhance wholeness in the multiple dimensions of people's lives, relationships, and society.

5. Although this workbook is written in explicitly Christian language, its exercises and ideas can be reworded readily and used in Jewish and Muslim settings. *Well Being* is ideally suited for use in many religious and secular settings because it is written in inclusive language.

6. *An Adventure in Healing and Wholeness*, 9.

Session 1

1. It's important to become aware of what your initial hopes are for this series. By referring back to these now and again, you can see how much you're able to use this experience for your healing and growth.

2. It's unfortunate that the word *health* often is used in our society to mean sickness. For example, "health care" usually really means sickness care. For this reason, I prefer to use positive terms such as well being, wellness, and wholeness in this workbook.

3. Quoted by Aaron Antonovsky in his insightful book, *Health, Stress and Coping* (San Francisco: Jossey-Bass, Inc., Publishers, 1982), 54. (I have paraphrased this definition to eliminate the sexist language.)

4. If you are struggling with heavy health problems, crises, or griefs, I trust you'll find some needed courage and inspiration when you read the remarkable true stories of Rosa Beyer, Wilma Rudolph, Helen Keller, Frank Smith, Clem Lucille, and Harold Wilke in *Well Being*.

5. This poignant passage has acquired new meaning for me as a man, thanks to the birth of three wonderful grandchildren in our family in recent years.

6. Traditionally, the church's task has been divided into four functions: *kerygma*, proclaiming the good news of God's love; *didache*, teaching; *diakonia*, expressing the good news in loving service; and establishing *koinonia*, the healing community.

7. Personal communication, December 1981.

8. Intentionality has taken some hits from critics in recent years. Someone observed, "If the road to hell is paved with good intentions, I wonder what the road to heaven is paved with."

9. From a filmed biography of Merton that I saw on Los Angeles Public Television, January 18, 1985.

10. If you have difficulty thinking of changes that give you hope, perhaps you'll find some hope in world developments such as these:

• The way both economic and ecological survival needs are pushing us to affirm, however reluctantly, our inescapable unity as one human family on a fragile but precious planet.

• The turbulent birth of new freedoms in South Africa and Eastern Europe.

• The dramatic ending of the Cold War with a blessed lessening of fears of global nuclear holocausts.

• The coming together of the planetwide environmental movements, governmental and nongovernmental; and a growing commitment to save the planet for all its human children and for its wondrously diverse flora and fauna.

• The flowering of whole-person health movements in many countries.

• The self-empowering ways women are redefining themselves and moving into leadership roles in politics, education, religion, and other professions.

• The availability of better health resources, contributing to an extended life span and opening up unprecedented opportunities for longer, more whole lives in more developed countries.

• The proliferation of self-other recovery groups that enable millions of formerly hopeless people to find well being by coping with a variety of life problems constructively.

• The incredible potentials of computers, videotaping, and cyberspace networks and other high-tech communication tools to enhance global communication and lifelong learning.

• The spiritual awakening of countless courageous people who have risked letting go of old authority-prescribed certainties and have found more freeing ways to deepen their spiritual lives.

• The flowering of Earth Day celebrations and the stimulation of earth-saving practices in countless places.

11. For a fuller discussion of using meditations, I recommend chapter three, "Guidelines for Using These Meditations," in Carolyn Stahl Bohler's book *Opening to God: Guided Imagery Meditation on Scripture* (Nashville: Upper Room Books, 1996).

Session 2

1. Trans. by David Magarshack (Middlesex, England: Penguin Books Ltd., and Baltimore, Md.: Penguin Books, Inc., 1958), 298.

2. If your primary interest is evaluating the spiritual health of your congregation, you can easily adapt this checkup for that purpose. Simply ask this question about each item listed: How effective is this congregation in helping its people maximize their spiritual-ethical health in this way?

3. If you have not known such a spiritually empowered individual personally, read several of the inspiring stories in *Well Being* about people whose faith gave them the power to live healthy lives. See the "windows of wholeness" about Rosa Beyer (p. 5), Hildegard of Bingen (p. 21), George Washington Carver (pp. 55–56), Frank Jones (p. 90), Dorothy Day (p. 155), Harold Wilke (p. 229), and Clem Lucille, my mother (p. 223).

4. Quoted by Douglas J. Harris in *Shalom: The Biblical Concept of Peace* (Grand Rapids, Mich.: Baker Book House, 1970), 13.

5. This center sponsored a wide variety of theory-generating conferences and professional training conferences, as well as other programs, all of which aimed at enabling participants and their churches to develop a spirituality that would enable people's souls as well as their minds, hearts, and bodies to find greater well being. When I retired, the governing boards of the Institute and the pastoral counseling training center of which I was clinical codirector for many years decided to join these two programs; they called the merged program the Clinebell Institute.

6. I am choosing to share a little about Erma's triumph over personal tragedy because I know in my heart that she would rejoice in the knowledge

that her journey through the dark night of the soul might bring a little hope and wholeness to people who hear it, as it certainly has to me. The folks you remembered in the learning exercise near this session's beginning were people whose religion served as wings that enabled them to fly. How many of them also found their spiritual wings in dark valleys?

7. Such tragedies are only the tip of the iceberg of sickness-causing faith and value systems in our society and world. Over the last few years, scams operated by "born again" financial planners are alleged to have cheated gullible Americans out of half a billion dollars.

8. John B. Cobb, Jr., *Theology and Pastoral Care* (Philadelphia: Fortress Press, 1977), 17.

9. "Prayer's Health Powers," *Fitness*, May/June 1994, 114. Dossey has a full report on his findings about prayer and healing in his book *Healing Words* (San Francisco: Harper San Francisco, 1993).

10. Even God's good gift of sexuality, one of the most pleasurable ways of getting high, can lose its spontaneity and joy and become a compulsive obsession.

11. If such holdover religious beliefs continue to burden your heart and mind, in spite of your efforts to find liberation from them, a few sessions with a pastoral counselor trained in helping people reduce such spiritual blocks can be a good investment that will increase the vitality of your religious life.

12. *Agape* is one of five Greek words for love in the Bible. It refers to the self-giving love of God that many Christians experience in Christ. We Christians have the God-given opportunity to become small, imperfect but effective channels of this love, enabling it to nurture healing and growth in ourselves and others.

13. Cited by Matthew Fox in his book on creation spirituality, *Original Blessing* (Santa Fe, N.M.: Bear & Co., 1983).

14. "Toward a Whole Theology," *Lutheran World*, January 1975, 14.

15. If you are having difficulty implementing your self-care plan, bear in mind that your plan will be more likely to work for you if it includes the following elements:
- A statement in which you spell out briefly for yourself how this spiritual self-care expresses your Christian lifestyle.
- Concrete, realizable objectives that you really want to achieve.
- Practical steps for moving toward these objectives.
- One or two attractive, achievable objectives that you'll begin moving toward immediately. In overcoming resistance to self-change, momentum from small, early successes often helps.
- A time line—when you'll begin and plan to reach various steps toward your objective.
- Rewards you'll give or withhold from yourself as you move toward or away from objectives.
- Playfulness as a continuing part of your plan. Activate your inner child to give your plan's implementation a playful touch to balance your serious intentions.
- Prayerful reflection as you shape your plan, keeping it energized by your spirituality.

Session 3

1. Published in "Anti-Slavery Examiner," September 1836.

2. If you feel overwhelmed by this checklist, bear in mind that your NS (need strengthening) items can help you identify your mind's growing edge. This means the place where you have the best opportunity, as well as perhaps the greatest need, to grow by using your mind's assets and gifts more fully.

3. For an illuminating discussion of EQ, see Daniel Goleman, *Emotional Intelligence* (New York: Bantam Books, 1995).

4. *Minding the Body, Mending the Mind* (Reading, Mass.: Addison-Wesley, 1987), 10.

5. To avoid the danger of blaming ourselves or others who do not get better when sickness comes, it is important to remember that usually numerous causes converge when people become ill. These include factors over which they have no control (for example, genetic vulnerability). Mental and spiritual factors may play small or large roles. Letting go of the blame-and-guilt game can

improve one's health by increasing the effectiveness of the immune system.

6. These suggestions are derived from my personal and professional experience with mental wellness issues.

7. *Between Health and Illness* (Boston: Houghton-Mifflin, 1984), 191.

8. These guidelines are from two sources—my personal and professional experiences with stress problems and from Joan Borysenko's *Minding the Body, Mending the Mind.*

9. The prayer was first delivered by Reinhold Niebuhr in a chapel service at Union Theological Seminary in New York City when I was in graduate school there. As it became widely used in twelve-step recovery programs, its author was forgotten until recently.

10. New York: NAL Dutton, 1981.

11. "A Case for Caregiving," The Carter Center, *Faith and Health*, Winter 1995, 1–2.

12. New York: Doubleday, 1989.

13. Cited in John R. McWilliams, revised Peter McWilliams (1995 ed.), *You Can't Afford the Luxury of a Negative Thought* (Los Angeles: Prelude Press, 1988), 44.

14. Found as number 454 in *The United Methodist Hymnal* but also in other hymnals.

Session 4

1. Frances Moore Lappé, *Diet for a Small Planet*, rev. ed. (New York: Ballantine Books, 1975), 1.

2. His world record was four minutes, six and eight-tenths seconds. Although this time is very slow by today's standards, it was a near miracle in the early 1930s when a four-minute mile was thought by many to be beyond human possibilities.

3. You may be wondering about Paul's statements about the body's being at war with the spirit in people. He used "body" in these passages as a symbol of impulses and primitive drives, not the physical body, per se.

4. Reported in *American Health*, March 17, 1987.

5. Alexander Lowen, *The Betrayal of the Body* (New York: Collier Books, 1969), 231.

6. *Spontaneous Healing: How to Discover and Enhance Your Body's Natural Ability to Maintain and Heal Itself* (New York: Knopf, 1955), 188.

7. *The Johns Hopkins Medical Letter, Health after 50*, July 1996, 1.

8. To teach yourself some of the hatha yoga movements, consult one of the guides that show photographs of how to do them. The one I have used is by yoga instructor Richard Hittleman.

9. Quoted in Robert Andrews, *The Columbia Dictionary of Quotations* (New York: Columbia University Press, 1993), 338.

10. Valley Forge, Penn.: Judson Press, 1977.

11. "Too much time on 'essentials,'" *Santa Barbara New Press*, June 25, 1996, A9.

12. Report on Headline News, Cable News Network, May 23, 1996.

13. If you have a special interest in addictions, see Howard Clinebell, *Understanding and Counseling Persons with Alcohol, Drug, and Behavioral Addictions*, revised edition (Nashville: Abingdon Press, 1997). It will give you in-depth information about treatment and prevention, including their vital religious dimensions. This is an updated version of the book, including a new focus on drug as well as alcohol problems.

14. Joyce Buekers has discovered that this partner approach works well in congregational and hospital well being groups.

15. These major stages of behavioral change have been charted helpfully by a research physician in *The Johns Hopkins Medical Letter, Health after 50*, July 1996, 1–2:
    (1) Precontemplation, when the negative consequences of a behavior such as smoking are at the periphery of people's minds.
    (2) Contemplation, when the idea of change is toyed with by the person.
    (3) Preparation, when the intention to change is joined with a plan of action.
    (4) Action, when actual steps are taken and people begin to feel empowered.
    (5) Maintenance, the stage of preventing or

recovering from relapses, which may last a lifetime.

16. Republished as *Primitive Remedies* by Wood-bridge Press Publishing Company, Santa Barbara, California, 1973.

17. *Primitive Remedies*; 19–22.

Session 5

1. *The Phenomenon of Man* (New York: Harper & Row, 1959), 265.

2. *The Intimate Marriage* (New York: Harper & Row, 1970), 179.

3. *Love and Living*, ed. Naomi B. Stone and Patrick Hart (New York: Farrar, Straus & Giroux, 1979), 34.

Session 6

1. Gabriele Uhlein, *Meditations with Hildegard of Bingen* (Santa Fe, N.M.: Bear & Co., 1983), 54.

2. San Francisco: HarperSanFrancisco, 1979.

3. Matthew Fox, *The Reinvention of Work: A New Vision of Livelihood for Our Times* (San Francisco: HarperSanFrancisco, 1994), 5. This landmark book points in crucial new directions that are essential for the health of work in the global economy of the twenty-first century. Its message is consistent with my understanding of the problems and possibilities of well being in work.

4. This list of wellness-nurturing rewards from work is limited by the fact that it reflects middle-class values and expectations derived from my background and experience. In this tragic time when the rich are getting richer and the poor poorer, it's important to be aware of the economic underbelly of our society. Television programs have encouraged the spread of middle-class economic expectations to people with non–middle-class economic opportunities. The *hopes* but not the *reality* of countless such people have been transformed by the tube. Yet the realistic hopes of millions of low-skilled people who live in the culture of chronic poverty are restricted to the first reward from work that I have listed—adequate income—but only if they are able to find and keep jobs. Remembering the special concern for the poor, both by Jesus and the Hebrew prophets, we would be wise as Christians to use whatever influence and political clout we may have to change the economic and political causes of widespread, injustice-rooted poverty, which exists even in affluent countries such as ours.

5. In my experience, the recent influx into theological seminaries of second-career students, many of whom are women, has increased the challenge and satisfaction of seminary teaching tremendously.

6. From a spiritual perspective, it is noteworthy that in Sharon L. Connelly's study of people who excel in their work and love it (what she called "work spirit"), all were found to have a sense of vision and larger purpose in their work. Many said that their unusual energy came from outside themselves and was channeled through them. From "Work Spirit: Channeling Energy for High Performance," reprinted from *Training and Development Journal*, May 1985.

7. Here are some key books on work wellness that I have found useful:
  • Richard N. Bolles, *The Three Boxes of Life: And How to Get Out of Them* (Berkeley, Calif.: Ten Speed Press, 1981). A rich compendium of life-work planning information and resources that emphasize the balance of learning, work, and leisure during all the adult life stages.
  • Matthew Fox , *The Reinvention of Work*.
  • Richard W. Gillett, *The Human Enterprise: A Christian Perspective on Work* (Kansas City, Mo.: Leaven Press, 1985). Explores critical ethical issues related to work—the public policy and theology of economic dislocation and unemployment, the militarization of the economy, racism and sexism in work, etc.
  • Alan Lakein, *How to Get Control of Your Time and Your Life* (NAL Dutton, 1989). A classic guide to doing what the title suggests.

8. See above for information on these two important books.

9. Lakein, *How to Get Control*; 1, 22.

10. These are two of the key books on humor and wellness that I have found useful:
  • Conrad Hyers, *The Comic Vision and the Christian Faith: A Celebration of Life and*

Laughter (New York: Pilgrim Press, 1981). Shows how comedy enriches and informs our lives and our religion.

   • Lawrence J. Peter and Bill Dana, *The Laughter Prescription: The Tools of Humor and How to Use Them* (New York: Ballantine Books, Inc., 1982), explores the use of humor in reducing anxiety, depression, and ill health as well as in coping with stress and communicating effectively, all with hilarious examples.

11. I need to level with you that this good advice, though true, is much easier to preach than practice. Changing type A behavior isn't easy. I easily push myself so hard with multiple expectations that I neglect the self-care I know I need. Even though my work pattern is geared toward trying to achieve what I see as significant objectives, there is enough work addiction in my pattern to make change both difficult and important to my well being.

12. *Women's Wit and Wisdom* (Philadelphia: Running Press, 1991).

13. San Luis Obispo, Calif.: Impact Publishers, 1980.

Session 7

1. A. Ray Grummon was like a second father to me. He was a major influence in my decision to become a clergyperson rather than an engineer as I had planned earlier.

2. I must add a comment from the "no good image is perfect" department. When I learned something about farming, my granddad, along with agricultural experts like my father, believed that turning the soil over by deep plowing was the best way to prepare the soil for seeding. Subsequent discoveries have demonstrated that, depending on the nature of the soil, avoiding deep plowing may be better for both the soil and the crops.

3. Unfortunately, many counseling and healing professionals are unaware of how frequently grief is a hidden cause. Many are not trained in using their therapeutic skills to treat blocked grief.

4. Lillian E. Watson, ed., *Light from Many Lamps* (New York: Simon & Schuster, 1951), 123.

5. I have been unable to locate the exact source, but it is good advice for any older people who assume that adventure is only for the young.

6. Perhaps getting "old" seems so mercifully distant that you feel you don't need to think about it now. If so, bear in mind that creative aging starts at birth.

7. Madeleine L'Engle, as quoted from a 1985 article in *The New York Times* (source: *The Beacon Book of Quotations by Women*, compiled by Rosalie Maggio (Boston: Beacon Press, 1992, 8).

8. For information on setting up and leading grief groups, see Howard Clinebell, *Basic Types of Pastoral Care and Counseling*, 227–30.

9. To locate such a pastoral counseling specialist, contact the American Association of Pastoral Counselors at 1-800-220-8041. The author was the first president and is now a diplomate in that association. (The cynic who said that "a specialist is someone who does everything else worse" was not aware of the competencies of most AAPC members.)

Session 8

1. If you are interested in an in-depth exploration of the application of this earth-caring approach by parents as well as by people-helping professionals, read my book *Ecotherapy: Healing Ourselves, Healing the Earth* (Minneapolis: Fortress Press, 1996). This is a guide to ecologically grounded personality theory, therapy, education, spirituality, and parenting.

2. Quoted in *Earthlight*, Winter 1994–95, 13.

3. Quoted in *Earth Island Journal* 11, no. 1 (Winter 1995–96), (Northern Hemisphere), contents page.

4. I am indebted to Peter Rukungah of Kenya who shared this proverb with me.

5. As I write (1997), one out of five American children live in poverty. Forty percent of the rivers and lakes are seriously polluted. Nearly 100 million Americans breathe air that is less than healthy. One out of every eleven children has unhealthy levels of lead in his or her blood. Eight million children and a half million pregnant women have no access to health care.

6. For clarification of any of these, be sure to read Chapter 4 in *Ecotherapy: Healing Ourselves, Healing the Earth*. There you'll find in-depth discussion of these and other ecologically damaging religious beliefs and values.

7. This diagram is taken from *Ecotherapy*, 7.

8. If you would like a full discussion of the meaning of the ecological circle with an account of how I awakened to its reality and power in an exotic setting—the tropical rain forest—read *Ecotherapy*, 3–9. But remember that such an awakening can occur in your own backyard or in your living room with a favorite houseplant.

9. *The Boston Globe*, April 14, 1996, 80.

10. Cited by Andrew M. Hodges in *The Deeper Intelligence* (Nashville, Tenn.: Thomas Nelson Publishers, 1994).

11. For a full discussion of this issue, see Patricia Byrnes, "Wild Medicine," in *Wilderness*, Fall 1996, 28–33.

12. Matthew Fox, Introduction, in Gabriele Uhlein, *Meditations with Hildegard of Bingen* (Santa Fe, N.Mex.: Bear & Co., 1983), 15.

13. For more about Rachel Carson's struggle and achievements, see Carson, *Silent Spring* (Greenwich, Conn.: Fawcett Publications, Inc., 1962).

14. From a Public Television interview around the time of the Earth Summit in Rio de Janeiro, Brazil, in June 1992. For a report of this unprecedented global earth-saving conference, see Adam Rogers, *The Earth Summit: A Planetary Reckoning* (Los Angeles: Global View Press, 1993).

15. This guided meditation is my environmental adaptation of two exercises by Joanna Rogers Macy (to whom I am indebted), in *Despair and Personal Power in the Nuclear Age* (Philadelphia: New Society Publishers, 1983), 141.

16. I am indebted to Gary Gunderson of the Interfaith Health Program of the Carter Center for this exercise.